CROMWELL'S
CROWNING MERCY

Oliver Cromwell (1599–1658) in an engraving of 1809 after the painting by Robert Walker. (Private Collection)

CROMWELL'S
CROWNING MERCY
The Battle of Worcester 1651

M ALCOLM A TKIN

WITH DRAWINGS BY S TEPHEN R IGBY

SUTTON PUBLISHING

First published in 1998 by
Sutton Publishing Limited · Phoenix Mill
Thrupp · Stroud · Gloucestershire · GL5 2BU

British Library Cataloguing in Publication Data
A catalogue record for this book is available from the British Library.

ISBN 0-7509-1888-8

Endpapers: Pikemen by Stephen Rigby

The original reconstruction drawings by Steve Rigby are available for purchase as limited edition prints. For further details contact Steve Rigby, c/o County Archaeological Service, Tolladine Road, Worcester WR4 9NB.

The title of this book derives from Oliver Cromwell's own assessment of the battle to the Speaker of the House of Commons in a letter of 4 September 1651.

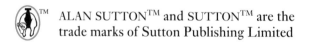 ALAN SUTTON™ and SUTTON™ are the
trade marks of Sutton Publishing Limited

Typeset in 11/12pt Ehrhardt.
Typesetting and origination by
Sutton Publishing Limited
Printed in Great Britain by
WBC Limited, Bridgend.

Contents

List of Illustrations

MAPS

Preface

There is now little sign of the violent battle that raged in and around Worcester on 3 September 1651: the remains of Fort Royal are still visible, as is the damage to Powick Bridge and musket-ball marks on Powick Church. However, they give only a fleeting impression of the magnitude of the battle that involved over 40,000 men at a time when the total population of Worcestershire was only about 57,000.

The battle was the final conflict of a series of civil wars that cost the lives of perhaps around 100,000 soldiers, and possibly another 100,000 civilians, and devastated the economy of Worcestershire and much of the rest of the country. The battle had repercussions that were felt as far away as the Scottish Highlands and the colonies of Virginia, New England and the West Indies. Today, the Civil War has taken on a romantic image. The reality is that this was a conflict that has been estimated to have cost the lives of 3.7 per cent of the population of England and 6 per cent of the population of Scotland.[1]

Despite the well-known role of the battle of Worcester in signalling the end of the wars, it has received scant attention in earlier general histories of the period. For many writers, the history of the Civil Wars has been that of the First (or Great) Civil War to 1646 and the rest has been a postscript. Of the battle of Worcester itself, the great nineteenth-century historian S.R. Gardiner, in his *History of the Commonwealth and Protectorate* (1903), set the tone for most later writers in considering that the odds were so far in Cromwell's favour that the outcome was inevitable and that its only importance was in the way that the campaign attracted popular support against the King: 'in this and in nothing else lay the significance of Worcester'. As a consequence, 'The military critic finds little to say about it'.[2] A contrary view was taken by Buchan in 1941, who described the campaign from Scotland to Worcester as 'the most brilliant pursuit in the history of British arms'.[3] General histories, such as those of Kenyon or Ashley, have been content to summarize the battle in a few paragraphs.[4] In recent years, the principal detailed accounts of the military events have been the concise pamphlet published by R. Holmes in 1985 and the chapter within the present author's *The Civil War in Worcestershire* (1995).[5] The battle has principally been seen as simply acting as a full stop to the wars rather than influencing subsequent events, yet the two cannot be separated.[6]

In particular, there has been little consideration of the nature of the involvement of Worcester, or of the effects of the battle on the local population, since the first seminal accounts of the battle published by the influential local historian J.W. Willis-Bund in 1905 and 1913.[7] Thus the battle has become something of an abstract event in the city's history, or one shrouded in myth. The present account, therefore, tries to convey something of its impact on the participants and the local population, who to a great extent were passive observers of events, but victims none the less.

One of the best known aspects of the battle has been the subsequent escape of Charles II. Few people cannot have heard of his concealment in the Boscobel Oak. Yet less thought has been spared for the fate of the thousands of ordinary prisoners who were imprisoned or transported. Scottish prisoners were transported abroad and their loss had a major impact on the home life, economy and political development of Scotland. The most detailed description to date has remained Gardiner's study in 1903, and the present account amplifies this. Sadly, the original sources are very sparse, focusing on the events themselves or on the fates of the notables. It is to be hoped that further study may reveal new insights, especially on the effect of the loss of so many men on the communities back in Scotland.

This was, indeed, a riveting campaign that excited the attention of the whole nation and, rarely for the English Civil Wars, showed a popular enthusiasm for the fight. The superiority in numbers that Cromwell enjoyed has only in retrospect made the outcome seem inevitable. The troops on the ground did not take the matter so lightly, however, and Cromwell had proved that it was possible to win battles with inferior numbers. The battle was, in the words of Cromwell, a 'crowning mercy'.[8] It represented the crowning achievement of his military career. It was also a mercy in bringing to an end (bar a few ineffective plots and risings) the fighting of the Civil War and gave an opportunity for conciliation and new attempts at restoring the stability that the country craved for. In the event these failed, and the King was eventually restored by peaceful consent in 1660. The book concludes with a look at how the news of this was received in Worcester and the attitudes of the former combatants.

The book uses the letters and accounts of people who fought at the battle, and the earliest histories of the events; some of these are reproduced in full within Appendix 1. Many of the sources are vague, and sometimes contradictory, reflecting the rushed and sometimes confused nature of the events. It should, however, be remembered that none of these sources was unbiased; they were influenced by whether they were written during the period of the Commonwealth, or after the Restoration, when there was a concerted attempt to claim to have supported the Royalist cause. They include letters from Cromwell and his generals, Harrison and Fleetwood. Colonel Robert Stapleton was particularly important in feeding first-hand accounts into the contemporary news-sheets which were produced within a matter of days to satisfy the demands of a news-hungry London. The Royalist accounts are more sparse and have generally survived as post-Restoration copies, but they are vital in showing a different perspective to the crusading vision of events as portrayed by the Parliamentarian chroniclers. One of the most important, *Boscobel*, was written by a local man, Thomas Blount (1618–79). There are also the more terse references to events in official documents such as the records of the Council of State. Often these merely hint at wider events and concerns. The flight of the King after the battle has continued to excite the popular imagination and many of those involved published their version of events, including the King himself. Some accounts were distorted by tricks of the memory; others were deliberately misleading, as with the stories promoted by the King prior to his restoration in order to protect those who had helped him. All were keen to promote the King in the best possible light, but it does seem that his bearing during those troubled weeks may have represented his finest moments.

These sources are illustrated through the use of modern reconstruction drawings by Steve Rigby as a means of seeing the events through the eyes of those who actually took part and of bringing the events to life. It is easy for modern histories to present the past merely in an academic and abstract way. This is not a story simply of campaign maps or artefacts; it is an account that is intended to reflect something of the pain and horror that is civil war.

Malcolm Atkin
November 1997

Acknowledgements

My first thanks must go to Bill Craig of the 'Heritage of Liberty' committee in the USA for originally suggesting that I write this. Work has been greatly assisted by the support shown by Hereford and Worcester County Council (and its successor Worcestershire County Council) through the Libraries, Recreation and Environment Committee under the chairmanship of Cllr Diane Rayner, and the County Librarian and Arts Officer, Michael Messenger. The staff of the Hereford and Worcester Record Office, Worcester Museums Service and Worcester City Library were, as usual, unfailing in their help and assistance. A special thanks goes to Tony Wherry, County Archivist, for permission to publish the documents in Appendices 1.2 and 1.4. The quotations from W.C. Abbott, *The Writings and Speeches of Oliver Cromwell*, vol. 2 (1939, reissued 1988) are by permission of Oxford University Press. I am grateful to those individuals and bodies who have given permission for illustrative material to be used, including Almonry Museum, Evesham, Worcester Museums Service, Hereford and Worcester Record Office, Worcester City Library, National Museum of Scotland, Andrew Noakes and, of course, Steve Rigby. Thanks are also owed to Dr Alistair Bantock of the Sealed Knot for encouraging the publication, and to Des Thomas of the English Civil War Society and Roundhead Association who first gave me the opportunity to sample the life of a musketeer in battle (and to Chris Scott who, as my file leader, ensured that I survived the experience). Final thanks must go to Susanne, my wife, for all of her patient encouragement, and also for providing the index.

ONE

Background

Say you have been at Worcester, where England's sorrows began, and where they are happily ended.

Hugh Peters, 1651

The battle of Worcester in 1651 was more than just another battle; it was the final stage in a series of civil wars that had affected not just England but Scotland, Wales and Ireland. Thus it was that Hugh Peters, the Parliamentary army chaplain at Worcester, described the battle as ending the nation's sorrows (see below, p. 120). For Cromwell this was a 'crowning mercy'. Expressing again what was clearly a widely held belief, this was a *mercy* in bringing to an end the fighting of the Civil War. But it was also the *crowning* triumph of his armies and a fitting end to his military career. One of the most significant aspects of the battle is the enthusiasm that was shown for the Parliamentary cause across large parts of the country, not least in Worcestershire. To understand this phenomenon it is necessary to review the course of the war since its outbreak in 1642.

The causes of the war have filled many a book and will be discussed here only as far as they illuminate the events of 1651. The reasons for the first outbreak of war are complex, entwining political mistrust, economic grievances and passions over religion at a national level. Overlapping these concerns was a further layer of local issues and loyalties. Towns, villages and families were all split by the conflict. Despite their differences, few relished the idea of war and many participants were simply swept along by the tide of events, however hard they tried to avoid it.

Worcester has a special place in the history of the Civil Wars. The skirmish at Powick, on the outskirts of the city, in September 1642 marked the start of serious fighting, and Worcester was the last English city in Royalist hands to fall to Parliament in 1646. In addition the county was an important strategic routeway for the armies of both sides as they manoeuvred for position.

Worcestershire generally was a well-off county. Unfortunately, this made it an attractive target for the armies of both sides during the impending war. In 1642, Worcester was the twelfth largest town in England with a population of around 7,000. It had successfully faced both economic and natural disasters, including recent outbreaks of plague. Now it was to be struck by the man-made disaster of civil war. At the heart of its importance was its role as a route centre and redistribution centre for raw materials and finished goods, especially textiles,

based on its position on the River Severn, with good road contacts east–west
linking London and Wales, and north–south linking Lancashire and Bristol. The
main employment of the town was still based around the textile industry,
although this faced increasing competition from other local towns and from
increasing decentralization into the villages. The textile industry dominated the
membership of the Corporation, followed by merchants (many of whom had
strong contacts with London) and then by those engaged in the food and drink
industries; tanning and leather-working were also important.

The history of town and countryside, citizen and gentry, were inextricably
linked. Worcester was an important market centre for its rich and varied
agricultural hinterland. It lay at the junction of cattle- and sheep-rearing in the
west, corn-growing in the south, hop-growing in the Teme valley and the market
gardening of the Vale of Evesham. There was also a thriving, if illegal, tobacco-
growing industry in the Vale. The county also had an increasingly important
industrial component: north Worcestershire contained an ironworking industry
based on the water power of the Stour which became especially valuable during
the war years.

As war drew closer, the partisans of both sides tried to win over the
uncommitted majority. The Royalist faction in the county was led by a small
number of influential county gentry, led by Sir William Russell of Strensham and
Colonel Samuel Sandys of Ombersley. From the start, such men (as the traditional
leaders of their communities) tried to exploit the innate conservatism of the county
in not wishing to disturb the balance between King and Parliament by raising
support for the King. But they failed to engender much active enthusiasm for
joining the Royalist cause, especially in the towns. There remained widespread
concerns over those reforms in the Church which seemed to bring it closer to
Catholicism, and to taxes imposed without consultation with Parliament. The
Ship Money and Coat and Conduct taxes were both resented and feared, because
they pointed towards a more absolutist monarchy.

Worcester, along with many towns at the time, was trying to assert its
independence from the rule of the county gentry, and this was reflected in its
political allegiance. Most of the influential clothiers of Worcester were
Parliamentarians and before the start of the war Worcester refused to support the
Commissions of Array and to allow Royalist recruiting parties to enter the city. In
early September 1642, the citizens and Trained Bands of Worcester delivered a
petition to the mayor, Edward Solley. They complained prophetically that
'Cavaliers and soldiers in divers parts of the kingdom (where they come) have
plundered the towns, bloodily killing the king's peaceable subjects, rifling their
houses, and violently taking away of their goods and in some places deflowered
women.'[1] Few, however, were prepared to take the step beyond such resentment
and grumbling towards active rebellion against their King. This long-standing
antipathy to the Royalist cause is important in considering the continued
difference in attitude between city and gentry in providing active support to the
Royalists in 1651.

Personal involvement in the war could simply depend on which side's
recruiting party found you first. Although around 7,000 men, amounting to

12 per cent of the population, may have been recruited into the Royalist army within the first year, the claim of Worcester and the county to any great loyalty to the Royalist cause depends more on the circumstance of being under Royalist occupation from October 1642 onwards rather than any great fanaticism. For those that remained at home there were incessant demands for money and supplies in order to pay the garrisons and the armies that frequently passed through the county on their way to battles elsewhere. In 1645, Colonel Bard warned of the consequences of not offering sufficient support. 'Know you that unless you bring unto me (at a day and hour in Worcester) the monthly contribution for six months, you are to expect an unsanctified troop of horse among you, from whom if you hide yourselves . . . they shall fire your houses without mercy, hang up your bodies wherever they find them, and scare your ghosts.'[2]

Increasing antagonism to the repeated Royalist tax demands, the requisitioning of men and supplies and the continued looting culminated in the rising of the 'Clubmen' in 1645. The Clubmen's original intention was to create a neutral third force to protect law and order ('foolish neuters' according to the then Parliamentarian, Colonel Edward Massey). Having failed to win any redress from the occupying power, by the end of 1645 the Clubmen (numbering over 2,000 men) were effectively operating in support of Parliament. The latter was steadily increasing its influence over the south and east of the county, raising taxes, recruiting troops and establishing committees of government under its own activist gentry such as Sir Nicholas Lechmere of Hanley Castle. Another event of 1645 that was later to prove of great significance was the movement through the county of the Scottish army, then fighting in support of Parliament. The Scottish army ravaged the countryside, looting food and desecrating churches, and bitter memories of this invasion remained in 1651 when the new king tried to use a new Scottish army to regain his throne.

The half-hearted attitude of the city of Worcester to the Royalist war effort was clearly demonstrated by the lack of cooperation shown by the citizens to the garrison during the two-month-long siege of 1646.[3] This was despite the writing of the now-famous slogan *civitas fidelis deo et rege* ('city faithful to God and King') on the transom of the drawbridge over the River Severn. The writer, whether it be local citizen, member of the garrison, reformado or mercenary, is unknown. The prominent local Royalist, Henry Townshend of Elmley Lovett, who was in the city at the time, offered an alternative view of the loyalties of Worcester, saying that 'the city began to grow so mutinous that many give out, they will throw the soldiers over the wall or club them if they should oppose this treaty, being now as all quiet people are weary of war, desiring their trading may go on'.[4] Townshend was particularly disappointed with the negative attitude of the leaders of Worcester society, as 'many of the best rank draw very backward' and refused to give active support to the Royalists. The main support from this quarter was confined to the same small knot of dedicated Royalist gentry that were to support the King in 1651. The names of Lord Talbot, Sir John Packington, Sir Ralph Clare, Sir Rowland Berkeley, John Washburn, Edward Pennel, the Blount family and Thomas Hornyold, as well as Samuel Sandys who surrendered at Hartlebury, will soon become familiar in this story. Eventually, on 23 July, the Worcester garrison had no option but to surrender, fearing that they were about to be betrayed by the citizens. The county had been bled dry economically and, whatever their personal loyalties were, the inhabitants simply wished the armies of both sides to leave them in peace.

Local Royalist families were to suffer greatly after the war was over; the activities of the Committee of Sequestrations, established to seize their estates, were vilified as the 'dismemberment of estates and ruin of families'.[5] The rates for compounding ranged from one-tenth to one-half of the pre-war value of the estates in question. In all, £28,219 14s 8d was raised from sequestered Royalist estates in the county during 1647/8.[6] Sir William Russell of Strensham (1602–69), a former Treasurer of the Navy, had been one of the most prominent supporters of the Royalist cause in the county during the First Civil War. He was a one-time governor of Worcester and had spent a fortune on raising troops for Charles I. A consequent seizure of his estates led to eventual imprisonment for debt until, in February 1649, his fine was reduced to £2,071. There is, therefore, an understandable lack of evidence to suggest that Sir William was prepared to risk his livelihood further and play any significant part in the Third Civil War, although he remained in contact with Royalist exiles.

The human consequences of war would still have been very evident in 1651. More men were maimed than were actually killed in the fighting and their maintenance had become a long-term obligation. At Bromsgrove, the Constable's accounts for 1649 record the passage of a number of maimed soldiers through the town who were given overnight accommodation. They included, for 28 March, '3 maymed soldiers Thomas Jones William Davis and William Laugher quartered over night and sent on with a pass. 1s 4d'.[7]

In March 1646, Lord Astley prophesied to his captors after the final defeat of the Royalist field army at Stow-on-the-Wold that the Parliamentary unity would disintegrate into factional disputes, saying, 'You have now done your work and may go to play, unless you will fall out among yourselves.' This prophecy proved accurate. The alliance of interests that made up the Parliamentary cause soon began to show tensions as Presbyterians and other moderates disputed with Independents and the radicals. Opinion polarized into monarchists (including those who had fought as Parliamentarians) on one side and republicans (infuriated by the plotting of Charles I with the Scots) on the other. The puritan Richard Baxter from Kidderminster, a former army chaplain in Whalley's regiment of horse, was shocked by the degree to which extreme views took hold of the army, with the most radical Independents calling for church and state democracy.[8] These divisions provided an impetus for a series of risings by Royalists and more moderate Parliamentarians that, along with an invasion by the Scots, together comprised the Second Civil War of 1648. Still economically exhausted by the war, and under the increasingly tight control of Parliament and its intelligence network, Worcestershire played no real part in these events. It is, however, likely that a small number of local Royalists were party to some of the rather ineffectual plots that characterized the period, and there was evidently some concern as to the loyalty of the county. It is, nevertheless, significant that no surviving document refers to Worcester as one of the targets of the conspirators, and this should perhaps have served as a warning to Charles II and his advisers of his chances of drawing any extensive support from the area in 1651.

About eighty discontented officers from regiments based around Gloucestershire met at Broadway, at the foot of the Cotswolds, in January 1648 to discuss what became known as the Broadway Plot. One of the leaders of the conspirators was Colonel Dud Dudley. Originally from Staffordshire, this Royalist ironmaster, with interests at Pensnet, near Dudley in north Worcestershire (now West Midlands), had played a notable local role in the First Civil War as one of the designers of the Worcester defences; he had also commanded the artillery during the siege of Worcester in 1646. But their plotting focused on the garrisons of Gloucester and Hartlebury rather than on Worcester. Exaggerated support was claimed from Bewdley, guarding the Severn river crossing, where two thousand 'capmen' (the manufacturers of the famous 'Monmouth' knitted caps) were said to be ready to rise. The total population was probably less than three thousand at the time, and there is no evidence of any actual support. The idea that Colonel Turton, the garrison commander of Hartlebury, might deliver the castle to the conspirators was also to be proved wildly in error by subsequent events. Parliament's intelligence (as in 1651) was far superior and, having got wind of the plot, they took swift action. Colonel Morgan was sent with his men from the Gloucester garrison to block the road to London in case there was an actual rising in the county. Nothing actually came of the plot but in June the Worcestershire Committee was authorized to raise fresh troops to quell any further insurrection.

The Parliamentary intelligence network continued to forestall any actual risings that might have been intended in the area. In July 1648, Colonel Turton appears to have had news of further plotting in Worcestershire, Shropshire, Staffordshire and Herefordshire. This information probably came through the noted Worcestershire industrialist and Parliamentarian Captain Andrew Yarranton (whom Parliament rewarded with £500 and sequestrations from a number of Royalist estates in the county and surrounds). Gunpowder was found behind the house of the parson of Wolverley, who was implicated in the plot. One of the leaders, Major Harcot, was arrested and taken to Hartlebury Castle where he was tortured by having lighted musket match placed on the soles of his feet until he confessed and identified his confederates.[9] Harcot's information allowed Colonel Dud Dudley to be captured but he subsequently escaped from prison in Worcester. Recaptured, he was taken to London and was ordered to be executed. Amazingly, he escaped the night before he was due to be shot and managed finally to escape to Bristol. He died in 1684 and was buried in St Helen's Church, Worcester.

One small local rising did take place in adjacent Herefordshire in August 1648 under Sir Henry Lingen, and some of the arms were supplied from the county. A Kidderminster joiner, John Brancill, had been employed by Edward Broade of Dunclent (two miles from Kidderminster) to make stocks for muskets to be used in the rebellion, but there is no evidence of any other support from Worcestershire. Parliament continued to keep its tight military hold on the

King Charles II (1630–85). He was aged only 21 at the time of the battle of Worcester, and had the difficult task of trying to unite a disparate army torn apart by jealousies. (Courtesy Worcester City Library)

county: Worcester and Hartlebury were re-garrisoned and yet more troops were raised from the area. The Second Civil War was brought to an end with the fall of Pembroke in July and the defeat of the Scottish army in August at Preston. One Worcestershire man who did take up arms in 1648 was Major William Pitcher who joined the rebellion in Wales. Pitcher had been a member of the garrison of Worcester that had surrendered in 1646 and therefore his participation in the

Second Civil War broke his parole not to take up arms again against Parliament. He was promptly tried and shot. This warning of the consequences of further rebellion would surely have been in the minds of county Royalists in 1651.

The principal result of the various plots and risings of 1648 was that Parliament finally lost patience with the captured King, who was now considered to be totally untrustworthy. He was put on trial for his life in January 1649. Some revulsion at the trial and subsequent execution of the King may have played a part in encouraging riots involving about two thousand people in Worcester against the Excise Tax in January 1649. There were, however, other reasons. Further riots against the tax in 1650 were deemed to have been caused by the violent attitude of Captain Prescott and some of the other Excise Sub-Commissioners who were consequently replaced.

When the First Civil War had begun, those opposing King Charles I had still proclaimed a loyalty to the principle of kingship. It was simply that the King was overreaching the limits of his power, or was being badly advised. Yet by 1649 the King of England, who believed he ruled by divine right, could be put on trial for his life and then executed. This radical step left many in the Parliamentary ranks uneasy and there was a further realignment of forces; in particular, the Presbyterian party edged closer to the Royalist cause. The execution of King Charles I was followed by the establishment of the Commonwealth as the victors of the First and Second Civil Wars tried to re-establish stability in the country. Meanwhile the nineteen-year-old heir to the throne, Charles II, was in a sorry and frustrating exile on the continent.

TWO

The Third Civil War

Charles had been forced to grow up quickly during the Civil War, especially following the imprisonment and death of his father, and had changed from being a high-spirited child to a figure of authority, though destined to be continually at the mercy of plots devised by scheming advisers and allies. His courage was unquestioned but his lack of experience (despite having been given titular command of the army of the Western Association in 1645) meant that he was obliged to rely on advisers who too often had their own agendas. In 1650, he decided to make his own attempt to win the throne by force. To do so, he had to forge a new alliance with the Scots, many of whom retained an emotional affection for the Scottish Stuart dynasty even though their army had fought on the side of Parliament in the First Civil War. The Scots had, however, come to believe that the alliance with Parliament had not served them well and therefore sought an alliance first with Charles I and then with his son, whose desperation appeared to be an opportunity to win good terms for their brand of Presbyterianism. The Earl of Argyle and the Covenanters proclaimed Charles II as King on the death of his father but at the same time made it clear that they would only support his restoration in return for his acceptance of the Scottish Covenant for a reform of the Church.

There were ominous signs of conflict even before Charles II sailed for Scotland. For the extreme Covenanters, this was a religious crusade with no room for compromise. But John Livingstone, one of the ministers in the delegation to the exiled Charles, wrote of his distrust of the King's real commitment to the Covenant. To Livingstone's horror, Charles was discovered kneeling to receive Communion, he tried to modify the oath of the Covenant, and he wanted to include 'malignants' (that is, non-Covenanting Royalists) in his army. The King left Holland in *The Skidam* and landed in Scotland at Garmouth-on-Spey, north of Aberdeen, on 24 June 1650. He then spent some time under what amounted to house arrest in Dunfermline. There he was subjected to four-hour sermons until he actually signed the Covenant. He was even forced to condemn his father as guilty of the bloodshed of the Civil Wars, and his Catholic mother, Queen Henrietta Maria, as an idolatress. This was an uneasy alliance that divided Scottish opinion, and it also antagonized his potential supporters amongst the English High Church and Catholics. Finally, in January 1651, Charles was formally crowned King of Scotland at Scone.

The news that he was attempting to raise an army in Scotland to fight for his throne generated little enthusiasm in England, despite the encouragement of Royalist agents. The economy was beginning to improve after a series of disastrous harvests in 1647–9 and wages were rising. One sign of increased confidence from Worcestershire is the evidence of a renewal of gentry house-building, such as Sir William Cooke's new mansion at Norgrove Court, Feckenham, built in 1649. Few wished to see the country thrown into turmoil again.

Parliament had taken steps to prevent any rebellion in support of the new king by forbidding public meetings such as horse-races, hunting and football matches which could be used as a cover by any conspirators. Where definite plans of revolt were uncovered, as in Norfolk in December 1650, the ringleaders were promptly hanged to deter others. Another warning of the strength of the Commonwealth was the expansion of the New Model Army by the creation of six new regiments of horse and ten regiments of foot. By the end of the Worcester campaign, the New Model Army comprised eighteen regiments of horse and thirty regiments of foot. The army was sent into Scotland in June 1650, with Oliver Cromwell, newly returned from Ireland, initially as second-in-command under Thomas Fairfax. Fairfax, however, had no heart for the impending war against his former allies and resigned, leaving Cromwell (aged fifty-two) as 'Captain-General and Commander in Chief' of the Parliamentary army.

Cromwell was a very different character from the King and his young aristocratic generals. His life until the age of forty had been as a Huntingdonshire landowner and farmer. He had served briefly as an MP for Huntingdon in 1628 but began to come to prominence with the return of Parliament in 1640. By then he was already in the circle of puritan leaders and on the third day of Parliament presented the petition of John Lilburne, later to become the leader of the Levellers. He was described at the time in these terms: 'his countenance swollen and reddish, his voice sharp and untuneable, and his eloquence full of fervour'. He was an energetic and passionate man, driven by his puritan beliefs, who strove to reconcile his principles with expediency. Cromwell had seen no military experience before the outbreak of the Civil War, when at the age of forty-three he raised a troop of horse for Parliament. Thereafter he brought a new professionalism and discipline to the English armies and a calculating strategic mind. He came to Worcester in 1651 having never lost a battle in which he commanded and seemed to relish fighting against greater odds. This must inevitably have brought a confidence and sureness of purpose to the Parliamentary forces at Worcester that the Royalists simply could not match.

The initial campaign in Scotland during 1650 appeared to go the way of the Scots, and by the beginning of September it seemed as though Cromwell had been outmanoeuvred by the Scottish commander, David Leslie (his former comrade at the battle of Marston Moor). Cromwell was forced to withdraw to Dunbar, his army having taken heavy casualties through disease. At this stage, the Scots greatly outnumbered the Parliamentary army with a force possibly as large as 22,000 men against Cromwell's 10,500. It looked as though the latter would have to fight with their backs to the sea or try to manage a risky evacuation by the fleet. Cromwell, however, was determined to take the initiative and, on

3 September, rather than wait to be attacked he launched a pre-emptive assault on the Scottish army that was forming up in front of him. The New Model Army attacked as dawn was breaking and completely surprised the sleepy Scots, many of whom were still in their tents. The musketeers desperately tried to light their match before the enemy fell upon them: in just one hour, three thousand of the Scots were killed with a further ten thousand captured. The survivors of Leslie's army were put to flight and retreated to Stirling. Unfortunately, the Parliamentary army was unable to exploit their advantage as Cromwell fell seriously ill soon after. He wrote to his wife immediately following the battle: 'I grow an old man, and feel infirmities of age marvellously stealing upon me.'[1] A chill was followed by the dysentery that affected large numbers of his troops and was made worse by bouts of malaria. He did not fully recover until June 1651, but meanwhile both sides recruited fresh troops. In an ominous precursor of the battle of Worcester, and against Cromwell's wishes, the Scottish prisoners from Dunbar were treated very harshly, many being herded into Durham Cathedral and kept in appalling conditions. Sixteen hundred of them died within a space of fifty-eight days, and many of the survivors were transported to the New World.

Cromwell renewed the campaign in the spring, firstly by rebuilding the morale and discipline of his army and then trying, unsuccessfully, to draw Leslie out into open battle. He was determined not to risk another dreadful winter in Scotland. Eventually, on 20 July, General John Lambert was able to rout the Scottish army at Inverkeithing, Fife. The dead included between five hundred and seven hundred MacLeans (up to 90 per cent of their total strength), as well as their young chief, Sir Hector. This raised the spirits of the army and was followed by preparations for the capture of Perth to cut off the King from his supplies. Cromwell was now manoeuvring Charles into a trap in which he would be obliged to follow Cromwell's own preferences for action. There were three options. Charles could try to escape into the Highlands: this would commit Cromwell to a long campaign in inhospitable territory which, in the light of Cromwell's illnesses of the previous year, he may well have not survived. Or Charles could simply abandon his attempt to win back his crown and sail back to France, which would have prolonged the expectation of future invasion, encouraged continued plotting by English Royalists and required the maintenance of a large, expensive, standing army by Parliament. The third option might have seemed at first sight to be the most risky: this was for the King to invade England itself. This option was bolstered by Royalist hopes (encouraged by some of the King's advisers) of raising fresh English support from former Royalists and disillusioned Presbyterians. At the same time, however, this would give Cromwell and the Council of State (the 41-strong executive arm of the Rump Parliament) time to raise, supply and manoeuvre overwhelming forces against him.

Cromwell evidently had sufficient confidence in the likely failure of any large-scale rising in support of the King, and in his ability to bring Charles to final battle on a territory of his own choosing. If successful, and if the King could be killed, then it would end the threat of Royalist rebellion once and for all. The King's advisers also clearly saw the dangers in accepting this option, but Charles decided to gamble all on the prospects of a large-scale popular revolt in his favour. He had, after all, been frequently advised that there were indeed large numbers of supporters in England ready to rise on his behalf. Plans for some form of rising in the country had certainly existed although the expected scale of support is not known. Correspondence from King Charles was intercepted which led, on 29 March, to the arrest of a key Royalist agent, Thomas Coke. Coke promptly revealed the names of his associates which resulted in the arrest of those implicated Royalists and Presbyterians. In his plan, Charles also hoped to outrun the cream of the New Model Army that could be expected to follow him from Scotland, and only have to face inexperienced troops and militia based in England. Thus it was that the King decided to head from Carlisle to Worcester and use the latter as a base to try to rally further support before moving on London.

Worcestershire was as important strategically in 1651 as it had been in the First Civil War. Above all, it controlled the bridging points on the east–west route from Wales to London. Wales had been a major source of recruitment for King Charles I during the First Civil War and might conceivably be so again. Charles knew that ultimately he would have to seize the capital to win back his father's throne, but in the meantime the agricultural base of Worcestershire would supply his army and the ironworking industry of north Worcestershire would re-arm it. In addition, the county had the emotional cachet of containing the last Royalist garrisons in England to capitulate at the end of the First Civil War.[2] The King was also hoping to capitalize on the expected personal loyalty of the people of adjacent Gloucestershire to their famous former governor of Gloucester, the Presbyterian Edward Massey, who had now joined the Royalists as second-in-command of the English contingent.

King Charles and his advisers had, however, miscalculated hopelessly on the degree of support that they might receive. Parliament had forestalled the Royalist–Presbyterian plot in England, arresting many potential supporters. It was also able to raise willing fresh troops and mobilize the local militias, whose eventual performance in action probably surprised everyone. The King received very little support from the English people, who could not face the prospect of another war and who were especially provoked by a detested foreign army acting on behalf of a covenanted king. They also had too healthy a respect for the strength of Cromwell's army and his generalship to risk joining a cause that they believed was already doomed. Richard Baxter of Kidderminster (1615–91) summarized the feelings of many in considering that Charles's march into England was more a sign of defeat in retreating from Cromwell than an advance to reclaim his throne: 'The success of Cromwell at Dunbarre and afterwards had put a Fear upon all Men, and the manner of the Scots, coming away, persuaded all Men that Necessity forced them, and they were look'd upon rather as flying than as marching into England; and few Men will put themselves into a flying army which is pursued by the conquering enemy.'[3]

Many of the Scots were equally concerned. The Duke of Hamilton described the march into England as a 'desperate venture in which people were laughing at the ridiculousness of our condition'.[4] David Leslie, the veteran commander of the cavalry and King Charles's second-in-command, was even more melancholy, 'for he well knew that army, how well soever it looked, would not fight'. His spirit had

Richard Baxter (1615–91). This puritan preacher from Kidderminster argued against the campaign in Scotland but did not join the Royalist army in Worcester because of 'sore eyes'. (Almonry Museum, Evesham, with permission)

been broken by the defeat at Dunbar in the previous year in which he saw fate in 'the visible hand of God' and his depression continued throughout the Worcester campaign. Many men simply refused to follow at all from Scotland and more soldiers deserted on the march south. This was despite the considerable efforts of Charles who had made a determined effort to cultivate the loyalty of the common soldiers in the army (at times to the great suspicion of their officers). With such difficulties, compounded by a lack of provisions, it is not surprising that a Parliamentary report described the troops as being mutinous, kept moving only by the promise of fresh supplies when they eventually reached Worcester. Meanwhile, General Monck had been left in Scotland with six thousand men to mop up Scottish resistance and destroy any power base for the King to return to, even if he succeeded in avoiding Cromwell.

Estimates vary, but King Charles was forced to rely almost entirely on a tired and poorly equipped army of about 11,000 to 13,000 Scottish troops, comprising about 3,000 to 4,000 horse and about 7,000 to 9,000 foot. This was after losing about 13,000 dead and captured at Dunbar in September 1650 and another 2,000 men at Inverkeithing. When the Scots, under their same general David Leslie, had invaded England in 1645 in support of Parliament, they had caused havoc over large parts of Worcestershire, stealing livestock, trampling crops, breaking up church fonts and looting property, and were still remembered with great bitterness, especially along the line of march that the soldiers took once again in 1651. They had caused further devastation in the north of England during their invasion of 1648 in support of Charles I. A blacksmith from the region later declared that the King deserved to hang 'more than all the rest for bringing in the Scots'.[5] Now, to help whip up fresh anti-Scottish feeling, the news-sheet *Mercurius Britannicus* listed every Scottish invasion of England since that of King Malcolm in 1071. National pride was at stake. The Hereford Parliamentarian Miles Hill had published a pamphlet in 1650 on the depredations committed by the Scots in their siege of Hereford in 1645: it was no coincidence that the King received no support from Hereford in 1651. To counter such fears, the King had ordered the Scots not to plunder on this occasion when they entered England. It seems that the King's policy was generally respected, despite assertions by Whitelock that 'after Warrington the Scots began to plunder extremely'.[6] There were certainly some claims for damages. Lieutenant-Colonel Brooke (of the militia) asserted that the Scottish horse had eaten whole fields of corn from his estates in Cheshire.[7] One Royalist officer claimed, however, that on 12 August some soldiers had been shot for stealing apples from orchards and even for taking a pint of beer without paying for it (Appendix 1.3).[8] Colonel Whiteley went further in this proclamation of saintliness and claimed that 'a flock of geese may feed all night in our camp and not one be missed in the morning'.[9] The opinions of these men were obviously biased but even the Kidderminster clergyman Richard Baxter accepted that the Scots behaved better than on their last foray into the county.

The efforts to avoid plunder might go some way to explain the poor condition of the Scots when they reached Worcester, many suffering from dysentery. In any case, the parliamentary armies were not blameless in this respect. Lady Anne Thornton of Nether Witton in Northumberland objected to having to quarter

2,450 horses and men from Cromwell's army on her estate for just a single night. She added that apart from having to feed the horses, the men had spoiled 30 cartloads of hay in making up their bedding, had accidentally burnt down a barn and had killed 16 sheep. She later received £95 5s 6d in compensation.[10] Any effort to restrict plundering, which many of the soldiers would have regarded as normal practice to supplement a paltry diet, had little practical effect in encouraging support. The spectre of a foreign, plundering army was too fixed in the popular mind and was relentlessly encouraged by Parliament. Major General Harrison exhorted the Committee of Yorkshire to provide support 'that the good of the land may not be devoured by such caterpillars'.[11] King Charles also miscalculated in his hope that Massey would attract his former supporters. Massey had won a fearsome reputation for his raiding parties into Worcestershire in the First Civil War and in the event proved incapable of attracting any personal loyalty from the region.

Even the support that the King was able to attract showed little signs of unity. His army was an uneasy union of long-time English Royalists and disillusioned Presbyterians, and the Scots divided between 'Covenanters' and 'Engagers', lowlanders and highlanders. The former Parliamentarians in the King's retinue included not only Edward Massey but also, briefly, Colonel John Birch and his brother Samuel. Birch had been responsible for the capture of Hereford in 1645 which would not have endeared him to local Royalists, and even Massey described him as 'a vile man'.[12] Both Massey and Birch were Presbyterians who had been expelled from Parliament in Pride's Purge of December 1648. There is, however, no evidence that Birch actually fought at Worcester. Thomas Lord Bruce, himself a Royalist, disdainfully referred to the army as 'That mongrel Scotch army'. The 'Covenanters' adhered to the Scottish National Covenant of 1638 to resist any change to the Presbyterian Church. The impetus to the movement had been the attempt of King Charles I and Archbishop Laud to introduce a version of the English Prayer Book. The Covenant became a symbol of resistance to English interference in Scottish affairs. The 'Engagers' were those Scots who, feeling betrayed by the English Parliament after having helped it win the First Civil War, had formed an alliance with Charles I in 1647. In return for military support to win back the throne, Charles I had acceded to the Solemn League and Covenant (as negotiated with the English Parliament in 1643) but only agreed to establish Presbyterianism in England for a three-year period. This expedient was regarded as a betrayal of the National Covenant by the Scottish Kirk for whom the war was a religious crusade founded on strict principles.

It was only following the disaster at Dunbar in 1650 that the Covenanters had been forced to swallow their religious principles and to accept the 'Engagers' and 'malignant' Royalists, even Catholics, back into the ranks of the army. They did not do so with good grace and equally it must have been difficult for Charles to conceal some satisfaction at the decline in influence of his religious tormentors. No doubt exaggerating, resentful Covenanter leaders even claimed that Charles was so pleased to see the decline of influence of the Kirk party that he had fallen on his knees to praise God for the defeat of his army at Dunbar.[13] Even now, many of the Scots would not take part in the campaign. Some of the western

The Scottish soldiers were exhausted by the time they reached Worcester and refused to march further. They were poorly equipped and in a low state of morale. Nevertheless they were the only men prepared to support their king in any great numbers. (Stephen Rigby)

clans, including the Camerons and MacDonalds, saw their priority as defending Scotland rather than invading England. This was not least because they feared leaving their lands at the mercy of neighbouring clans that remained at home![14] Others in the Kirk party such as the Earl of Argyle saw the defeat as a sign of divine displeasure and refused to support the King further.

The Scottish generals – Leslie, Hamilton and Middleton – and the young English commander, the 23-year-old Duke of Buckingham, were wracked with their own personal jealousies that greatly reduced the efficiency of the army. The young King had been able to take personal command after the Kirk party lost political control, but did not have the experience to unite his young generals (whose average age was only about thirty-three years). The inexperienced Buckingham believed that he had rights of seniority, as commander of the English contingent, when the army entered England, and therefore sulked when the Scottish generals retained their influence. Clarendon wrote how Buckingham refused to attend council meetings, would not speak to the King and did not change his clothes, 'nor did he recover his ill humour whilst the army stayed at Worcester'.[15] Neither could Charles temper the recklessness of generals such as Hamilton against the caution of others like Leslie. In many respects, this was a cause lost well before the army reached the gates of Worcester. As such, their mere presence is a tribute to those men who did follow Charles out of a simple loyalty to their monarch.

Cromwell was determined to crush this invasion completely and so prevent the possibility of civil war breaking out once again in England. He had the ability to raise forces that would massively outnumber the Scots and, in contrast to the army of King Charles, the Parliamentary army was well disciplined and (at least against the threat of an invading army) united in purpose in what was now both a political and religious crusade. Unsuitable officers that faltered were weeded out so that one wrote from Scotland in June of 'great and daily' change of command. Those who remained were the most able as well as the most dedicated. This tightening of the command structure naturally caused some unease and it was said that 'a man must have a good footing' in the army to survive.[16] Colonel Berry took a strong line on discipline when he assumed command of his regiment of horse in 1651 with a number of court martials and even an execution, but discipline was not enough: Cromwell claimed to be able to pay for regular supplies as his army moved south and so avoid the traditional expedient of 'free-quarter' (although he had suffered from problems in paying his troops whilst in Scotland). On 18 August he wrote from Ripon to the mayor and corporation of Doncaster advising them that he would be requiring bread, cheese, butter and meat to be supplied when his army arrived but that 'the country shall receive ready money'.[17] In this he had the enormous advantage of the Council of State to help organize logistical support. By contrast, King Charles was let down by English supporters in his increasingly desperate pleas for funding.

As the pursuit of the Scottish army began, Cromwell stayed with the slow-moving artillery and nine regiments of foot, together with two regiments of horse. One report put the total number in this army at about 10,000 men.[18] They began a march from Perth down the east side of the Pennines, parallel to the route taken

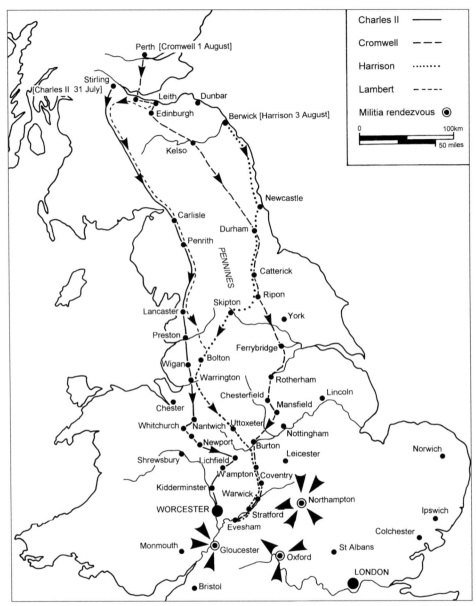

Map showing the route of the Scottish and Parliamentary armies, August–September 1651.

by the Scots from Stirling. He sent on ahead his commissary-general John Lambert with 4,000 of his best horse to shadow the rear of the Scottish army. Lambert was ordered to 'attend the motion of the enemy, and endeavour the keeping of them together, as also to impede his march'.[19] His task was then to rendezvous with the 3,000 horse and dragoons from the militias raised in May under General Thomas Harrison, and those men of Colonel Nathaniel Rich, Colonel Sanders and Colonel Barton who together comprised the reserve units based in northern England. This latter force was now moving westwards across the Pennines from Newcastle. Their immediate role was to box in the left flank of the Scots, to 'flank them, straighten their provisions, and do service as you can see opportunities upon them'.[20] With Lambert to the rear and Harrison to the east, the Scots were to be shepherded down the west coast and, above all, prevented from making a break towards London. Any attempt to bring the Scots to battle would, however, wait until Cromwell felt in a position to bring the maximum number of forces to bear.

Lambert and Harrison met at Haslemoor in Lancashire on 14 August with a combined strength of about 12,000–14,000 men. A total of 3,000 had joined from the Lancashire militias alone.[21] More joined from Cheshire. In preparation for the impending campaign, Cromwell had written to Parliament on 4 August warning that the King might try to escape into England and suggesting, therefore, that they raise the militia.[22] These men would both reinforce the New Model Army and forestall any Royalist support in the country. The news of the King's march into England, and Cromwell's evident intention to allow this to happen, had caused some initial panic which was overcome as the Council of State issued a flurry of orders to local officials, mobilizing the militia nationwide and providing for the defence of key towns. General Fleetwood (Cromwell's second-in-command) had been recalled to London in February 1651 following his election to the Council of State. He was now ordered to raise new troops from the Midlands, and to cover any attempted breakout of the Scottish line of march towards the capital. London mobilized 15,500 men of the Trained Bands under General Skippon to defend the capital if need be. In addition, ships were sent to watch the ports of France and Flanders to warn of any reinforcements from the continent.[23] The *Charles* was ordered to patrol the coast off Milford Haven and round to the Severn.[24] Thus there was a closely coordinated plan for defence in considerable depth. However, Worcester was as far as the government was prepared to allow the Royalist army to march southwards, with a mobilization at Gloucester as the ultimate anvil against which the Scots would be crushed.

The reaction of the government towards anyone contemplating joining the Royalist army was also made abundantly clear. On the day that Charles entered Worcester (22 August), the conspirators Love and Gibbons were executed in London. Four days later Charles and his abettors were declared rebels and traitors; commissions of martial law were issued to officers in Lancashire, Chester, Shropshire and North Wales to try anyone found guilty of giving assistance to the invaders. Arrests were quickly made; Cromwell was himself ordered to proceed against a Captain Young of Worcester 'for an example and terror to others'.[25]

Cromwell was eventually able to concentrate an army at Worcester with a total strength of about 30,000; the men were later disparagingly termed by the Royalist historian Blount as the 'scum and froth of the whole kingdom' but were to prove their worth in battle.[26] They included seasoned troops of the veteran New Model Army regiments and newly raised regular regiments; about one-third was made up from county militias that had poured in to rendezvous from counties including Essex, Suffolk, Cheshire, Oxfordshire, Gloucestershire and Worcestershire (see Appendix 2). Other militias were kept in mobilization points that encircled Worcester. This rapid mobilization reflects a genuine enthusiasm to support the Commonwealth against foreign invasion and is one of the most notable features of the campaign. The effort was not without problems. As the first of the militia units had been mobilized in May for the campaign, Cromwell and Harrison shared concerns as to the value of such troops and they had to be stiffened with regular officers.[27] But many men were experienced veterans, and in action they were later described as performing 'with singular good service'.[28] The Cheshire militia were singled out for especial praise by the Council of State for their 'cheerful readiness' to appear in such large numbers.[29] The Essex militia ran part of the way to Worcester so as not to miss the battle. The enthusiasm was not universal. Although some Surrey units may have fought at the battle, the Surrey militia under Sir Richard Onslow were reported to have dallied on their march until they knew who had won.[30] Cromwell reported to Parliament that he did not know what side they might have supported if they had actually arrived in time, contradicting the later history of Whitelock who claimed that the regiment had 'marched hard' to come to the battle.[31] Robert Wood, who later stood as an MP for Surrey in 1654, was criticized as being 'a profane swearer and bad life who refused assistance in sending forces to Worcester'. Wood's supporters countered by saying that he had sent a man and a horse.[32]

While Cromwell and the Council of State were coordinating the massing of their army, Charles moved further into England; but it was no victorious entry into his kingdom. The Royalists were being sucked deeper and deeper into a void with ever-increasing problems of supply and no ready place of sanctuary. The troops were forced to take shelter where they could and were tired, wet and hungry; their clothing and shoes were falling apart. On 16 August the King reached the River Mersey at Warrington. There was a brief skirmish around the bridge but Lambert (to the frustration of Harrison) would not risk his main force until the total Parliamentary army was properly gathered. Lambert and Harrison withdrew to Knutsford in order to protect the road to London and the King was therefore allowed to proceed southwards. The Earl of Derby arrived shortly afterwards with a small force of only 250 foot and 60 horse from the Isle of Man to support the King and they remained in Lancashire to try to raise further support. The local Parliamentary commander, Colonel Robert Lilburne, took this threat seriously and there were a number of skirmishes with the recruiting parties. Significantly, Derby was now able to recruit without the spectre of a foreign army around him and successfully raised around 1,500 men, although this was far short of the promised total of 7,300. Hopes of recruiting further support were dashed when Derby was decisively defeated at Wigan on 25 August. Here,

Lilburne's 800 men, comprising his own exhausted regiment of horse and the garrisons of Chester and Liverpool, were outnumbered. Nevertheless, about sixty Royalists were killed and another 400 taken prisoner; Lilburne was reported to have lost only ten men. This crushing victory encouraged more overt support for Parliament from the local population. Lilburne reported that 'The country begins now to bring in prisoners and show themselves to me, but before but a few appeared.'[33]

Meanwhile, the Scottish army had continued on its march into Cheshire in an increasingly sorry state. At Nantwich it was described as being 'discontented and sick', with the King being forced to go 'cap in hand' to beg it to go on; the King had to order Nantwich to pay £3,000 within a day towards the costs of new shoes and other provisions for the army.[34] Coming into Shropshire, they bypassed Shrewsbury where the governor, Colonel Mackworth, pointedly refused access to the 'Commander-in-Chief of the Scottish army' rather than acknowledge the King, and then moved from Wolverhampton into Worcestershire.

Cromwell's men were in not much better shape. The speed of the march from Scotland, with soldiers marching 20 miles a day in their shirt sleeves and using carts to carry their equipment, left some of the men exhausted and sick. They marched 300 miles in three weeks, having taken only one day's rest. Conditions were not helped by violent storms with hailstones as big as musket balls that killed birds at Towcester. The Council of State had to make special provision for the sick to be left behind in counties stretching from Northumberland down to Leicestershire. By 26 August, Cromwell had also worn out his draught horses from the artillery train and 100 more had to be commandeered from Northamptonshire at a cost of £300 18s 2d.[35] Plans were already being made for the impending battle. On the same day, expecting to have to undertake a long siege of Worcester, he also ordered 'five thousand shovels, spades and pickaxes, thirty tons of match and four hundred barrels of gunpowder' to be sent to Gloucester in readiness.[36] Suppliers offered to provide the tools at the rate of 15d per spade and shovel and 2s 8d per pickaxe but, possibly having experienced earlier army contracts, they were careful to insist that this was on the condition of payment in cash rather than by credit.[37]

How then would Worcestershire react to the gathering conflict? The county was clearly seen as a potential target for the Royalists, although there is little surviving evidence for the basis of this belief. Some lack of enthusiasm for the Parliamentary cause can be gathered from the fact that only sixteen out of the seventy-two members of the City Chamber turned up to hear the formal reading of the Engagement 'to be true and faithful to the Commonwealth of England' on 14 February 1650.[38] But this was a long way from risking all in open rebellion. On 13 January 1651, the Council of State ordered 'That special care be taken for the security of Worcester, Gloucester and Hereford, that all dangerous and suspicious persons be removed, and an account taken of all arms and ammunition.' All weapons and ammunition were to be confiscated.[39] One person upon whom suspicion fell was Sir William Russell of Strensham, who was accused of passing information under an assumed name to the royal court on the continent.[40] There was, however, no evidence from Coke to suggest that Worcestershire was

*Parliamentary
cavalry shadowed
and harassed the
Scots as they
marched further into
England. Here, a
troop of horse
prepare to ambush a
Scottish column.
(Stephen Rigby)*

specifically implicated in his plot, although his arrest evidently spurred further precautionary measures locally. In March, the Council of State ordered that the city be made indefensible. Whereas the town defences of Gloucester (solidly loyal during the First Civil War) were ordered to be restored, at Worcester they were ordered to be levelled 'for special reasons' as there were 'some designs on foot by the enemy against that place'.[41] The demolition work was to be supervised by Nicholas Lechmere of Hanley Castle and Baron John Wylde of Droitwich. One bonus accrued from this action was that the government netted a profit of £23 from the sale of materials. In April, the Council of State also questioned whether the defences of nearby Madresfield House outside Malvern (a garrison fort of the First Civil War) had been made untenable, as discussed the previous year.

This was a society in which movement was tightly controlled. Parliament prevented some former Royalists from returning to Worcestershire, including (on 19 May) another former Royalist governor of Worcester, Colonel Samuel Sandys of Ombersley (1615–85). This was the sort of person who could have been expected to act as a local focus of support for the King (as, indeed, he did for the rest of the period of the Commonwealth). Conversely, John Washburn of Wichenford was refused permission to leave the county in 1650. He had only just paid a fine of £797 10s to redeem his estates after taking part in the 1646 siege of Worcester. The intention of these measures was clearly to neutralize the area against any possible attempt to rise in support of the King.

Nevertheless, at least some elements of the local community were considered loyal to the government. On 31 March, the Council of State appointed Colonel John James of Astley as garrison commander to raise and command the horse and dragoons of the Worcestershire militia.[42] A levy of troops from Gloucester was also put under his command.[43] These men were to play an important role in ensuing events.

THREE

The Armies

What was the nature of the armies now moving towards Worcestershire? Civil War armies were ponderous bodies. During the march down to Scotland both sides were concerned to get the troops moving as quickly as possible. The bulk was composed of infantry, organized in regiments with a theoretical strength of *c.* 1,200 men but more usually *c.* 700 and even as low as *c.* 300. Two-thirds of these consisted of musketeers, armed mainly with 12-bore matchlock muskets but with an increasing number (particularly those guarding the artillery) armed with the more modern firelock (flintlock) muskets, which were safer than the matchlocks in that they did not rely on the musketeers carrying lengths of lighted match. Huge quantities of match would be required to supply a major battle such as Worcester. By 1651 up to 20 per cent of musketeers may have been armed with firelock muskets. When the London Trained Bands re-equipped in 1650, one-third of the muskets were firelocks. The muskets fired a soft lead ball *c.* 1⅓ oz (38 g) in weight, although there was considerable variation – hence the importance for every musketeer to carry his own bullet mould to ensure that the shot would fit his own particular weapon (otherwise the soldier would have had to chew or clip the ball to size). The muskets had a range of up to *c.* 150 yd (137 m) but were probably accurate to only *c.* 50–60 yd (46–55 m) in the hands of most soldiers. This was, however, less important when being fired *en masse*. The most devastating tactic was to fire by 'Swedish salvee' (salvo). The ranks of musketeers would double up to provide a body of men only two or three ranks deep who would kneel, stoop and stand in a tight formation, with the men on the ends of the line turning to fire towards the centre of the target. The individual inaccuracy of the weapon then became irrelevant and the combined, simultaneous, firepower at a range of perhaps only 20 yards could tear a hole in any enemy formation. The disadvantage was that it then left one's musketeers vulnerable whilst they reloaded and was therefore only used by troops confident of victory and often as a preparation to a final charge. The normal rate of fire for an individual would have been around two rounds per minute but a disciplined formation could maintain an almost continuous fire against the enemy by firing in successive ranks. The ammunition was carried either in bandoliers comprising, typically, twelve flasks each containing a loose charge of black powder or, increasingly by 1651, as preformed paper cartridges carried in leather pouches or haversacks. The cartridges had no great advantage in terms of speed of loading but made resupply easier during the course of a long battle such as Worcester. Fresh supplies of powder would have been kept to the rear in small barrels called 'budge barrels'. The dangers of carrying loose powder in bandoliers is graphically illustrated by an incident at Worcester during the battle for Fort Royal. A Scottish musketeer was attempting to refill his bandolier from a supply of powder that he had scooped up into his bonnet. Whilst he was kneeling on the ground to do this a second musketeer came up and, not realizing what was happening between his legs, stood over the first man and fired his weapon at the enemy. The inevitable happened. A spark from his pan ignited the powder below and both men suffered horrific powder burns, as the following account of the incident describes.

A Souldier in the time of service being in the Fort-Royal at *Worcester*, hastily fetched his bonnet full of Gun-powder; and whilest he was filling his Bandeliers, another Souldier carelesly bestrides it, to make a Shot at one of the Enemies which he saw lying *perdue*. In firing his Musket, a spark flew out of the Pan, and gave fire to the Powder underneath him, and grievously burned the Hands, Arms, Breast, Neck and Face of him that was filling his Bandeliers. And as to himself, he likewise was burned and scorched in all the upper part of his Thighs, *Scrotum*, the Muscles of the *Abdomen*, and the Coats of the Testicles to the *Erythroides*, so that the Cremasters were visible. And indeed it was to be feared, that, when the Eschar should cast off from his Belly, his Bowells would have tumbled out.[1]

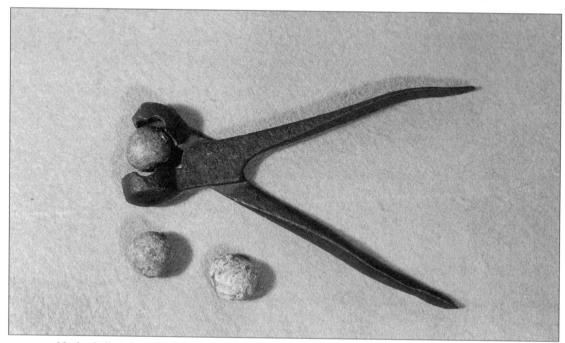

Musket balls and mould. Soldiers would either make their own musket balls or have to trim mass-produced balls in order to make them fit their own weapon. (Courtesy Worcester Museums Service)

The well-organized supply of the troops with ammunition during the course of the battle was critical to the success of the parliamentary troops. A musketeer is here being given a fresh supply of pre-made cartridges by an NCO. (Stephen Rigby)

The musketeers wore no armour although their thick woollen coats gave important protection against powder burns from their own weapons. Although they carried a short, cheap, sword (a 'tuck'), if the battle came to hand-to-hand combat they were more likely to reverse their muskets to use the heavy butt ends as very effective clubs, with their hands gripped around the hot gun barrels. During the Civil War, officers despairingly complained that the soldiers used to blunt their swords by using them to chop firewood and on occasion tried to take them away to issue them only before a battle. Swords in peacetime were, however, a status symbol normally only carried by the gentry and so the right of the soldier to carry them was jealously guarded.

The musketeers were protected from cavalry by blocks of pikemen carrying 16–18 ft (4.8–5.4 m) long pikes made of ash with an iron spear point. As a common means of attack on a block of pikemen was to try to cut off the spear points of one's opponents, the points were protected by 4 ft (1.2 m) long 'langets' or strips of iron which were riveted onto the shaft below the head itself. The unwieldy pike was still considered the more 'honourable' weapon and certainly required the most burly men in the regiment to handle it. Pikemen originally wore armour consisting of back and breast plates with 'tassets' covering the thighs, but it was not proof against musket balls and by the time of the battle of Worcester it is likely that few of the pikemen wore armour beyond their iron 'pot' helmet.

In open battle, the regiments would form up in ranks six to eight deep, divided into a number of divisions. Skirmishing parties (or 'forlorn hopes') would be placed ahead of the main formation. According to theory, three regiments might be grouped together within a 'tertia', with three of the latter comprising a brigade. In practice, a brigade could comprise a much smaller unit. Each regiment would consist of a 'stand' of pikes in the centre, flanked by two equal bodies of musketeers. However, the use of the pike was declining and it is not certain how many pikemen were included within the regiments at the time of the battle of Worcester. Reference was indeed made to the 'push of pike' during the battle, but this may well have been merely a euphemism for hand-to-hand fighting. If pikemen did engage with the enemy foot in close combat they may well have simply dropped their pikes after the shock of the first thrust and fought with swords instead.[2] They would have advanced in close formation with their levelled pikes held shoulder high and aimed at the faces of the opposing ranks of pikemen. This was as much a test of nerve as anything else as the men saw rows of iron points heading steadily towards them, but once the pikes had passed their target they became quite useless as a weapon and the urgent need was then to cut down their opponents with the sword before they could retreat and re-form. Sir John Smythe had described the tactic in 1591. His advice was 'with one puissant charge and thrust to enter and disorder, wound, open, and break the one with the other'.[3]

The cavalry were then, as ever, considered the more socially superior. They consisted of light horse, wearing a thick buff leather coat with breast and back plate over the top, iron 'lobster pot' helmet and armed with sword, pistols and/or dog-lock carbine. The heavy cutting sword was the primary weapon. The pistols

Trooper's armour found in a barn at Lulsley, Worcs. This is reputed to have been used at the battle of Worcester. (Private Collection)

and carbines were both 24 bore (that is, they fired a lead ball of just over ½ oz or 14 g) but the pistols were only effective at point blank range. Both the Scottish and Parliamentary armies received fresh supplies of sets of cavalry armour during the war, although it is possible that some troops at the end of the Civil War fought only in their buff coats. The better quality examples of buff coat would have been sufficient to turn a sword blade but not a bullet. In July 1651, Cromwell complained that equipment for the horse in Scotland was in short supply and ordered 1,000 back and breast plates and 1,500 'pots' (helmets). The cavalry was organized by troops of sixty men into regiments of 400–500. Their task in battle was to first drive off the enemy cavalry and then try to encircle the enemy's foot and attack it in the flanks and rear, causing sufficient confusion for the infantry to break up the enemy formation from the front. They charged at a fast trot, boot to boot and with drawn swords, usually three to six ranks deep. The opposition cavalry would counter this with a countercharge, also at the trot.

There was also a hybrid type of mounted infantry – the dragoons, who rode into battle but were equipped as musketeers with firelocks and fought on foot. In a pitched battle they were intended to strike at the flanks of an enemy. Although they were considered to have a poor status, with mounts to match, the dragoons were to form an important part of the Worcester campaign through their greater mobility and were used as advance guards and scouts. The Scots also mounted many of their infantry as dragoons to speed up the march south, a practice also considered by the Parliamentary generals. There were reports that Cromwell had considered mounting 5,000 foot whilst at Chesterfield but this was rejected for fear of antagonizing the local population who would have been expected to supply the mounts. As an emergency measure preceding the battle of Worcester itself, some Parliamentary infantry were mounted behind troopers in order to reinforce the bridgehead at Upton-upon-Severn as quickly as possible.

Although their equipment was on the whole similar to that of the English forces, Scottish units were also notable for the inclusion of lancers and longbow-men. Disparaging comments were made about these on the march southwards but no mention is made of their use during the actual battle of Worcester. The highland levies were the poorest-equipped of the Scottish forces but one should not simply imagine the stereotype of a plaid-clad warrior carrying only the traditional arms of broadsword and small shield ('targ') and engaging in wild charges. Stuart Reid has convincingly argued against the existence of a specific 'highland charge'.[4] Wherever possible, the highlanders would have been re-armed with musket and pike (as references in the battle show); their greatest problem at Worcester was probably their shortage of ammunition, which encouraged closing to hand-to-hand combat as the only practical alternative to being shot down at a distance.

Scottish artillery at the battle, under the highly experienced General of Artillery, James Wemyss of Caskierberran, was limited, comprising only sixteen light leather cannon. Although possessing the great advantage of mobility, as this type of gun was drawn by a single horse, it had to be used with care and was regarded as a limited-shot weapon for supporting an assault, or in a last ditch defence rather than for maintaining a long bombardment. Mounted in pairs or in

Scottish leather cannon, made by James Wemyss. They are made from an iron tube strengthened by iron rings and closed at the breech with an iron plug. The barrels were then bound in hemp rope before being sewn into a leather sleeve. The guns were usually mounted in pairs or in fours. (Photograph: National Museum of Scotland)

fours, they would fire a solid cannon ball of *c.* 1½ lb (0.7 kg) or anti-personnel case-shot. The artillery at Worcester may have been reinforced by the abandoned larger cannon of the Parliamentary garrison, although these should have been 'spiked' by the retreating troops to prevent them being used. Unfortunately, in any case, it is doubtful whether the Scots would have had enough trained gunners to fully crew the cannon, or sufficient powder for a prolonged action. Nevertheless, the Scots managed to provide a sustained bombardment at the opening stage of the battle at least.

Massey's supporters mistakenly gave credit to him for the supply of the leather cannon. He had, however, been developing a new type of 'firepike' (leather bottles fastened to the end of pikes and filled with a burning, spitting, material) which were intended to deter charging horses and were considered particularly useful in street fighting. It is probable that these were used at Worcester, although no mention of them has survived. The Parliamentary artillery train was undoubtedly superior to that of the Scots although its exact size is not known. Cromwell had been forced to leave his heavy siege guns and mortars in Scotland with Monck.

Instead, he is likely to have brought his field guns consisting of 9 lb (4 kg) demi-culverins, 5¼ lb (2.3 kg) sakers and smaller guns, pulled by teams of up to four horses or oxen. Their range was up to 1,800 paces with a normal rate of fire of 10–15 rounds per hour. The columns of Fleetwood and Lambert also brought their own artillery to the battle. Although there is no record of any heavier siege guns being brought to Worcester before the battle on 3 September it is very likely that arrangements to provide these were also well in hand.

Early Civil War battles could be confusing affairs as there was no distinction in the uniforms of the two sides. The cavalry wore plain buff coats; the infantry regiments were distinguished by a variety of coloured woollen coats; and officers wore a variety of civilian dress. To reduce the obvious scope for confusion, armies would adopt field signs (a sprig of greenery, ribbon or piece of paper in a hat, or a coloured armband) to differentiate the troops on the day. The Worcester battlefield in 1651, however, would have seen more of contrast between the Venice red coats of the New Model Army and the 'hodden grey' coats and blue bonnets of the Scots national army. This distinction would not have been universal: the Scottish supply system had broken down and many would have replaced worn-out clothing with whatever they could find. Five Worcester clothiers were forced, on 2/3 September, to provide £453 1s 5d worth of red cloth to re-clothe part of the Scottish army which may well have been intended for the red-coated King's Lifeguard. There was no symbolism in the colour as red was the cheapest colour to dye. It is unlikely that there was time to make this cloth up into uniforms before the battle and the poor tailors were not paid for this cloth until 1675. The Parliamentary army probably looked only marginally better dressed than the Scots. Soldiers could expect little more than the single issue of a coat and a shirt. After a campaign such as that in Scotland, living, sleeping and fighting in clothes that were rarely washed or changed, they would have looked very ragged. Thus it was that prisoners from the battle of Worcester were routinely stripped to provide replacement clothes for their captors (see p. 126 below). It is also unlikely that the Parliamentary militia units had been issued with formal uniforms; they therefore fought in a mixture of uniforms from the earlier Civil Wars and civilian dress, identified (as with the Worcestershire militia) by coloured ribbons in their hats or on their arms.[5]

The Scottish national army comprised both regular lowland regiments and some highland regiments such as the Ross clan. Other highland clans fought as independent units (the MacGregors having made a point of asking to serve as a united clan). Some of these clans may have worn the great belted plaid with its dull-coloured tartans (although there was no system of clan tartans as such at this time), but most probably dressed similarly to the lowlanders. In 1650, Sir Arthur Haselrigg was not able to distinguish highlander prisoners by their dress – only by their hardiness in surviving the terrible conditions of the prison at Durham Cathedral. An important distinction does, however, have to be made between the highlanders that fought in regular formations and the more undisciplined clan levies. It is likely that the latter remained very poorly equipped and of little value in a formal battle (their main use being in skirmishing and plundering) although it was the latter that King Charles regarded as his favourites, appealing as they did to his romantic nature.[6]

The Parliamentary New Model Army had been created in 1645 to unify the command structure and avoid the earlier problems of relying on local levies. By 1651, many regiments had acquired a local identity. The Lord General's regiment, for example, was largely recruited from Lancashire (although reinforced with 500 Londoners during the Worcester campaign). In a break with tradition, the officers were appointed for their skills rather than their social status. Contemptuous Royalist claims that the army was only officered by tradesmen were greatly exaggerated, although of the regimental colonels at Worcester, Pride had been an employee of a brewer, Cooper and Goffe had been salters and Horton a servant. Such criticisms were not simply confined to Royalists. The somewhat snobbish Lucy Hutchinson referred to General Harrison as 'but a mean man's son, and of a mean education, and of no state before the war'.[7] The costs of maintaining the army had risen to £157,000 per month by August 1651.[8] By the end of that year, the daily pay of the troops was as follows:

infantry	10d	(4p)
dragoon	2s	(10p)
cavalry trooper	2s 6d	(12.5p)
ensign	3s	(15p)
lieutenant	4s	(20p)
surgeon	6s	(30p)
captain	8s	(40p)
major	13s	(65p)
lt.-colonel	15s	(75p)
colonel of foot	£1	(£1)

The wages of cavalry officers were slightly greater and varied more throughout the period. They also included an allowance for their horses.

The wages of the common soldier were therefore no better, and probably worse, than that of a labourer of the time. The soldiers would, in addition, be expected to provide much of their supplies out of their wages. Income was supplemented by the proceeds of 'lawful plunder' which ranged from stripping the possessions of prisoners and the dead, to sacking a town taken by assault. Evidence of both can be found in the aftermath of the battle of Worcester.

The costs of the army were greatly increased during the Worcester campaign through the mobilization of the militias. The pay for some of the militia units was still outstanding in 1656. To offset the accelerating costs, the government sought to demobilize these units as soon as possible after the battle of Worcester; many of the men would in any case have been anxious to return home for the harvest and sowing of fresh crops. Around one-third of the force created in 1651 was made up of re-formed militia units. The militias had not generally enjoyed a high reputation in the earlier phases of the Civil War, but those of 1651 were stiffened with large numbers of veterans and regular officers. They performed a critical role in the battle. This godly army would undoubtedly have remembered their catechism from the First Civil War as being 'the Instruments of Justice, and the Executioners of God's Judgements' (Psalms 149, vv. 7, 9) as they fought a new holy war against the Royalists and foreign invaders.

The need to feed and supply such a large army was a nightmare for the Parliamentary commissariat under Lambert and Whalley who had to arrange for sufficient supplies to be ready at intervals along the line of march. The campaign was as much a triumph of organization as of military might. Orders were continually sent out to local committees to arrange for bakers' ovens to work day and night to ensure that bread and biscuits (hard tack) were ready for the arrival of the troops. This was an organization that the invading Scots could not hope to match. The intention throughout the Scottish campaign was that each soldier should carry one week's rations in his canvas or leather snapsack, with additional supplies loaded onto packhorses. The rations consisted essentially of bread, or biscuit, and cheese (although Cromwell also ordered meat to be ready at Doncaster; see p. 17 above). In 1654 the troops were issued with 1 lb of biscuit per day and probably ½ lb of cheese. The rock-hard biscuit would probably have been dissolved to make a kind of porridge. The soldiers would be expected to supplement this by purchasing meat out of their pay – if they could avoid the temptation of looting additional food on their route of march. Water bottles were not supplied as an official part of equipment, although the daily ration of drink according to Sir James Turner was one bottle of wine or two pints of beer. The troops on the Scottish campaign had been supplied with pewter bowls in an attempt to improve hygiene (they were easier to clean than the wooden platters with which the soldiers would have otherwise supplied themselves).[9] Whilst on the march, the troops would probably have been dispersed to billets in the towns, villages and farms through which they passed rather than making camps. Tents were not generally provided for the English common soldiers at this time unless at a siege (although more commonly used by the Scots), and where billets were not available then they would have been forced to make temporary shelters or simply to sleep in the hedgerows.[10] Some of Cromwell's army may have brought tents with them from Scotland, as these were issued in August 1650, but many of these were probably left with General Monck. Tents were ordered to be brought to Worcester – but these did not arrive until after the battle.

The senior officers of the armies at the time of the Third Civil War were distinguished by their youth. The average age of the generals of the Royalist/Scottish forces was thirty-three years as compared to thirty-eight years in the Parliamentary ranks. Cromwell, at fifty-two years, was one of the oldest generals. They were well acquainted: many of the King's generals, including the senior Scottish commander, David Leslie, had formerly fought on the side of Parliament in the First Civil War. Some of the older commanders had also seen previous military service on the continent. King Charles at twenty-one years, and the Duke of Buckingham at twenty-three years, were the youngest and least experienced generals – and yet the fate of the country rested on their shoulders.

FOUR

The Occupation of Worcester

THE INVASION OF WORCESTERSHIRE

As the Scottish army began its march southwards, the Worcestershire militia had obeyed Parliament's orders and rallied on Pitchcroft field, Worcester, under the garrison commander, Colonel John James, and Captain Andrew Yarranton.[1] One of the members of the militia was John Nicklis of Evesham who fought, was captured and taken into Worcester, and then escaped.[2] When the destination of the advancing army became clear the decision was taken to use the militia to try to slow up the Scottish advance in order to allow reinforcements for the vastly outnumbered Worcester garrison of 500 men to gather. Ironically in view of the earlier orders of Parliament, the defences of Worcester were also ordered to be repaired with the hope of denying the King and his increasingly dispirited army any shelter until Cromwell was ready to engage. On 15 August the Council of State praised the militia commissioners for their efforts in assuring 'the good posture' of the county and encouraged them to be ready for the impending contact with the Scots, who were by now on their way from Wolverhampton.[3] Local tradition has it that the Scots entered the county at Tenbury Wells and camped on the river meadow; King Charles is reputed to have stayed at the Swan Inn.[4] This may, however, have been a confusion with the Scottish invasion of 1645. The first definite record of the Scots in the county is their arrival near Kidderminster on 21 August. Events then moved very quickly.

The militia rose to the challenge of the invasion. Yarranton first tried to demolish the stone bridge at Bewdley in order to block any river crossing across the Severn and hinder any support arriving from Wales. One party of five men from Presteigne did join the Scots at Bewdley: Nicholas Meredith, John Bull, Thomas Gomey, William Taylor and Andrew Higgins had ridden there to meet General Montgomery and present him with some wine. They then joined the Duke of Buckingham's troop in Worcester.[5] The Scottish columns fanned out through the fields beside Kidderminster and passed through Hartlebury. They were now only 10 miles north of Worcester. As the forward units of the Scots approached, Whitelock says that 'the country forces [i.e. the militia] made a gallant resistance and beat back the enemy several times'.[6]

Initially it seemed as though the citizens of Worcester might, like those of Shrewsbury, try to resist a Scottish siege. Potential opponents, such as Lord Talbot of Grafton (later the Earl of Shrewsbury) and Sir John Packington of Westwood, Droitwich (who had fought at Edgehill and the 1646 siege of Worcester), had been arrested to hinder any Royalist mobilization and were now imprisoned within the city.[7] Volunteers from the city had also set to with the garrison in order to repair quickly the recently levelled city defences. This probably consisted of the patching of the city walls, cleaning out some of the wide ditches that fronted them (although apparently not on the east side) and blocking the gates with banks of earth and stone. General Harrison wrote three letters within the space of twelve hours on 21 August urging them on and promising reinforcements. At least a part of the city therefore decided to 'hazard our lives in the keeping of the City and did what we could to strengthen the walls, and the well-affected in the City and County came in to us willingly engaging themselves and in the expectation of assistance from the Major General [Harrison] according to his promises'. The Parliamentary faction was focused on the County Committee and was led by the former governor, George Milward (a wealthy clothier), Simon Moore (vicar of St Peter's, rector of St Michael's Bedwardine, Master of St Oswald's Hospital and one of the county magistrates), Edward Elvins (another clothier and former sheriff), Gervase Buck (a Justice of the Peace from near Kempsey), Captain William Collins, Richard Inett and Andrew Yarranton (the engineer and agriculturist, now commander of the militia). Two other men, the clothiers Thomas Hackett and John Higgins, were also described as being 'well-affected not approving that a man take up arms against Parliament'.[8]

But as night fell, resolve was crumbling within the city at the prospect of a battle being fought on their doorsteps. There would still have been stark memories of the long siege of 1646 and the citizens were anxious to persuade the troops of both sides to move off elsewhere and leave them in peace. On the evening of Thursday 21 August, with the King having passed through Kidderminster, the mayor and sheriff requested a meeting with the garrison commander, Colonel James and the County Committee to discuss 'the peaceful entry of the enemy into the city'.[9] There was a heated debate, but eventually those advocating armed resistance until the arrival of Cromwell's army (led by Edward Elvins, the clothier Major Fowlke Estopp and Captain Theophilus Alie, commander of the garrison in 1648) were outvoted by the rest of the Chamber. Instead, with the sound of gunfire coming ever closer, the citizens prepared to surrender and thereby avoid the destruction that would inevitably accompany an assault or siege. The Scots were evidently coming prepared for a siege: sixteen cartloads of ladders were brought up with the rear of the army.[10] The city's hope now was that the Royalist army would only rest in Worcester temporarily and then continue its march elsewhere.

Despite the decision of the council not to oppose the entry of the King's army when it eventually arrived, the militia still fought on throughout Friday 22 August, still hoping for reinforcements and determined to buy further time for Cromwell to gather his forces together. But even the last minute arrival of five troops of Welsh horse from Harrison could not restore the confidence of the city. Other foot requested from Hereford had not yet arrived and it was clear that there would be no further reinforcements before the imminent arrival of the Scots. Yarranton's militia fought a skirmish with the Scots at Ombersley, only 5 miles outside the city. With the help of the Welsh horse there was further skirmishing up to the outskirts of the city, probably in the area approaching St Martin's Gate which was now the main access point into the city from the north. Fore Gate on the more obvious approach route of the Scots had already been blocked, or 'mured up', by the garrison. The horse and dragoons of garrison seems at this stage to have been scattered into small units to harry the advance as best they could. With the Scots at the very gates of Worcester, some troops were reportedly again sent to Bewdley to raid the quarters of the Scots in the rear, taking advantage of the fact that the Scots had not occupied the west side of the Severn. They reported some success, killing two quartermasters and taking some prisoners. By now, Cromwell's army was in Nottinghamshire and preparing to rendezvous with the Midlands forces.

The odds were, however, hopeless for the Worcestershire and Welsh troops fighting with their backs to the walls of Worcester. With the Scottish advance guard at the gates of the city, the regrouped garrison now had little option but to withdraw. The leading civilian Parliamentarians also prudently decided to retreat to Gloucester with them. In order to impress the fast-gathering Scottish army, some amongst the citizens began to fire on the thirty-strong rearguard of the retreating garrison. With great presence of mind, troops under Captain Boyleston of Bewdley were quickly ordered to load up the contents of the ammunition magazine (seven firkins of powder) and take this to safety in Gloucester. It might also be presumed that they had tried to 'spike' the heavy artillery in the city, although this is not documented. The advance guard of the Scots entered the city on the night of 22 August, whilst King Charles probably stayed outside the city walls at the Whiteladies, Barbourne, in order to make a grand entrance in the daylight. Did Charles perhaps reflect that this was the ninth anniversary of the date in 1642 when his father raised his standard at Nottingham to formally commence the Civil Wars? After allowing time for the city to prepare due ceremony, he entered the city at noon on the next day with an escort of 500 horse and dragoons and was greeted with all pomp and ceremony, according to Clarendon, 'with all the demonstration of affection and duty that could be expressed'. His recent attempts to defend the city against the King set aside, the mayor, Thomas Lysons (d. 1675), was knighted in gratitude for his support. Not all went well. The surgeon Richard Wiseman describes treating a townsman who was shot with a pistol at point blank range through the mouth during the entry of the King. Unfortunately he does not give the circumstances and so it is not possible to say if this was part of an over-enthusiastic salute (although this seems unlikely as the pistol was loaded with ball), an accident or even an attempt to assassinate the King.[11] The Council of State was furious at this turn of events and regarded the surrender of the city as treachery on behalf of the citizens. In reality, this was a simple matter of local pragmatism with the city council probably desperately hoping that the King would soon be on his way again.[12]

As the Scottish army advanced through Worcestershire the local militia tried to slow up the advance in order to allow the parliamentary forces to concentrate against them. On 22 August

there was a skirmish at Ombersley. The Scottish army was notable for including units of lancers. (Stephen Rigby). Inset: modern Ombersley.

In the meantime, the city tried to curry favour with the occupying army by identifying the homes of Parliamentary supporters. The son-in-law of Thomas Hackett, alderman Richard Carwadine (another clothier), had his house in St John's burnt down. Cromwell later interceded on behalf of Thomas Soley of St Andrew's parish, a member of the local militia, whose clothes had been stolen from his house after he had fled to the Parliamentary army.[13] Simon Moore was also compensated after he 'suffered great losses by the Scotch army at Worcester'. On 13 September he was awarded £20 out of the surplus from the sale of lead arising out of the demolition of the Cathedral bell tower in 1647. Thomas Writer (Wrighter), a tanner and maltster of All Saints parish, claimed that he lost £2,000 during the occupation. A long-time supporter of Parliament (removed from the city council in 1644), he was, however, also an excise officer and therefore his treatment may have been seen as an opportune means of settling old scores.[14]

The King's problems continued. A local preacher, Rowland Crosby from St Swithin's, managed to antagonize the Scottish Presbyterians at the Sunday service in the Cathedral by enthusiastically praying for the King as 'supreme head and governor' of the Church.[15] There were at least nine Scottish ministers with the army and this advocacy of royal power in ecclesiastical matters, whilst a traditional English Royalist value, proclaimed the very principles against which the Covenanter Scots were fighting. This dispute would have done nothing to improve the unity of the King's army in the days before the battle.

The Scottish troops were exhausted by their 300-mile march and by now were hungry, footsore and very poorly equipped. They had only had one day's rest since leaving Scotland and it was said that King Charles had not changed his shirt during the whole of the march to Worcester.[16] Major-General Harrison had ordered all horses, cattle and other livestock to be cleared from the route of the Scots to deny them any support and, with Lambert, had continually harassed the route of the Scottish march. The burden of resupplying the army now fell heavily on Worcester and the surrounding area, and patrols were sent out to try to raise men, money and provisions. William Penn was later accused of being a captain in Lord Talbot's troop of Worcestershire horse that tried to recruit in the Belbroughton and Chaddesley Corbett areas. Most of this would have been achieved by compulsion but one local Royalist, Roger Love of Bromsgrove, was happy to provide £400 for the cause. The first need was to house and feed the arriving troops. The city's housing stock was already under pressure from the effects of the First Civil War, when a large part of the suburbs had been destroyed. Worcester had a population of about 7,000; the number of people in the city was, therefore, almost trebled overnight. The army would have relied on requisitioning supplies and free-quarter with the citizens, who no doubt had little hope that they would ever be repaid.

Most of the troops were housed within the city, either in billets or camped within the large open spaces that still remained within the medieval defences. The main force of cavalry camped outside the city walls on Pitchcroft, with only small parties at outlying positions such as Madresfield and Upton-upon-Severn. Whitelock makes a reference to the Scots entrenching themselves in the fields west of Worcester, although it is clear from later events that few troops were permanently stationed south of St John's.[17] By contrast, Clarendon complained that proper defences to take advantage of the lie of the ground, river and city were not made.[18] Within Worcester, it is likely that large buildings such as the Cathedral, Bishop's Palace, Deanery, town hall (Guildhall) and city churches would all have been commandeered as barracks. The inhabitants of the parish of St Michael's Bedwardine (which includes the area of the Bishop's Palace, Cathedral Close and castle) later claimed that they had borne one-tenth of the burden of housing the troops. To make matters worse, some of the Scots had brought their wives with them in the baggage train. There were reported to be up to 1,000 camp followers, although this may be an exaggeration.[19] Soldiers were not given any allowance for their dependants and campaign life would have been very hard for them as they scratched a living by cooking, laundering and nursing. If their husband was killed then they would try to find a new man to support them as quickly as possible. At Worcester, their distinctive appearance, wearing plaid shawls patterned with early tartan checks, is likely to have caused a local stir. Some Scottish women even dared to go bare-headed, leading to the risk of being branded as a whore if captured.[20]

The headquarters of the army was established at what is now known as the Commandery, just outside the medieval Sidbury Gate (but within the line of the Civil War defence leading up to Fort Royal), and the King's quarters were off the Cornmarket (beside St Martin's Gate) in what is now known as King Charles's House. The tower of the Cathedral became an observation post.

Apart from the woollen cloth for uniforms, new shoes and stockings had to be found for the footsore army. The shoes should not be equated with the modern army boot but were more like casual shoes with thin soles that would not have survived a long march very well. Fortunately, the area had a strong leather-working tradition.[21] The citizens also had to provide food, with £183 14s 4d being spent on veal, mutton, lamb, chicken, rabbit, pigeon, duck, eggs, butter, hams, bread, fruit and wine. On the night before the battle alone, the city spent £7 5s 4d on wine for the troops. On the day of the battle itself, they spent £6 4s 8d on food and a further £6 6s 0d on nine gallons of sack and over eleven gallons of claret as the hard-pressed Scots fortified themselves. Candles were also supplied to light the camps and billets. As the occupation continued an increasing proportion of the basic resources of the city would have been diverted to the needs of the army, leaving the civilian population with rising problems themselves of dealing with lighting, heat and food. The accounts were only presented in 1655 and, as this was when the city was firmly back under Parliamentary control, the council naturally claimed that it had been 'enforced and compelled' to entertain the 'Scots King'.

Despite the hopes of the city, it was clear from the preparations of the army that this was to be no passing visit. Indeed, by this stage they were probably incapable of marching further and Clarendon tells how 'neither officer nor soldier was in any degree willing to quit them [their quarters in the city] till they should be thoroughly refreshed'.[22] Instead, it seems that the King hoped to use this as a base from which to rally further support, confident that he could resist a siege. Over the next two weeks the troops continued the work of the former Parliamentary garrison in restoring the defences. At least one Scottish officer was not impressed by the state in which he found the defences, describing them as 'only an old broken wall, and a fort, in a manner slighted' (see Appendix 1.3). The fort was probably the remains of the castle mound south of the Cathedral.

Nehemiah Wharton had described the defences at the start of the Civil War in 1642 as 'The wall in the forme of a triangle, the gates seaven, the bulwarkes [towers] five, but much decayed: no castle, only a mount of earth . . . This citty hath also a stronge stone bridge over Severne, consistinge of six arches, with a gate in the middle of the bridge, as stronge as that on London Bridge, with a percullis.'[23] Attempts had been made to strengthen the defences throughout the course of the war but the tendency was to allow them to fall into disrepair as soon as the immediate crisis passed. Even during the course of the siege of 1646, the citizens showed a marked reluctance to work on the defences.[24] The defences that Wharton saw were repaired, with the main additions being the start of the construction of an earthwork (rampart and ditch) on the east side of the city, protecting the approach road from London and incorporating a sconce on what is now Fort Royal Hill. Four-sided bastions were built around the gates on the north and east sides of the city defences, and later on the new defence constructed south of the castle. They provided a rudimentary form of the contemporary Dutch system of defence in allowing flanking fire along the line of the walls, and protecting the medieval gates. According to the map of 1660, a bastion was also built on the St John's side of the bridge across the River Severn in order to protect the crossing.

It is not clear what the Scots added to the defences but Nicholas Lechmere of Hanley Castle described their activity as being 'beyond imagination'.[25] The centrepiece of their work was certainly the rebuilding of Fort Royal – 'a very fair and large fort' according to the Parliamentarian Colonel Stapleton – on an extension of the east defences.[26] The new Fort Royal was a large star-shaped sconce built to command the high ground of Red Hill and the London Road, on the east side of the city. The shape of the triangular artillery bastions on the corners of the sconce can still be seen within Fort Royal Park, and its ramparts survived into the 1960s. Eighteenth-century plans show an outer defence line on the east side, including a small diamond-shaped bastion. The line of this became Fort Royal Road. A ditch was also dug across the line of the London Road itself (the seventeenth-century line of which ran a little to the south of the present route, which is eighteenth-century in origin). Men from Ripple were commandeered to help build the fort, described as still unfinished and only 'half-raised' at the time of the battle. Six months later they were recalled to help finally level it.[27] The short life of the fort is confirmed by the limited archaeological evidence. The fills of the V-shaped ditch as excavated in 1969 showed an absence of tip-lines from erosion or sedimentation and this, together with a complete absence of any artefacts, suggested that there was no time lapse during which the ditches would typically have been used as rubbish tips.[28]

The occupation of the city by the Scottish army was a major upheaval for Worcester. The troops were exhausted by their long march and in no mood to leave its comforts. This caused enormous problems in housing and feeding the army. Detail from an eighteenth-century engraving of Worcester (1764).

Worcester Cathedral from Fort Royal. The tower was used as an observation post during the battle and the cathedral itself was subsequently used as a prison to hold the captured Scots.

Fort Royal was linked to the main city defences by two lines of bastioned earthworks. The northernmost joined the medieval city defences south of Friar's Gate whilst the southern line ran down to the River Severn, enclosing the site of the castle. The relationship of these to Fort Royal suggests that they formed part of an earlier plan, although the ditches may well have been cleaned out or even increased in scale in 1651. Sections were excavated across this southern line of defence in 1966 and 1991 on Severn Street. They revealed a V-shaped ditch with concave bottom, 8–10 m wide and 2.4 m deep, very similar in form to that found on the north side of the city on 'The Butts' which was also re-dug in the Civil War period. There the ditch was over 16 m wide and 3.5 m deep, with a 5.5 m wide berm. Although open during the course of the battle, typically no military finds were found within them, because any finds were from the layers of soil that were thrown in to backfill the ditch and therefore post-date the battle.[29]

Despite frequent orders to do so, the defence ditch on the east side of the city seems not to have been cleaned out during the seventeenth century. Excavations in 1966 revealed the ditch as a 10–16 m wide and 2.5–3.5 m deep flat-bottomed drainage ditch, filled with water and mud. This would in itself have been a formidable obstacle and it was clearly felt unnecessary to try to dredge it. In contrast to that on the north side, there was no berm, and the ditch was dug immediately outside the city wall.[30] At the time of the battle, much of this ditch, and the city wall behind, would have formed part of an inner line of defence within the new earthwork enclosing Fort Royal.

The Scots also fortified the castle mound as a platform for artillery. The ruinous remains of the curtain wall on top of the mound would have offered some protection, whilst the sides of the mound were turned into a massive pincushion with protruding 'storm poles' to hamper an assault. The medieval city walls were c. 1.8 m thick and had been lined with a bank of earth at least 2 m wide in the First Civil War in order to strengthen them against cannon shot. The gates leading into the city were also blocked, possibly by temporary barricades such as the cart pushed across the carriageway of Sidbury Gate, or by more permanent earthen mounds. Fore Gate, on the north side of the city, was described as being 'mured up' (probably by the former garrison to block the approach of the Scots from that direction). It is also possible that a clear passageway for troops was created around the inside of the city defences by the demolition of buildings backing onto the walls (as in the 1646 siege), as Stapleton and Cromwell both refer to the burning of outhouses.[31] Whitelock goes further in saying that the Scots burnt down the suburbs, which would have been normal practice during a siege in order to provide a clear field of fire.[32] This would also have given the King the opportunity to charge and to 'scour' the enemy away from the walls with his cavalry as he planned, albeit unsuccessfully, to do during the actual battle. Although there may well have been some fresh demolition, a large part of the city's suburbs would still have been lying as waste ground from the First Civil War. Some demolition was probably undertaken simply to obtain firewood!

It is possible that much of the defence work was done under the supervision of local carpenter-turned-builder Henry Baldwin who made part of his considerable fortune out of Civil War defence work. In contrast to the failure of his fellow citizens to win payment for supplying the army, Baldwin was not averse to using his contacts in the military to ensure payment for his work, and the city later claimed that it had been forced to pay £4 to him only 'with compulsion of the souldiers'. Other local people were commandeered to assist in the war effort. On Sunday 24 August King Charles ordered the citizens of Salwarpe parish, next to Droitwich: 'You are hereby required to send out of your parish 30 able men to

An exact Ground-Plot of ye City of
WORCESTER
as it stood fortifyd 3 Sept 1651

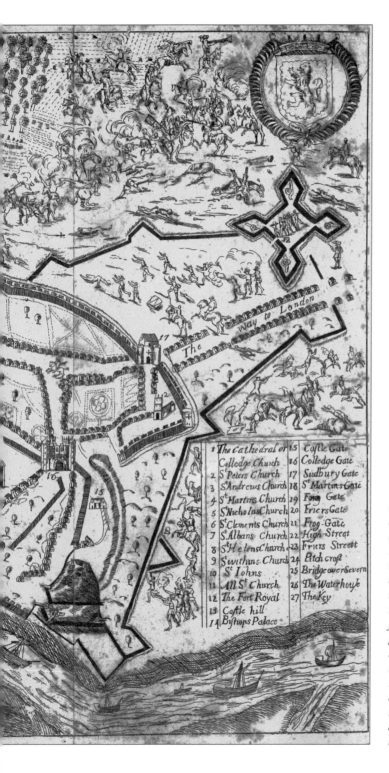

1	The Cathedral or Colledge Church	15	Castle Gate
		16	Colledge Gate
2	St Peters Church	17	Sudbury Gate
3	St Andrews Church	18	St Martins Gate
4	St Martins Church	19	Fore Gate
5	St Nicholas Church	20	Friers Gate
6	St Clements Church	21	Frog Gate
7	St Albans Church	22	High Street
8	St Helens Church	23	Friers Street
9	St Swithins Church	24	Pitch cross
10	St Iohns	25	Bridge over Severn
11	All St Church	26	The Waterhouse
12	The Fort Royal	27	The Key
13	Castle hill		
14	Byshops Palace		

The Vaughan Map of 1660, showing the defences of 1651. The Civil War defences of Worcester had been built up from 1642 on the basis of the derelict medieval defences. Great efforts were made to rebuild the defences in the weeks before the battle – first by the Parliamentary garrison and then by the Scots. The major addition was the rebuilding of Fort Royal. This protected the east side of the city and was linked to the main city defences by a bastioned line of earthworks.

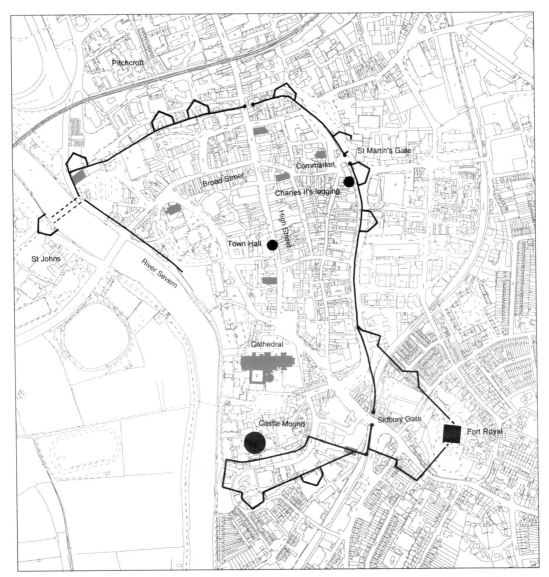

Map of the Civil War defences of Worcester, based on the outline published in Young's map of 1795 and the Vaughan Map of 1660. Fort Royal not shown to scale. (Background based on the Ordnance Survey 1:1250 mapping, with permission of the Controller of HMSO)

work at the fortifications of this city, and in regard of the necessity to begin tomorrow morning (Monday) at five o'clock, whereof you and they are not to fail, as you tender our displeasure.'[33] They were ordered to bring spades, shovels and pickaxes with them. In addition, troops were sent out on Monday 25 August to complete the demolition of Bewdley Bridge and to destroy the bridges across the rivers Teme and Severn at Powick and Upton-upon-Severn, thus creating an island of defence against the expected arrival of Cromwell's army.[34] The route into Wales via Bransford Bridge was, however, left intact as a possible escape route until the evening of Monday 1 September.[35]

One difficulty that the Scots could not resolve was the shortage of artillery and ammunition. It is possible (though unlikely) that Fort Royal and the castle were defended by cannon left behind by the retreating Parliamentary garrison, although the gunpowder stocks had been removed. The Scots would otherwise have been reliant only on their sixteen leather cannon and would have been hard-pressed to distribute these around the key points of the defences. However, the city did have a number of powder mills for making fresh gunpowder, and they were probably by the river to take advantage of water power from the Severn. There was also a 'powder house' for storage in the north-east corner of All Saints' churchyard, beside Angel Lane. Such a location minimized damage to neighbouring properties in the event of an explosion. Lead was stripped from roofs to melt down into musket balls and the city was also obliged to provide iron bars to the value of £7 18s 1d and 2 lb of the best steel to help the Scots re-arm. This was, however, not to prove enough.

THE FAILED MUSTER

If King Charles had thought that he was entering a stronghold of Royalist support then he was soon to be sadly disappointed. The prisons were broken open and known Royalists released, including Francis, Lord Talbot, Joseph Evett of Woodhall and Sir John Packington.[36] The latter had been held at the Crown Inn on Broad Street. It was now the King's turn to try to mobilize local volunteers on the Pitchcroft. There had indeed been some show of support in the county. Roger Love of Bromsgrove had tried, enthusiastically, to ring the church bells as a signal to mobilize support until stopped by the vicar, John Hall.[37] With regal confidence, the King summoned all able-bodied men in the county from sixteen to sixty to assemble with their horses fit for service and the best weapons and arms that they could procure. His first bold call to arms upon arriving in the city berated the traitorous Parliamentary faction:

> Whereas by the traitorous plots and conspiracies of many rebellious people of this Kingdom assuming to themselves the name and power of a Parliament the fundamental free and known laws of this kingdom have not only been endeavoured to be utterly subverted And to this end the said rebellious persons under their deceitful device and pretence of liberty and freedom from tyranny committed have seduced and drawn into their conspiracy many other people and subjects of this kingdom and raised forces to effect the same whereby they not only committed the most horrid Act of murder upon our late dear royal father their undoubted lawful head & sovereign of the rightful & long established government of the kingdom by many successors of ages and by the undoubted & known laws of the same but also do yet still persist in the same wicked plots &

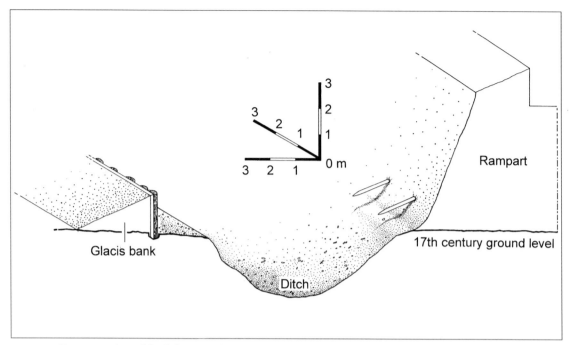

Reconstruction of the defences on Severn Street, based on excavations at Kings School in 1966. The ditch was 8–10 m wide and 2.4 m deep. Storm poles have been shown protruding from the rampart as an additional hazard.

rebellion against us our crown & dignity And utterly to extirpate all royal government of this kingdom and the laws liberties & freedoms of the same and to bring general vassalage servitude of all the true and loyal subjects of this nation under the tyrannical yoke of the said rebellious people calling themselves a Parliament And of a rebellious Army raised & continued by their Complottment together, who have to that purpose entered into our realm of Scotland and done much hurt & spoil to our subjects the people of that nation whereof it hath pleased god with a revengeful eye to look upon that their rebellion And to give us assurance of his mercy & providence over us several late successes against them at the pass at Warrington & here at Worcester, both respectively they endeavoured to keep against us but have been defeated of the same and yet nevertheless they continue the same their rebellion and are come back to hinder our settlement in our throne of government of this kingdom And do daily raise what forces they can to destroy our royal person And the just laws and freedoms all our true & loyal subjects of this realm of England for prevention whereof And to free all our true hearted and well affected subjects to us and our government from the misery & slavery of bondage under such tyrants & rebels who have truly manifested their wicked intentions of their hard pressures of our loving subjects by many years continuance hitherto.

Despite this call, the muster on 26 August was very poorly attended, as the majority of the county evidently tried to avoid being drawn further into the conflict. Clarendon commented that even the 'well-affected' gentry simply chose to remain at home.[38] This failure must have been recognized as a serious blow to Royalist chances of success and evidently disheartened Charles. He issued another declaration in a more conciliatory tone, referring now only to 'unhappy differences' rather than 'traitorous plots', stressing reconciliation to all but the regicides and offering to restore Parliament's liberties and freedoms:

We shall not rip up the causes of the unhappy differences betwixt our Royal father & the two houses of Parliament. It shall be our study that they may be for ever buried and that our subjects of England and dominions of Wales, may return to their obedience they owe us as their lawful king and to the ancient & happy government of the kingdom by king Lords & Commons wherein they and their ancestors have lived, so long, so happily without the effusion of more blood with these thoughts we are now returning into our kingdom of England with an army (by the blessing of God) able to protect our loyal subjects who shall join with us and assist us in doing justice upon the murderers of our royal father and to defend us from the violence of such as will continue the expulsion of us from our full Rights the subversion of the lawful government of the kingdom, and the oppression of our good subjects in England by arms & exorbitant imposition.

In a more immediate effort to win over support from the approaching army of Cromwell he offered to pay all arrears of the pay of the Parliamentary army if they would come over to him, and made it clear that his intention was that the Scottish army should leave the country as quickly as possible. There was, however, a flaw in his plan. It depended on local support being forthcoming to feed the men on their return journey.

Unfortunately for the King, this second declaration still failed to win over any substantial support from the county. Massey's attempt to raise support from the Gloucestershire border also failed miserably, as did the King's messengers to neighbouring towns. None of the city council who had surrendered to the King, and very few other Worcester men, are documented as having played any role in the battle; what support there was mainly came from the county gentry and their tenants or labourers. Two citizens who did join the muster were the Worcester clothiers Walter Heming and William Clarke, who had recently deserted the Worcestershire militia for the Scots.[39] Another local man was Charles Woodward, who was later accused of being a quartermaster in the King's army.[40] In all, only 23 of the local gentry and 140 men were listed as being present at the muster.[41]

Here appeared —
Francis Lord Talbot now Earl of Shrewsbury, with about 60 Horse
Mr Mervin Touchet, his Lieut. Collonel
Sir John Packington [of Westwood, Hampton Lovett]
Sir Walter Blount [of Sodington]

The failure of Worcestershire to support the muster on Pitchcroft was a great disappointment to the King, who had been promised large-scale support from the English. (Stephen Rigby)

Sir Ralph Clare
Sir Rowland Berkeley [of Cotheridge]
Sir John Winford [of Astley]
Mr Ralph Sheldon of Beoly
Mr John Washburn of Witchinford with 40 Horse
Mr Thomas Hornyold of Blackmore Park with 40 Horse
Mr William S[h]eldon of Finstall
Mr Thomas Acton [of Burton]
Captain Benbow
Mr Robert Blount of Kenswick
Mr Robert Wigmore of Lucton
Mr Edward Pennel the Elder [of Woodston in Lindridge]
Captain John Kingston
Mr Peter Blount
Mr Edward Blount
Mr Walter Walsh [of Abberley]
Mr Charles Wash (sic)
Mr William Dansey [of Stoke Prior]
Mr Francis Knotsford

Francis, Lord Talbot, Sir John Packington, Sir Ralph Clare, Sir Walter Blount, Thomas Hornyold of Hanley Castle and Ralph Sheldon of Beoley had all been members of the Royalist Committee of Safety during the First Civil War. At least one-quarter of the named individuals had been present at the siege of Worcester in 1646; many were also Catholic. Some of those listed were able to bring a retinue with them: John Washburn and Thomas Hornyold each brought forty men. Lord Talbot, newly released from prison, summoned sixty men under his lieutenant, Mervin Touchet; they included Colonel William Carlis, a Staffordshire man (who later took up residence at Hallow, Worcs), who was described as being major to Lord Talbot, and Richard Kemble who was his captain lieutenant. William Penn of Belbroughton was also later accused of being a captain in the troop.[42] This troop of local men were later to play a key role in the final stages of the battle and in assisting the escape of the King.

Not surprisingly, a number of those listed as being present tried after the battle to claim that they were either not there at all or had attended only under duress. It is therefore now very difficult to disentangle real and false alibis. In some cases, witnesses conveniently went missing before hearings. Even Lord Talbot tried to excuse himself by saying that he was only at Worcester because he had been held under arrest there. A similar excuse was given by the 31-year-old Packington who, although seen at the muster wearing a sword, claimed to have been an unwilling recruit. He had written before the battle: 'I am resolved not to meddle; for I have already burnt my fingers. I will not again thrust them into the fire.'[43] No witnesses could be found to contradict his story and Cromwell certainly believed that he had not actually fought in the battle; instructions were therefore given that he was not to be treated as a prisoner of war. Packington did, however, remain at the heart of Royalist conspiracies in the county up to the Restoration, and he lost his lands no less than three times for his support of the Royalist cause. The eighteen-year-old orphan John Romney of Knightwick was living with his uncle in Worcester at the time of the arrival of the Scots. Some of them had been billeted on the house and he claimed he had been forced to join the muster because he was 'terrified by their threats'. His story was also believed although he was later implicated in Booth's rising of 1659 and his estates seized.[44]

Sir Rowland Berkeley of Cotheridge (1613–96) claimed that he had never attended the muster at all. He composed his alibi in two letters written to his father-in-law (the Royalist Sir Thomas Cave) after the battle. He claimed in a letter of 8 September that he had 'cavilled not on either side' and followed this up on 12 September with a statement that before the battle he had resolved 'not to meddle' and had therefore stayed at home at Cotheridge, ignoring the King's summons to attend the Pitchcroft muster. According to this version of events, on the morning of the battle, he claimed that he had been seized by cavalry acting on the King's orders. He then claimed to have spent the rest of the day dodging the fighting.[45] A very different story was composed in the eighteenth century to suggest that he had actually fought at the battle and escaped arrest after leaving the King at Barbourne Bridge. Sir Rowland was said to have exchanged his lathered piebald horse for a similar, but fresh one, from a nearby farm and then took to his bed. When soldiers arrived he claimed that he was ill and that his distinctive horse clearly had not been ridden that day.[46] The truth of what actually happened on that day may never now be known – the balance of probability is that Sir Rowland did take some part in the battle, although embroidered by later romantic invention. Parliament was not convinced by his excuses and, as a consequence, he received the third largest fine amongst the Worcestershire gentry for his alleged part in the battle (£2,030).

It is more certain that the noted Kidderminster Presbyterian theologian, Richard Baxter, did refuse a summons from the King to attend, claiming problems with sore eyes. King Charles had chosen a local man, Colonel Greaves of Mosely (who had fought for Parliament in the First Civil War but who had been removed from command in 1647 and was now a 'gentleman of the royal bedchamber'), to try to persuade Baxter to join him. Baxter later admitted that he suspected the outcome of the impending battle and so doubted if he could have provided much assistance. One other notable omission from the list was Sir Henry Lyttleton of Frankley. Given his later history as a thorn in the side of the Protectorate it is surprising that he was not more involved in 1651, and the Committee for Compounding clearly thought so too. None the less, charges of him assisting the Scots had to be dropped in March 1652 through lack of evidence.[47] But it was not simply the gentry who came to the muster; indeed, Clarendon complained that few of the gentry who had previously written letters of support actually joined the army at Worcester, although 'some common men' who had previously served in the Royalist armies loyally rejoined the colours.[48] Whether out of conviction or simply for adventure, the servant of John Higgins joined the King's army, albeit without the approval of his master.[49]

In all, there may have been around only 2,000 English troops within the King's army at Worcester. Charles had pinned many of his hopes on the Earl of Derby's

Map of 1795 showing the plan of Fort Royal and part of the east defences of the city, after the map of 1660. Note the additional defence just to the east of Fort Royal. The line of this ditch became Fort Royal Hill. The sconce built on top of the castle mound is also shown.

ability to recruit supporters – expecting that 7,000 men could be raised from Lancashire. In the end he had managed to raise only about 1,500 men, who were totally crushed by Lilburne at the battle at Wigan on 25 August. The wounded earl arrived at Worcester with only a handful of supporters. In the war of insults between King and Parliament, the Council of State referred to these English Royalists as 'the trash of the people'.[50] The English troops were under the command of the Duke of Buckingham, with Edward Massey as second-in-command and Samuel Tavert as Quartermaster General. As a consequence, the Royalist forces of 13,000–15,000 men had an overwhelmingly Scottish complexion, recognized by the King who fought under the Scottish rather than English standard – 'proud Scotland's royal shield, the ruddy Lion ramped in gold'.[51] His army in the field was characterized by the Scottish regimental flags bearing the St Andrew's cross and Covenanter slogans, in contrast to the St George's cross carried by their Parliamentary counterparts. This in itself must have reinforced the opinion that this was more of a national conflict between England and Scotland rather than between the new King and his Parliament.

FIVE

The Encirclement of the Scots

FINAL MOBILIZATION

Whilst Cromwell was marching south with his army, the Council of State had taken charge of the mobilization and supply of troops from the rest of the country. Strong nerves had been called for. Lucy Hutchinson reported how the Council of State initially panicked at hearing the news that Cromwell had allowed the King to march into England. There were even some rumours that Cromwell had betrayed the Commonwealth by conniving with the invasion. 'Some could not hide very pale and unmanly fears, and were in such distraction of spirit, that it much disturbed their councils.'[1] Eventually, Lucy says, 'they at length re-collected themselves, and every man that had courage and interest in their counties, went down to look to them'.[2] Cromwell may well have been counting on the Scottish invasion to focus the minds of those who had not given full support to the campaign whilst in Scotland. He had previously complained of the difficulty of recruiting experienced officers to the regiments in Scotland. Some men, like Sir Thomas Fairfax, had felt uncomfortable with a pre-emptive invasion of their former allies. Richard Baxter refused to pray for the success of the Scottish campaign and wrote to soldiers 'to help them to understand what a crime it was to force men to pray for the success of those that were violating their covenant and loyalty, and going in such a cause to kill their brethren'.[3] Now, however, that the threat was coming closer to home there was a new sense of common purpose in defeating the foreign invader. Fairfax was reconciled to Cromwell; he had taken the field in Yorkshire at the head of the county militia and now offered to raise additional troops. Continued nervousness at the tactic of allowing an enemy to penetrate deep into England without apparent check is evident in the repeated commands by the Council of State that Lambert should maintain close contact with the Scottish army to prevent it breaking out towards the capital. Tensions within the Parliamentary cause continued to surface in isolated incidents, however. Lucy Hutchinson's husband, the governor of Nottingham, Colonel Hutchinson, had been given a commission to raise a regiment of horse for the Scottish campaign and had immediately sent three

John Lambert (1619–84), who shadowed the Scottish army on its march and commanded the crucial attack on Upton-upon-Severn. From an engraving of 1672. (Courtesy Worcester City Library)

troops from his former soldiers to Cromwell intending to follow with the rest of the regiment. However, on being told that his men had been dispersed among other regiments, he decided instead to use the rest to secure Nottinghamshire. He also ordered the demolition of Nottingham Castle because according to Lucy he feared that Cromwell's army might eventually come to use it against the people. Although done with the approval of the Council of State, this 'heartily vexed' Cromwell.

The regicide Thomas Scott and Richard Salway (Stanford-on-Teme grocer and former mayor of Worcester) were employed to liaise on the ground between the Council of State and the army. Orders went out from the Council of State to the army and militia commissioners all over the country as they tried to anticipate the King's movements. The most urgent need was said to be for new foot.[4] By 23 August, three new regular regiments of 3,000 men had been raised under Colonel Cobbett, Major Blake and Colonel Duckenfield.[5] Militia troops were mobilized from all over the country. Some were held back to maintain security in their home counties but others were marched off to rendezvous with the main field army or to be held in reserve (see Appendix 2, p. 175). By 21 August, Middlesex had raised two troops of 60 horse and 500 foot; Cheshire had raised over 2,000 foot in three regiments; Essex had also raised a brigade of three regiments of foot (up to c. 3,000 men) with further bodies of dragoons and horse that were left in the county. The local magnate, Lord Grey, had been put in charge of mobilizing the Northamptonshire, Leicestershire and Rutland forces with his own regiment of foot; by 25 August he had raised 1,100 horse. He reported a shortage of pistols for his men but was told to 'make bold' with any arms found in the possession of suspected Royalists.[6]

The various movement orders had to be emended en route as intelligence was updated as to the location of the Scottish army, and a stream of messengers was sent out by the Council of State to the marching columns. The destination for the contingent from East Anglia was changed in turn between 18 and 24 August from St Albans to Dunstable to Buckingham and finally to Oxford. Not surprisingly, the order for the Worcestershire militia to march off and join the Midlands rendezvous was cancelled once the destination of the Royalists became clear.

General Fleetwood was in charge of the mobilization of the militias in central England, stiffened by a number of regiments of the New Model Army including his own and Gibbon's regiment from Nottingham, and supported by Lord Grey, Heane at Oxford and Desborough (summoned from the West) at Reading. Oxford and Northampton became the main rendezvous points. The troops from Sussex, Surrey, Hampshire, Berkshire and Kent were ordered to join the East Anglian contingents from Norfolk, Suffolk, Essex and Cambridgeshire at Oxford on 24 August. The troops from Leicestershire, Rutland, Northamptonshire, Warwickshire, Oxfordshire, Lincolnshire, Bedfordshire, Huntingdonshire and Buckinghamshire were to gather at Northampton on 22 August with Fleetwood's own regiment of horse and the new foot regiments of Gibbon and Cobbett (newly raised out of Barkstead's London regiment).

Another rendezvous was held at Gloucester for the troops of the county, South Wales, Monmouthshire, Herefordshire and Wiltshire on 25 August under the command of the governor, Sir William Constable.[7] There, as well as feverishly working on the defences, the citizens proudly claimed that within two days they had mustered and armed 700 militia, consisting of 200 of the better-off (those able to provide their own arms) organized as a company under the mayor, Anthony Edwards, with another six companies of 'handicrafts men and other labourers and servants'.[8] Impressed by this show of loyalty, the Council of State offered to pay £200 towards the costs of those who were too poor to pay the normal charges for service.[9] Around 6,000 men had already been mobilized in Monmouthshire at Chepstow on 14 August, when Craddock arrested suspect gentry and their horses throughout the county and commandeered their horses.[10] The Gloucester forces were to be used as a final block to the advancing Scots and, behind them, further troops were collected at Bristol from units based in the south-west in order to protect the coast. As the ultimate Royalist target would have to be the capital, 15,000 troops of the Trained Bands were held there under General Skippon.

All did not go smoothly. Some troops, such as the Lincolnshire and Cambridgeshire militias, missed their rendezvous and were sent to a reserve location at Mansfield. There were particular worries over Colonel John Twistleton's regiment of dragoons from Kent that had inexperienced officers and became seriously afflicted by disease. Both factors necessitated the replacement of some officers and may have been a factor in the regiment not reaching Worcester.[11]

The Council of State had to ensure that the men were paid. They ordered that county militia committees find one month's wages in advance with one week's wages for the common soldiers to be paid immediately and another three weeks' pay to be held by the officers until the rendezvous. They also had to organize ammunition and supplies and, somewhat ominously, the transport of surgeons' chests.

On 22 August, as the Royalists entered Worcester, the Council of State formally passed over all responsibility for the campaign to Cromwell. The destination of the Royalists was now clear and Cromwell was close enough to liaise directly with Harrison, Lambert and Fleetwood over the final battle plan.[12] The Council of State continued to be heavily involved, particularly in continuing to express their concern that the Scottish army should be tightly hemmed in by Lambert and also in organizing supplies. On 27 August they warned the militia committees of Warwickshire, Shropshire, Gloucestershire, Herefordshire and Worcestershire to prepare provisions for the imminent arrival of the Parliamentary army (for which they would be reimbursed). The irritation aroused by the early surrender of Worcester is evident in the addition to the order sent to Worcestershire to collect supplies 'and thereby show how little you approve of what your revolting city hath done'.[13]

Cromwell now ordered selected troops from the rendezvous points to converge on Evesham, 13 miles south-east of Worcester, as the final mustering point before the battle. There were plenty to choose from, even though he had been obliged to leave part of his own army behind, sick and exhausted by their march from Scotland. Some of the militias can hardly have been in a much better state. The Essex militias reached Worcestershire via Dunstable only eleven days after receiving their orders.[14] There was the 13,000-strong combined army of Lambert and Harrison from the north; Fleetwood brought some of his newly raised militias from the Midlands, some probably attached to his own regiment and that of Gibbon, Cobbett and Grey from Northampton and Oxford. Heane, Desborough and Blake brought their regiments from Oxford, Reading and Plymouth respectively. By 27 August, Cromwell had amassed an army of *c.* 30,000 at the Evesham rendezvous. The strength and confidence of the army was such that another 5,000 men of the militia could be held in reserve at Coventry. Orders for Lilburne's troops in Lancashire to join the main army had also been countermanded in favour of them being deployed to deal with what was now expected to be a Scottish retreat following the eagerly awaited final battle.[15] They now moved forward into Shropshire and to guard Bewdley Bridge. Cromwell was also ordered by the Council of State to supply some of his officers to command additional militia forces that were sent into Lancashire behind them.[16]

The size of the artillery train is not recorded but was certainly far greater than that of the Scots. Apart from the artillery brought down from Scotland, the Council of State had ordered a second train to Fleetwood from London on 21 August, accompanied by 500 men detached from Colonel Barkstead's regiment.[17] (These men were later incorporated into Cromwell's own regiment of foot, and the officers were sent back to London.) There was evidently no shortage of resources, as a third train of artillery was dispatched to Lambert and Harrison on 24 August.[18]

The impact of the arrival of such an enormous force on the Vale of Evesham must have been staggering. Evesham had a population of less than 2,000 and the total population of the county as a whole was only around 57,000. By comparison, the Parliamentary army brought to the siege of Worcester in 1646 numbered only 5,000 men. The task of providing regular supplies for around 30,000 men would have been an enormous burden for the surrounding villages to bear, and large parts of the countryside must have been turned into a vast armed camp as troops arrived from all over the country. They would have been billeted throughout the local villages and farms or made shelters in the woods and hedgerows. In addition, there were likely to have been a considerable number of camp followers. Cromwell had encouraged wives to join the soldiers in Scotland to serve as nurses to the troops, and these no doubt followed their menfolk southwards. If the pattern of the First Civil War was repeated, the local people could have expected horses, carts and other supplies to have been commandeered by the commissariat. It was approaching harvest time and there must also have been fears as to what damage might be caused to the growing crops, or how difficult it might be to gather in the harvest if a long siege developed. Local people would have remembered instances of the troops of both sides trampling crops during 1642–6, commandeering draught animals, and markets having to be cancelled. On the other hand, some local people would undoubtedly have made a quick profit in supplying the army with food and other supplies.

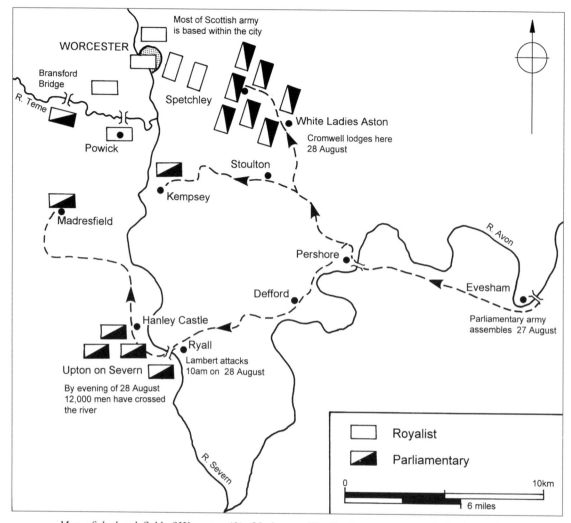

Map of the battlefield of Worcester (1), 28 August. The Parliamentary army had advanced from Evesham with one column seizing the river crossing at Upton-upon-Severn.

The plan of Cromwell and the Council of State was to cut off any further advance of the Scots, surround them and then annihilate them. The Council of State again had a special thought for the people of Worcester who were 'like to pay dear for their treason'.[19] The King had also called a council of war to discuss his tactics: whether to march out and fight this superior army in open battle, prepare for a long siege, march on London or march into Wales in the hope of raising more recruits. In reality, as the noose closed, the initiative was to be all with Cromwell.

THE FIRST ASSAULT

Putting aside the exhaustion of his army, Cromwell was determined to secure his position without delay. Any attempt of the King to break out towards London was blocked by the presence of the army holding the crossing over the River Avon at Evesham. The crossing of the River Severn 13 miles to the north of the city at Bewdley was also secured by Lilburne without opposition, but the key to ultimate success would be to cut off the Scots completely by crossing the Severn and occupying the south and west sides of the approaches to Worcester. This would prevent an advance towards the Bristol Channel or into Wales and provide the means to develop a pincer attack on the beleaguered Scots.

The nearest bridging point over the River Severn south of the city was at Upton-upon-Severn, 9 miles to the south of Worcester. At the time, this was a small village, defended by a force of *c.* 300 English and Scottish horse and dragoons from the 5th Cavalry Brigade under Edward Massey, who had made his headquarters at the home of Nicholas Lechmere at Severn End, Hanley Castle, 1 mile north of Upton, on 25 August. By 27 August, 150 Scottish horse were also quartered there. Lechmere, a prominent Parliamentarian and one of the militia commissioners, was a reluctant host who recorded in his diary how Massey, his former ally from the First Civil War, 'treated my people civilly, but threatened extirpation to me and my posterity for having joined the Parliament'.[20] The troops had demolished the span of the stone-arched bridge

Edward Massey (1620–74). Second-in-command of the English troops with the King, and commander at Upton-upon-Severn. (Courtesy Worcester City Library)

The tower of Upton church, now largely demolished. Lambert's dragoons were forced to shelter here whilst the Scots tried to burn them out.

nearest the town in order to hinder a crossing by the enemy but, as was normal in such instances (to allow the passage of the friendly troops), a plank had been left across the void. However, remarkably for a commander of the experience of Massey, no guard was mounted and this was to prove fatal to the whole course of the battle.

The advance guard of the Parliamentary assault force on Upton moved out of Evesham under Major-General John Lambert on 27 August. Passing down the main road from Pershore and Defford, they halted out of sight of the Scots around the village of Ryall, behind a low ridge just to the east of Upton. Lambert was able to reconnoitre the wide river crossing from the vantage point of the ridge. Unable to believe his luck at the lack of a guard, he decided to seize the moment. In the full light of day at about 10 a.m. on 28 August, Lambert ordered eighteen picked dragoons to shuffle across the bridge and establish a bridgehead. No doubt feeling extremely exposed and vulnerable, they successfully reached the other side but were eventually spotted and, coming under fire, were forced to take cover in the adjacent church. The Scots first of all fired their pistols through the church windows and then tried to set light to it in order to burn the soldiers out, but this all caused sufficient diversion for the rest of Lambert's dragoons to successfully ford the river $c.$ 150 m downstream on Fisher's Row and charge into the town to rescue their comrades. This crossing across the fast-flowing river was no mean feat for the horsemen: the Scots were outflanked and were forced to retreat along the main road towards Worcester.

In order to exploit the bridgehead at Upton, reinforcements were quickly summoned from General Fleetwood's brigade that was following on behind Lambert, including 300 infantrymen of Colonel Cobbett's foot sent down with the horse, each one riding behind a trooper. More horse, foot and two cannon followed.[21] The Scots were greatly outnumbered. Massey had built a shallow-ditched, rectangular earthwork with flanking ditch just outside Upton-upon-Severn and across the road to Worcester, with the line of a stream behind them, and it was probably here that he tried to make a last stand. It is, however, likely that the Scottish position was outflanked by horse charging down New Street into Hyde Lane to the west of their defences. Hidden first by the houses and then by the hedges that bounded the lane, then as now, they could attack the Scottish positions from the side and rear. Only six or seven of the Scots were killed in the action although many were no doubt wounded and captured. Massey himself was seriously wounded (with 'ray-shot' according to Clarendon) in the left hand, right arm and thigh in leading the rearguard. He managed to escape back to Worcester but was unable to take part in further action. Caution and discipline prevailed on the Parliamentary side: Lambert ordered a halt to the advance rather than risk rushing headlong into the Scottish army. The bridge was quickly repaired and the Parliamentary army regrouped to prepare for their advance towards Worcester.

By the end of 28 August, the Parliamentary forces on the west bank of the Severn around Upton numbered $c.$ 12,000 men (almost equivalent to the total strength of the Scottish army). The rest of the army had also been busy. As

Dragoons shuffling across Upton bridge at 10 a.m., 28 August. The seizure of the Severn crossing at Upton was one of the most significant episodes of the battle. (Stephen Rigby)

Massey's last stand at Upton. At least 'forty carbines were shot at him within half pistol shot'. He was reported to have been shot in the hand, head, right arm and thigh. His horse was killed under him. Nevertheless, he managed to escape back to Worcester on a borrowed horse. (Stephen Rigby)

Lambert was attacking the Royalist positions at Upton-upon-Severn the main Parliamentary force began to move forward out of Evesham ready to occupy the high ground on the east side of Worcester. The huge army came up along, and beside, the main road through Pershore (where Cromwell temporarily made his headquarters) and Stoulton to White Ladies Aston and Spetchley, whilst Cromwell rested overnight on 28 August at Mr Simons's house at White Ladies Aston.

Cromwell rode to Upton on 29 August from his new headquarters at Judge Berkeley's house at Spetchley, only 2 miles south-east of Worcester, to congratulate his men on their victory. He was greeted 'with abundance of joy and extraordinary shouting from his elated troops'.[22] From their camp around Upton-upon-Severn, scouting parties of horse and dragoons under Colonel Blundell were sent out to reconnoitre over a distance of 4½ miles north from Upton. A troop of dragoons under Major Mercer and Captain Chappell went to occupy Madresfield House, which was immediately abandoned by the Scots and became the army's advance position. This also ensured that the eventual advance could not be harried by Scots operating on the flank of the army. Lambert's men also

Surviving Civil War earthworks at Upton-upon-Severn. This is probably where the Scots made their last stand. A scatter of musket balls have recently been found beside the adjacent hedge line.

The people of Worcester awaited the final battle with great trepidation. At last there would be
some relief from the demands of the occupying army – but at what cost? A Covenanter preacher
remonstrates with Scottish soldiers carousing in a Worcester inn. (Stephen Rigby)

took the opportunity to plunder the mansion of the local Royalist Thomas Hornyold (who was in Worcester with the King) at Blackmore Park, north of Hanley Swan.

Cromwell's plan of battle was broad in scope and left little to chance. It consisted of a series of defensive lines that would block any ability of the Scots to manoeuvre and prevent any possibility of reinforcement. One mixed mounted column of New Model Army horse and militia under Colonels Twistleton and Kendrick, including elements of the Worcestershire militia and Welsh troops, was sent westwards to Bransford Bridge on the Teme in order to prevent any escape of the now encircled Scots into Herefordshire and Wales. The arrival of the Parliamentary troops was clearly not seen as a prelude to offensive action at this stage, as the Scottish outpost there left the bridge intact until the evening of 1 September. Five troops of Worcestershire dragoons and the Worcestershire horse, with two troops of Rich's regiment of horse, were also sent north to Bewdley to block any escape into Wales or northwards. Further afield, the nearby towns of Gloucester, Ludlow, Hereford and Bristol had also been fortified to prevent a Scottish entry in case of a break-out and other forces were collected at Bristol. Welsh troops stood by to prevent a break-out to Milford Haven. If these precautions failed then the reserve at Coventry was in position to cover any likely escape route into the Midlands. To the north, Sir Arthur Haselrigg was moving into position in Westmorland and Cumberland to 'utterly extirpate and destroy them' if the Scots did somehow manage to break through the Parliamentary lines.[23] The King had therefore been totally isolated.

On the east side of the River Severn, the rest of the army now moved forward into their final battle positions on the high ground surrounding Worcester. The Scots tried to harry the advance as best they could from roadside ditches, hedgerows and trees. Both Royalist and Parliamentary accounts agree on the scene as Colonel Stapleton reported how 'Some small pickerings there was and poppings of musqueteers behind the hedges but nothing considerable was attempted.'[24] The troops now waited for the main stage of the battle to commence and took the opportunity to rest as much as they could. Sadly, the tents that had been ordered for the men failed to arrive before the battle and many would have made what shelter they could in the woods and hedgerows. As soon as the outcome of the battle became known to the Council of State they promptly cancelled the order for the tents but promised that they would 'think of another way of satisfying those honest soldiers'.[25] In the meantime, the families of these troops also had to wait for news of the battle, which was now recognized as being imminent. In Essex, the family of Colonel Thomas Cooke at Pebmarsh spent the day of 2 September in prayer and heard during the evening that Cooke and his men were well at Worcester. The next day, Wednesday 3 September, the Revd Ralph Josselin of Earls Colne (a former Parliamentary army chaplain) visited the home of Sir Thomas Honywood at Markshall where he reported, 'Spent this day in prayer at my Lady Honywood's. much company there, and god's presence with us, our expectacions god will advance his glory in our salvation.'[26] The Essex men had good need of those prayers on that day.

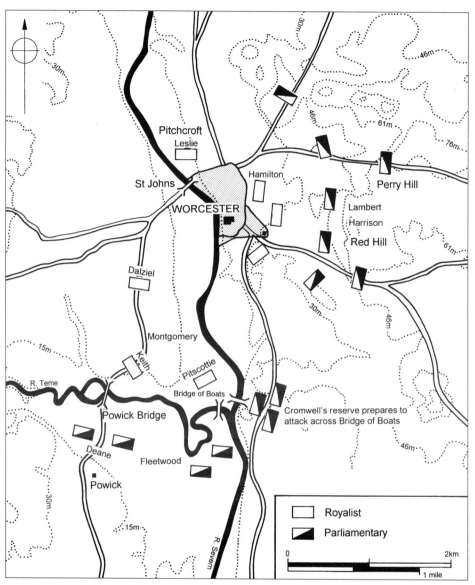

Map of the battlefield of Worcester (2), 12–3 p.m., 3 September. Fleetwood and Deane try to cross the River Teme. Success only comes when Cromwell's reserve charges the flank of the Scots across the pontoon bridge built over the Severn.

SIX

The Storm Breaks

The Parliamentary lines now extended for a length of *c.* 8 miles around the city. By Friday 29 August, on the east side of the city, the opposing forces were within only 'half musket shot' (*c.* 50 m) in some places and the two sides continued to engage in sporadic skirmishing. Cromwell was kept well informed as to movements of the King's army: scouts were sent out to provide fresh information on the disposition of the troops and he also had a number of spies operating within the city. On Sunday 31 August, Lambert led a patrol to probe the city defences, leading to a brief but ferocious exchange of fire. The main body of the Scots were based behind the shelter of the medieval defences and within the earthwork leading out to Fort Royal, with some foot and horse (probably including the 7th Cavalry Brigade under the Duke of Hamilton) also drawn up outside the defences facing Perry Hill. Clarendon implies that these troops were under the overall command of Middleton.[1] His rival, Leslie, commanded the main cavalry force drawn up on Pitchcroft to the north of the city wall. The jealousy between these two generals may later have proved fatal to the Royalist cause. There were also outposts flung out at Powick and Bransford in order to warn of any attack from the west side of the Severn.

Cromwell's main army had occupied the arc of high ground dominating the city to the east of Fort Royal from Elbury Hill in the north (where the troops no doubt kept a close watch on Leslie's cavalry), through Perry Hill and Red Hill to Bund's Hill in the south. This was a mixture of veteran New Model Army and militia foot, with the main body of the New Model Army horse behind them. They would have made temporary siege camps in the fields and woods. There is no evidence as to how far they created formal siege lines, using the equipment ordered up from Gloucester, but it is likely that there was a mixture of local trenches and surface defences created with gabions (large wicker baskets filled with stones and earth). Blount refers to a breastwork at the south end of Perry Wood, which was probably a dried-up former water course that would have formed a natural defence for the troops.[2] There was a rectangular enclosure on the top of Elbury Mount, measuring 200 × 100 × 150 yd, until it was destroyed for the construction of a reservoir in the nineteenth century, and this may well have been a Civil War encampment. English troops of the period were notorious for disliking to dig trenches – the task was often left to commandeered local civilians or punishment details. Serious crimes such as the losing of one's horse or arms, or of retreating before coming to hand-to-hand combat, were punishable by being sent to the pioneers.[3] The reported discovery of

During an abortive sally against Charles Fairfax's regiment of foot on Red Hill, Major Knox mistakenly leapt a hedge into a stand of pikes and was killed. (Stephen Rigby)

large quantities of musket ball, and clay pipes of the period during the construction of new housing on Red Hill in the 1950s is a pointer to the presence of the army lines, but unfortunately no records of the discoveries were kept.

The battle proper began with a fierce artillery barrage, the Parliamentary cannon firing *pell-mell* into the city. This was designed to give the defenders a taste of what they might expect if they did not surrender, but also served the purpose of testing the Scottish firepower. The Scots rose to this challenge and returned the fire from Fort Royal 'as if they never feared to want for powder or bullets'.[4] The bravado was no doubt commendable, but the reality was that their supplies were very limited and would be badly needed in a short while.

The Scots also retaliated by a night raid of over 1,000 men and 250 horse onto the main Parliamentary positions on Red Hill and the outpost on Bund's Hill. Such an attack was called a *camisado* because they wore white shirts over their armour as an identification signal. Unfortunately their plans had been betrayed by a local tailor called William Guise who was reported to have lowered himself over the city walls by a knotted rope in order to reach the Parliamentary lines, and Parliamentary troops were consequently waiting in ambush. As hidden musketeers opened fire from behind the hedges, the Scots, under General Middleton and Sir William Keith, lost about ten men on Bund's Hill. Their bodies were found on the road the next day. A further half-dozen soldiers were taken prisoner. On Red Hill, against Charles Fairfax's regiment of foot, Major Knox was killed 'coming very boldly up, and leaping over a hedge, rushed upon a stand of pikes, and so (as his victors termed it) lost his life in a vapour'.[5]

This first failure to repel the besieging army seems to have convinced more local people as to the likely outcome of the forthcoming battle and now 'the country came in freely to the Parliament's army' in a desire to be seen to have supported the winning side.[6] William Guise was not alone in acting as a spy from within the city: after the battle, Parliament rewarded a 'little maid' with £100 for her efforts and another £40 to others, but Guise was less fortunate. He was arrested the next day and hung from the signboard of the Golden Cross Inn in Broad Street.[7]

The wounded Earl of Derby managed to limp into Worcester on Sunday 31 August with a handful of survivors from the battle of Wigan. This evidence of fresh defeat cannot have reassured the citizens as to their fate. Even Massey's servant deserted to the Parliamentary lines. Until then, some in the city may have still held out some hopes of Royalist success. After all, Massey himself had successfully defended Gloucester in 1643 with a garrison of only 1,500 men against a Royalist army of 30,000. His experience, however, was now lost to the army and was to be sorely missed. Stapleton (though not an unbiased source) described how the citizens now 'curse the cavaleers, and repent that ever they deserted the Parliament'. The Scottish infantry were also described as mutinous, fearing (not without reason, as events showed) that the cavalry would leave them to their fate. The Royalist historian Clarendon described the whole army as being 'in amazement and confusion'.[8] On the same day, Cromwell called another council of war to finalize his battle plan. This was to be no rushed affair, but was characterized by a long period of build-up during which we can be sure that Cromwell had carefully considered his tactics and options, as the final battle was orchestrated with enormous confidence.

Landscape at the junction of Teme and Severn where the boat bridges were to be constructed.

On the west bank of the Severn, the next four days were spent in bringing up supplies and gathering together twenty pontoons, planks and poles that would be used to build bridges for an assault across the rivers Teme and Severn. Local shipwrights, carpenters and carters are also likely to have been pressed into service to assist at this stage, and local people may even have been forced to help drag the pontoons up the River Severn. Robert Ward in his *Animadversions of Warre* (1639) describes such pontoon bridges in the Netherlands where they were built to be wide enough for four men to march abreast. There, the 20–30 ft (6–9 m) boats were anchored in the water, weighed down and tied to each bank to restrict movement; on a fast-flowing river such as the Severn, however, they must have been dangerously dragged by the current. One bridge would enable Fleetwood's men to follow the Scots across the Teme whilst the bridge across the Severn would allow support to be summoned from the main Parliamentary army on the east of the city.

Supplies continued to be gathered from the surrounding countryside. On 1 September, the city of Gloucester sent nearly 16,000 loaves of bread from eighteen bakers, forty barrels of 'stronge beere' (at a cost of £20) to the army and a barrel of better quality 'double beer' for Cromwell (worth £1). Other supplies

Charles Fleetwood (1618–92), who commanded the assault on the west side of the Severn. (Courtesy Worcester City Library)

included hides to cover the powder barrels.[9] No doubt much of the time of the musketeers was spent in preparing the thousands of cartridges that would be required for the battle, with NCOs distributing match and flints.

The main battle was set for Wednesday 3 September. The time of the attack may well have been delayed until the anniversary of Cromwell's victory at Dunbar in the previous year, so as to unsettle the enemy. The delay would also have ensured that the troops were recovered from the exertions of the march to Worcester. As a recognition sign, Cromwell ordered his troops to show nothing white (that is, they tucked their shirt collars inside their coats); from this we may presume that, as at Wigan, the Royalists were wearing white ribbons on their arms or in their hats as their field sign. At Wigan, the Parliamentary army had worn green recognition signs.[10] The Parliamentary watchword at Worcester was, as at Dunbar, 'The Lord of Hosts!' – however, it was reported that the Parliamentary army was finally brought to battle so quickly that less than one-third of the troops had actually been told this.[11] Undoubtedly they would have also used other traditional Parliamentary battle cries such as 'No King but King Jesus' or 'God and the Right'. The watchword of the Scots is not recorded – at Dunbar, it had been 'The Covenant!' If used at Worcester, the call is likely to have drawn only a half-hearted participation from many of the English contingents. Thus at Wigan, the call sign had simply been 'Jesus!' Cromwell himself would command the Parliamentary reserve of crack New Model Army troops, able to direct and observe, and throw his men into the battle as and when needed.

Wednesday was a fine and clear day. The first move was to go to General Fleetwood's troops on the west bank of the Severn who were to try to bring the Scots into open battle on the flood plain below Worcester. Fleetwood's army moved up from its base at Upton-upon-Severn at dawn in two columns. Many of the units were probably from the militias, assembled by Fleetwood in the Midlands but with each column formed around a core of New Model Army units. Local tradition tells of Fleetwood's cavalry taking a final opportunity before the battle to water their horses at the foot of the ridge leading up to Powick, beside the Upton road in Carey's Brook. The discovery of a number of (undated) burials nearby suggests that they may have been disturbed by a minor skirmish. By midday all was ready. The smaller westernmost column, consisting of Cobbett's and Haynes' foot with Matthew's foot in reserve and with Fleetwood's horse, all under the command of Major-General Richard Deane, tried to dislodge the highlanders under Colonel Keith from their outpost on the ridge at Powick. The church would have been a focal point of the Scottish position, acting as an observation platform, and consequently was a target for Deane's men. The marks of the shot from a small cannon (robinet or falconet) are still visible at the base of the tower of the church. The shot is closely grouped, suggesting that the tower was being used as a sighting target by the Parliamentary gunners, and possibly to dislodge Scottish observers from the top of the tower. That the latter tactic failed is suggested by a grouping of smaller shot higher up the tower as if the advancing troops closed to open fire with muskets at the tower window and parapet. Discretion may then have taken the better place of valour as the Scots beat a hasty retreat. Deane's men fought the Scots back with great difficulty through the

Powick church from the south. The tower bears the scars of cannon fire.

Small cannon ball impressions on the tower of Powick church.

network of hedgerows, ditches and lanes to Powick Bridge and the adjacent mill (a predecessor of the present building). The enclosed ground gave the cavalry little room to manoeuvre, whilst there was plenty of cover for the Scottish musketeers that lined the hedgerows. When the Parliamentary troops finally reached the bridge, they found that the two stone arches nearest the city had been demolished to block the crossing. The Scots would also have been able to use the mill as a vantage point to pour fire on the advancing troops. The fighting was described as 'very hot, but the Lord gave our men to gaine ground of the enemy, till we had beaten them out of the ground'.[12]

The larger eastern column, consisting of the two New Model Army regiments of Gibbon and Blake and including the militia regiments of Marsh and Grey, had considerable difficulty in their advance. The pontoons had to be towed against the strong current of the Severn for a distance of *c.* 8 miles. Those destined for the Teme bridge were presumably pulled from the west bank of the Severn whilst parties of men would also have been on the east bank to pull up the majority of pontoons intended for the Severn crossing. It is likely that much of this heavy labour was undertaken by local civilians. They finally reached the confluence with the Teme by about 2 p.m. The fields on the opposite side of the Teme seem to have had little defence at this stage, with possibly only 300 highlanders under the command of Major-General Colin Pitscottie. The high, steep-sided, banks of the river were, however, a considerable defence in their own right. The Scots had not begun to deploy their forces out of the city until Deane had reached Powick and for the second time in the battle the Royalist guard proved to be very lax. King Charles was reported by Clarendon to have been on his horse for most of the night whilst awaiting signs of an attack.[13] He probably spent the morning

View across Powick bridge. The narrow lane and hedgerows prevented the cavalry from operating freely and there was bitter hand-to-hand fighting.

Powick bridge, showing the repair of the two arches nearest the city (right of picture) which were demolished by the Scots to hamper the parliamentary advance.

inspecting and encouraging his troops and had held a council of war on the tower of the Cathedral. According to one of his officers, he was planning an assault on the east side of the city and evidently did not consider the possibility of a major Parliamentary attack from west of the Severn. Thus the Scottish cavalry were concentrated to the north of the city on Pitchcroft, ready for an attack to the east. As it was, concluding that Cromwell did not intend to come to battle that day, he had then retired for some lunch.

The news of the final advance on Powick brought panic to the city. Charles was almost knocked down by some of his cavalry 'running in so great disorder, that he could not stop them, though he used all the means he could, and called to many officers by their names'.[14] Sir Rowland Berkeley told a similar story of the King not being able to find the officers to bring up their men to the battle.[15] A good many were probably scattered around the inns of the city, also enjoying their lunches. King Charles again made the long climb to the top of the Cathedral tower with his staff to gain a panoramic view of the whole battlefield. Having assessed the new situation and with the foci of action no doubt highlighted b

Hilt of 'mortuary type' sword found at Powick. (Courtesy Worcester Museums Service)

growing clouds of smoke billowing around the Teme from the musket fire, the King hurriedly ordered up reinforcements from the highlanders quartered around St John's and in the city. He then rode out to inspect the situation on the ground for himself. Powick Bridge was ordered to be held at all costs. Around 2,000 men, in two infantry brigades, were now quickly brought up, under the overall command of Major-General Robert Montgomery, with Colonel Sir William Keith and Major-General Pitscottie as his front-line brigade commanders and with Major-General Thomas Dalziel's brigade in reserve outside St John's.

THE BRIDGE OF BOATS

The eastern column had towed their twenty pontoons into final position to create one bridge across what is now the 35 m wide Teme and a second 'within pistol shot' *c.* 45 m to the north of the river confluence on the 80 m wide River Severn. It was said to have taken only half an hour to construct the bridges and seems to have met little opposition from the highlanders still assembling on the far bank.[16] Both rivers were low after a hot summer, although the flow was probably greater than that of today. The completion of the bridging was a tremendous achievement in the midst of a battle. The troops and boatmen must have sweated to manoeuvre the pontoons into position (possibly five on the Teme and the other fifteen on the Severn), lay the decking across and build ramps to allow easy entry and exit for the horses.

A 'forlorn hope' of troops had been put across the river to protect the bridges before the main body of Pitscottie's highland brigade took up their positions, but they were unable to push the Scots back far enough to open up the bridgehead. The main focus of the attack at this stage would have been the pontoon bridge across the Teme. Although this river was narrower than the Severn, the steep bank made the crossing more difficult. Fighting had developed all along the river bank from the hedged landscape around Powick and Wick to the more open flood plain at the confluence of the Teme and Severn. The discoveries of cannon balls on the meadows to the east of Manor Farm give some impression of the firepower that was poured across the river. It is likely that the buildings of Manor Farm, on the shoulder of higher ground overlooking the flood plain and commanding the road into Worcester, provided Keith with a command post for the Scots. The flood plain may have been *c.* 1 m below the present ground level, due to subsequent silting, and it would therefore have been more marshy than at the present time.

The steep banks of the Rivers Teme and Severn made the crossing on the bridge of boats a hazardous undertaking.

The New Model Army cavalry under Cromwell charge across the 'bridge of boats' on the River Severn. This opened up the bridgehead for the parliamentary army to pour across the river floodplain and drive the Scots back into the city. (Stephen Rigby)

Seeing that the battle was becoming bogged down, Cromwell brought down his reserve of three crack brigades of regular horse and foot from the main army on Red Hill. These comprised Cromwell's sixty-strong Lifeguard and part of his own regiment of horse, Hacker's regiment of horse and the foot regiments of Ingoldsby and Fairfax. Previously hidden from the Scots by the shoulder of high ground on the east bank of the Severn at Timberdine, and taking advantage of a natural ravine *c.* 180 m to the north of the confluence and another easy slope to the south, they suddenly stormed down onto the narrow flood plain and across the swaying pontoon bridge across the Severn. The river banks were less steep here, making the crossing less of a scramble for horse and man alike but still no mean feat. Cromwell was reported to have been the first man across the bridge. The bridge can hardly have been very stable for such a large number of men and horses to cross. There would also have been a great danger of the troops bunching on the narrow flood plain whilst waiting to cross and therefore risking being easy targets.

Once the breach had been made, and a proper bridgehead established, Cromwell ordered the regiments of Goffe and Deane, followed by those of Blake, Gibbon and Marsh and finally Lord Grey's regiment, to cross the pontoon across the Teme.[17] The number of regiments that had to be summoned is a testimony to the ferocity of the resistance mounted by the highlanders. None the less, over a period of around half an hour they managed to force back Pitscottie's highlanders across the flat open ground of the flood plain on to the slight ridge behind. The MacLeods, MacNeils and Gunns, along with Pitscottie's own regiment of foot from the Fife area, fought a desperate retreat, fighting doggedly from hedgerow to hedgerow and

Fighting throughout the fields and lanes of Powick was at 'push of pike'. This may have been a euphemism for hand-to-hand fighting with the pikemen dropping their pikes after the first charge and fighting on with swords. (Stephen Rigby)

often at the 'push of pike' (that is, hand-to-hand fighting), through Manor Farm and back down on to the road leading into Worcester. Most of the troops were probably musketeers, who would have fired their weapons and then used them as ferocious clubs. The surgeon Richard Wiseman treated a number of skulls fractured by musket butts. What pikemen there were would have fought in blocks with their pikes levelled, trying at first to thrust their pike points as hard as they could against the enemy and overrun them. Many men would simply have been knocked over and trampled rather than have been wounded. But before the lines of pikes became inextricably intertwined, the men would have dropped their pikes and fought on with their short swords. It is likely that the highlanders, who may in any case have been the most poorly equipped part of the army, saw such hand-to-hand fighting in the lanes as their best hope of survival by not allowing the Parliamentary troops to attack in open formation and use their superior fire-power. Otherwise, with the Scots' ammunition running low, the Parliamentary troops could afford to stand back and shoot the highlanders down at will.

As the battle raged, the clouds of smoke from the muskets would have spread like a cloud of sulphurous fog across the battlefield, hindering the King's view from the city and adding to the confusion. The colourful 6 ft square battle flags carried by each company of foot and the 2 ft square cavalry guidons were vital in such circumstances in acting as rallying points for the troops. As Carlton has pointed out, the noise of the battle in that altogether much quieter world would have been even more disorientating than it would to modern ears.[18] But above the noise of explosions would have been the relentless succession of orders shouted by the Parliamentary sergeants and officers and signalled by the beat of the drum, for the blocks of musketeers and pikemen to gain ground towards the city. Such an advance would have depended greatly on the discipline of the troops under fire and the ability to keep moving up supplies of match and ammunition to replace the exhausted bandoliers, or to distribute fresh handfuls of cartridges. The charges on a bandolier could easily be used up within the hours of intense fighting, and the barrels of the muskets would soon become uncomfortably hot. However, if, as seems likely, the Scottish supply system crumbled under the weight of retreating men, then its musketeers would soon have run out of ammunition.

A standard method of advance was for each successive file of musketeers to advance, fire and then retire to reload behind the next line stepping forward to fire; having reloaded they would themselves advance ready to fire once more. This tactic produces an almost continuous wall of fire creeping steadily towards the enemy. To break an enemy charge, or as a final preparation before their own charge, divisions of musketeers might be drawn up in close formation to fire a mass volley or 'Swedish salvee'. This could rip huge gaps in the opposing lines (but left the troops defenceless until they could reload). In these circumstances of noise, smoke and the need to focus on the orders of one's officers the common soldier quickly lost any sense of the wider tactical position. Each man probably had only a narrow tunnel of vision and concern. They must concentrate on following the orders to form up in whatever formation was required and ensure that their muskets were safely loaded for the next command to 'Present' and 'Give

Fire!' Once the command structure was broken, or when a soldier lost his bearings in his formation by his adjacent comrades being shot down, then there was every prospect of a rout. This was, of course, what the firepower of the Parliamentary army was aiming to create amongst their enemy.

Further to the west on Powick Ham, Colonel Haines, supported by the regiments of Cobbett and Matthews, was now able to take advantage of the support coming from his right flank on the far side of the Teme. He was thus finally able to force a bridgehead on to the fields lining the north bank. His men waded the river *c.* 1 mile to the west of Powick Bridge, and eventually took the bridge from Colonel Keith's highlanders. Keith himself was captured there. One can imagine the files of musketeers creeping along the low parapet walls (since rebuilt) of the bridge for shelter and trying to throw planks across the void of the demolished arches whilst under fire. Further to the west, dragoons also managed to cross the river at the now partially demolished Bransford Bridge. The seizure of these crossing points followed by an emergency repair of the broken bridges now allowed Fleetwood's cavalry brigade, waiting impatiently behind Deane's column, to come into action. Having crossed the Teme, the cavalry regiments of Kendrick, Twistleton and Fleetwood were able to cut off any attempt to flee westwards, and they then proceeded to drive the beaten Scots back towards Worcester. The Parliamentary army now poured across the Teme without hindrance. The Scottish retreat became a rout down the road leading into St John's, which the second line of defence, consisting of two brigades of foot and cavalry (possibly the 2nd Cavalry Brigade), under the now seriously wounded General Montgomery, failed to hold as they ran out of ammunition. Lieutenant-Colonel Shaw of Dunfermline's Horse and Norman MacLeod of Berneray were knighted in the field for their valour in desperately trying to stem the Parliamentary advance. The Scots were pushed back into the final reserve of Dalziel which was occupying the higher ground around St John's. Although the majority of Scottish troops were still uncommitted within the city and to the north on Pitchcroft there was no attempt to send further reinforcements. The King clearly did not have the confidence, or organization, of Cromwell in being able to move his army quickly about the battlefield. This is despite the fact that the cavalry were drawn up outside St Clement's Gate, which was adjacent to the bridge over the Severn, and therefore in a good position to support the beleaguered highlanders. But the cavalry, under their demoralized general Leslie, had little enthusiasm for the battle.

The road into St John's was said after the battle to have been lined with the Scottish dead all along its route. One can imagine the scene: the Scots fleeing desperately, with the Parliamentary forces advancing steadily behind them, pouring wave after wave of musket fire into their backs, or firing against blocks of pikemen that still tried to block the charges of the cavalry; the cavalry in turn cutting down any stragglers that fell behind or tried to break away, getting behind the retreating troops to catch them as between anvil and hammer. As Cromwell declared, 'We beat the enemy from hedge to hedge, till we beat him into Worcester' (Appendix 1.1).[19]

SEVEN

The Final Phase

SCOTTISH COUNTER-ATTACK

Despite the Parliamentary successes on the west bank of the river, the battle was not yet won. Cromwell admitted that he had engaged half his army on the west bank against 'but parties of theirs'.[1] Contemporary estimates put the number of Scots involved in the fighting so far as around 2,000–3,000 (see Appendix 1.3). The main Scottish army of *c.* 10,000 men had not yet been brought into action and there may have been up to 7,000 men within Worcester and *c.* 3,000 horse to the north on Pitchcroft. They had been positioned both to receive what had been expected as the main Parliamentary attack on the east side and possibly to make a pre-emptive assault of their own. Back on the tower of the Cathedral, King Charles saw a chance to turn the tide of the battle. He sought to relieve the pressure on his highlanders by launching a counter-attack on the east side of the city, thinking that Cromwell had over-weakened his forces on this side by drawing off his three brigades to cross the boat bridge. Cromwell's army was now divided and linked on the battlefield by a single pontoon bridge. They therefore no longer had such an overwhelming force on the east side of the Severn (perhaps *c.* 15,000 men), although they still outnumbered the Royalists. Charles was to show in the ensuing action that he would not simply command from the rear. Although his reputation is now as a flamboyant figure, in the battle he was dressed simply and soldierly with back- and breastplate over a buff coat, and with grey breeches. Only the Order of the Garter, worn around his neck, made him stand out from the other officers.[2] One of his soldiers gave his own assessment that 'certainly a braver prince never lived; having in the day of the fight hazarded his person much more than any officer of his army, riding from regiment to regiment' (see Appendix 1.3, p. 167).

So it was that at around 4 p.m. Charles attempted a pincer movement on the Parliamentary gun positions on Red Hill and Perry Hill. Perhaps if he could punch a hole in Cromwell's right wing then there would be a chance, if not for victory, then at least an escape out on the road to London. The King led one column of foot out of Sidbury Gate on the right, with another under General Middleton (later joined by the Duke of Hamilton) coming out of St Martin's Gate on the left. In support were the Duke of Buckingham and Lord Grandison with the English cavalry. The mixed force of lowland regiments (including Sir Alexander Forbes's foot), highlanders and English gentry faced, in the main,

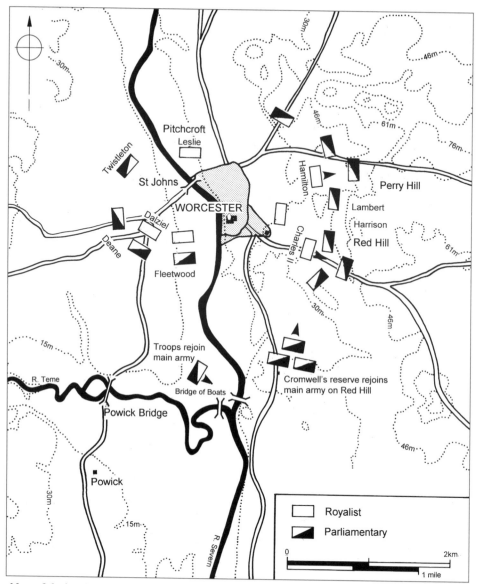

Map of the battlefield of Worcester (3), 4 p.m., 3 September. The King mounts a counter-attack on the east side of the city.

inexperienced militia troops from Essex and Cheshire, stiffened by the New Model Army regiments of Pride and Cooper and with the cavalry further to the rear. It is also likely that the recently arrived 'country people' from Worcestershire had been placed here. The Parliamentary troops were under the command of Lambert (who had his horse shot from under him) and Harrison. The three regiments of the Essex militia, under Sir Thomas Honywood, Joachim

The Royalist cavalry under the Duke of Hamilton charged up this open ground to storm the Parliamentary gun positions on the crest of Perry Hill.

Matthews and Thomas Cooke, found a new resolve in the heat of battle although the day before they were 'so amazed at the shot from the cannon, that some of them fell flat on their faces'.[3] The King had some initial success and reached his target of the gun positions on the crest of Red Hill, despite murderous fire from the sides of London Road as his men charged uphill out of the city. On the left, on Perry Hill, the Parliamentary troops had fortified the cutting of a natural watercourse and dug a trench across the top to protect their gun positions on the open ground beside the wood. The defences were lined with musketeers and with a body of cavalry drawn up at the summit. None the less, Hamilton charged through the medieval fields with their ridge and furrow that bounded Perry Wood and stormed the summit of the hill. After a fierce fight he captured the cannon there and the fighting spread into the wood. For a time, as the blue saltires of the Scottish banners could be seen to move forward, the King might have been forgiven for thinking that victory was within his grasp.

But the Scots had neither the reserves of manpower nor sufficient ammunition to press home their advantage. The advance slowed down as the foot began to run out of powder and shot. In the end, the desperate soldiers were forced to try to fight on using the heavy butt end of their matchlock muskets as clubs. The day might have been saved, but Leslie refused to commit the main cavalry reserves waiting to the north on Pitchcroft, beyond the left flank of the attack. Sir Rowland Berkeley was in no doubt that one of the critical factors that cost the King his victory was the cowardice of the Scottish cavalry.[4] Leslie felt the subsequent charges of betrayal very keenly. It may be that he was reluctant to support his rival Middleton and was certainly in a depressed and confused mood,

For a time, the course of the battle looked in the balance as the Scots and the English Royalists stormed Red Hill. Then they ran out of ammunition and were forced to retreat as Cromwell brought up his reserves of cavalry. Taking fresh heart, the Essex militia counter-attacked in a fury and gave no quarter. (Stephen Rigby)

Sir Alexander Forbes, commander of Fort Royal. He was wounded in the charge with the Duke of Hamilton. (Courtesy Worcester City Library)

R.White sculp

WILLIAM DUKE of   HAMILTON and
Castle Herald Marquis   f Cliddisdale Earle of
Arran Cambridge and   Lanerick Lord of Aven
and Innerdale one of his   Ma.tie most Hon.ble Privy
Councell and Knight of the   most Noble order of y Garter
Borne Anno. 1616 and   died of his wounds
After Worcester Fight Año   THRO VGHE   1652. Año Ætat. 35.

*The Duke of Hamilton (1616–51). He commanded the charge on Perry Hill and died of
wounds at the Commandery after the battle. His family were refused permission to return the
body to Scotland and he is buried in Worcester Cathedral. (Courtesy Worcester City Library)*

but he may also have been worried about his cavalry being caught in a pincer movement by the Parliamentary troops on Elbury Hill charging down into his rear as he moved away from the security of the river.

Seeing the danger, Cromwell rushed back from the west bank of the Severn with his regular cavalry to reinforce the militia on Red Hill. The movement of large bodies of troops back and forth across the battlefield at such critical times displays the tactical awareness and self-assuredness of Cromwell in the battle. This must have been one of the most tense parts of the battle. Hacker's horse led the charge. This was probably where the commander of Cromwell's Lifeguard, Captain Howard, was wounded as he 'did interpose very seasonably and happily at a place of much danger, where he gave the enemy (though with his personal smarts) a severe check when our foot, for want of horse, were hard put to it'.[5] Despite all the urgings of King Charles, the out-gunned Scots were finally forced to retreat as Cromwell was able to commit 'reserve upon reserve' to the battle.[6] There had been heavy casualties amongst the commanders of this stirring venture. Sir Alexander Forbes (the commander of Fort Royal, now riding with Hamilton) was shot in both calves and lay in Perry Wood all night before being taken into the city; Middleton was also wounded. Sir John Douglas was killed, whilst Hamilton, his horse killed under him, was also fatally wounded from a 'slug shot' to the leg. He was taken back to the Commandery where, after the battle, the King's surgeon and Cromwell's surgeon argued over the merits and dangers of amputation. Consequently, the operation was finally carried out too late to save his life and he died on 8 September, aged thirty-five. His last letter to his wife from his death-bed began thus:

The Commandery, just outside Sidbury Gate, was the headquarters of the Duke of Hamilton during the battle. He died there of his wounds on 8 September.

Dear Heart,
You know I have long been labouring, though in great weakness to be prepared against this expected change, and I thank my God I find comfort in it, in this my day of tryal; for my body is not more weakened by my wounds, than I find my spirit comforted and supported by the infinite mercies and great love of my Blessed redeemer, who will be with me to the end and in the end . . .[7]

THE CAPTURE OF THE CITY

The return of Cromwell's regular cavalry gave the militia fresh heart. With 'The Lord of Hosts' ringing in their ears as both a battle cry and a prayer they turned to the offensive. Steadily, as more and more troops were brought into the battle, they forced the Royalists back to their sconce at Fort Royal. Royalist accounts tell of King Charles himself leading the rearguard as his cavalry tried to hold off the Parliamentary advance in order to give as many men as possible the chance to escape back into the city and to regroup there. Although being closely pursued, the crush of men trying to retreat forced him to dismount, so he climbed the ramparts of Fort Royal in a last attempt to urge his men forward in another counter-attack.[8] Some Parliamentary troops were forced to retreat with some loss but then, in a ferocious charge, the Essex militia under Colonel Cooke (given an honorary doctorate by Oxford University for his part in the battle) stormed the ditch and earthen rampart of the fort 'to the very mouth of their cannon'. The Scottish banner was ripped down and replaced by the St George Cross of

Model of Fort Royal. (Courtesy Worcester Museums Service)

Fort Royal from Worcester Cathedral. The fort was designed to protect Worcester from the surrounding high ground. Once captured, its guns became a terrifying weapon against the city.

England. In no mood to take prisoners, the militia massacred the fort garrison and those other Scots who had taken shelter within its defences. Up to 1,500 men were reported to have been killed in this part of the battle. The King, therefore, had a very narrow escape before being dragged back into the city by his aides.

The capture of Fort Royal now threatened the flank of the Royalist army outside the city walls and signalled a general retreat of the King's army.[9] According to reports in the *Mercurius Politicus* of 4 September, Cromwell tried to offer the Scots a chance to surrender. He 'did exceedingly hazard himself, riding up and down in the midst of the fire; riding, himself in person, to the Enemy's foot to offer them quarter, whereto they returned no answer but shot'.[10] In a more likely version of events, Scott and Salway said that Cromwell had sent a messenger who was the person actually shot at.[11] In any event, this was the last chance for mercy before the city was stormed. The fort cannon were now turned upon the city and shot was poured into the backs of the retreating Scots as they tried to squeeze back down the built-up road, past the Commandery and through the three-storey-high Sidbury Gate. The latter was blocked by an ammunition wagon. According to one version of events, this had been overturned by an Elmley Lovett carrier, John Moore, to protect the retreat of the King, but it is more likely that it

Sidbury Gate in 1651, from the
Vaughan Map of 1660.

had been overturned by the Scots to make a temporary barricade across the gate. The Parliamentary cavalry were close on the heels of the Scots, with Major Swallow from Whalley's regiment of horse (formerly commander of the famous 'Maiden Troop' of Cromwell's original Ironsides) taking the honour of being first through the gate, closely followed by the men of Croxton's Cheshire militia together with General Harrison and his horse. Meanwhile the Essex militia regrouped and continued their steady advance down from Fort Royal to mop up the other Scottish troops trapped outside the city walls. It seems, therefore, as if the militias were being used as the shock troops, with the regular infantry of Pride, Cooper and Lambert following behind as a solid reserve. It is likely that the bulk of the cavalry was still being held back to keep a watch on Leslie's cavalry, surely expecting them to be committed at any time.

As the Parliamentary troops entered the city in the failing light, Richard Baxter described how the Scots were 'trodden down and slain in the streets': Cromwell's men were clearly in no mood to show mercy and the fighting in the narrow streets was extremely bitter. Now back in the city, King Charles stripped off his cumbersome armour in Friar Street to allow him to move more freely in his buff coat. Seizing a fresh horse, he desperately tried to rally his cavalry in the city and on Pitchcroft to 'scour' the enemy from around the walls, but to no avail, for according to one officer 'they were so confused that neither threats nor entreaty

From being a key part of the defence of the city, the capture of Fort Royal made it a terrifying weapon in the hands of Parliament. The garrison was massacred and the guns

turned upon the city. (Stephen Rigby)

would persuade them to charge with His Majesty'. Leslie himself was described as riding 'up and down as one amazed or seeking to fly'. The cavalry, confirming Leslie's opinion made on the march south that they would not fight, had clearly disintegrated as an effective fighting force. The officer described how 'we of the horse, trampling one upon another, [were] much readier to cut each other's throats than to defend ourselves against the enemy'.[12]

Around the same time, the Scottish reserve in St John's, under Dalziel, finally collapsed and surrendered. There was nothing now to prevent Fleetwood's cavalry from charging into the city, over the Severn Bridge at St John's. Unlike the other bridges, this had been left intact as it was needed to allow the free movement of Scottish troops in and out of the city, but there seems to have been no organized attempt to defend it. This is despite the depiction on the map of 1660 of a bastion defending the bridgehead and a substantial gatehouse with drawbridge on top of the bridge itself (see p. 46).

As the battle raged, part of the Parliamentary army on the west bank of the Severn, their job done, were now ordered to re-cross the boat bridge and rejoin the conflict on the east side of the river. This force included Cobbett's foot. The task of these already footsore and battle-weary soldiers was now to advance through Diglis to attack the south defences of the city, below the castle. The castle was strongly defended and no doubt fire was poured down on to the attackers from their leather cannon. Nevertheless, Cromwell's men broke through the earthen rampart and ditch (on what is now Severn Street). With cavalry now also pouring across the bridge from St John's, the Scots were forced to try to defend themselves from attacks on three fronts. There is no record of how effective Massey's 'firepikes' might have been in distracting some of the charging cavalry, but the Scots were overwhelmed by superior numbers and firepower and were relentlessly pushed back towards the quay where most laid down their arms. The main force of Scottish cavalry, lying outside the city defences on Pitchcroft, had played little part in the battle but now broke in a panic and tried desperately to escape northwards whilst there was still time to do so. In the city, the King was said to have been almost knocked down by his own men as they retreated past him so that 'all was confusion; there were few to command, and none to obey'.[13] The Parliamentary attack was relentless: Sir Rowland Berkeley described how they 'fell to storming without any reserve'.[14]

Charles managed to retreat to his quarters in the Cornmarket, beside St Martin's Gate (now 'King Charles's House') and to prepare his own escape, which would be covered by two diversionary charges down Sidbury Street and the High Street led by the sixty-year-old Earl of Cleveland, Sir James Hamilton and Major Carlis (later King Charles's companion on his flight). Lord Talbot's troop of Worcestershire horse formed the core of the counter-attack. The local Royalists Thomas Hornyold and Peter Blount are also said to have taken part in this sacrificial act of loyalty. Such an offensive action at this stage in the battle caught some of the Parliamentary troops unawares. According to one Scottish cavalry officer, many of them were already distracted by looting and were therefore cut down by the Royalist horse (see Appendix 1.3, p. 167), who nevertheless suffered heavy casualties. Sir James Hamilton and Captain Kemble were seriously wounded

The battle ended with a phase of vicious hand-to-hand fighting in the streets of Worcester. (Stephen Rigby)

and others killed as they were trapped between the Parliamentary horse pouring through Sidbury Gate and those coming down Broad Street from St John's. For some on the Royalist side, the realization of the scale of defeat and the bloodshed that was now to fall on the city went against nature itself as 'the Dusk of which Fatall Evening, when the ashamed Sun had blush't in his setting, and plunged his afrighted Head into the depth of the Lucklesse Severn'.[15]

King Charles's House on New Street / Cornmarket. These were the King's quarters during the battle.

Most of the citizens of Worcester had played no direct part in the battle and must have sensibly locked themselves within their houses, but as the climax of the battle now raged around them there was little that could be done to protest their innocence. As Cromwell's men poured through the city they were accompanied by the sounds of house doors being kicked in, shots and screams as the troops looked for survivors and their expected reward of plunder. The Scottish mercenary Sir Andrew Melvill was knocked from his horse in the final stages of the battle and was about to be stripped of his finery by soldiers when an officer tried to claim him, or rather his clothing, as his own prize. Seeing this booty about to be taken away from him, one of the soldiers simply shot Melvill in the stomach in order to spoil the clothing and spite the officer. Melvill was considered of no consequence in this act of casual barbarity but was left to die, thrown over a gun carriage. In the morning another English officer took pity on him and he was taken to a poor woman's house to be cared for, but Melvill's troubles were not over. The house was then looted by Parliamentary soldiers who even took the bed he was resting on. He was dragged from the house and left to die in a ditch, with a corpse thrown on top of him. Fortunately the old woman and her daughters rescued him and tended his wounds over the next three months until he was able to travel in hiding to London and thence to the continent. Melvill's brother was less fortunate: he was one of those transported to the West Indies.[16] Despite his injuries, and his return to mercenary service on the continent where he was wounded yet again, Sir Andrew reached the ripe old age of eighty-two.

THE ESCAPE OF KING CHARLES

The King only just managed to escape. Dragoons under Major John Cobbett (detached from Skippon's London regiment) broke through the front door of Charles's quarters as he was hurrying out of the rear door. This was reportedly after knighting Colonel Lachlan Mor Mackinnon for saving his life. Cobbett paused to take the King's Garter and Collar of All Saints left in the quarters and this may have bought the King a valuable breathing space.[17] The adjacent St Martin's Gate was the only exit from the city in Royalist hands and the King was slowed down by the crush of horsemen around him as they too tried to flee. Nevertheless, they would have at least shielded him from the rapidly approaching Parliamentary horse as he galloped northwards. Once beyond the city walls he was joined by the remnants of Leslie's cavalry in full flight, pursued by Whalley's horse. There was the briefest of pauses at Barbourne Bridge to decide a route to take. Remembering the failure of General Leslie to move out of Pitchcroft during the battle, Charles complained bitterly, 'We had such a number of beaten men with us, of the horse, that I strove . . . to get from them; and though I could not get them to stand by me against the enemy, I could not get rid of them now I had a mind to it.'[18]

The infantry had no such chance to escape but some of the King's men hung on grimly. A small group of English gentry fought on at the town hall until killed or captured. At the castle, the Earl of Rothes and Colonel William Drummond

Sir Andrew Melvill was shot by disgruntled parliamentary soldiers simply to spoil his clothes. (Stephen Rigby)

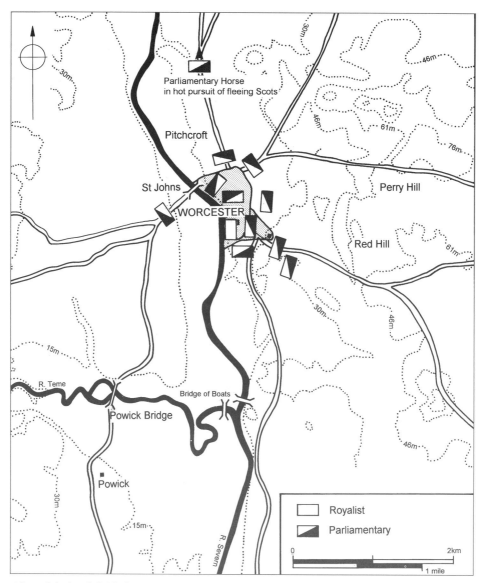

Map of the battlefield of Worcester (4), 10 p.m., 3 September. The Scots are forced to surrender.

managed to hold out with their 1,300 exhausted Scots until about 10 p.m. when the survivors were finally forced to lay down their arms. Colonel Wogan was reported to be the last man to escape the city, when close to midnight he broke out with a party of fifty men. The battle of Worcester had lasted ten hours in all. Despite the overwhelming odds, Cromwell described the latter stages of the battle 'as stiffe a contest for four or five houres as ever I have seen' (Appendix 1.1).[19] Cromwell's men were in no doubt over the higher justice of their cause: 'The

Lord gave our men to gaine ground of the enemy, till we had beaten them out of the ground: the charges was very hot for a while, but the Lord owned us in this contest, and the enemy fled before us.'[20]

The battle of Worcester was the last time that Cromwell commanded his troops in the field, crowning a career in which he never lost a battle. It was in many ways the battle that best demonstrated his skills as a strategist. He manoeuvred the Scots into a hopeless position and then devised and conducted a crushing plan of battle that demanded a cool tactical overview. The confidence of Cromwell is clearly seen in the daring construction of the pontoon bridges in the midst of the battle and the shifting of large bodies of men from one flank to another. The efficiency of the supply system to deliver fresh ammunition and water to the troops must also have been critical. A thought should also be spared for the troops that had to accomplish these orders. Although it is unlikely that any were engaged in continuous action during the course of the ten-hour battle they would have become exhausted, dehydrated and maintained principally by the adrenaline of the moment.

With the end of the battle comes exhaustion. (Stephen Rigby)

EIGHT

Aftermath

Initial reports claimed that 2,000–4,000 Scots had been killed in the battle. Many more were wounded and a considerable number of these must have died in the following days and weeks. Most of the survivors were captured. By contrast, Parliamentary losses were put at only *c.* 100–200 men, including Quartermaster Moseley.[1] Many were from the Cheshire militia who had led the assault in Sidbury Gate. The more seriously wounded on the Parliamentary side were taken to the Savoy and Ely House military hospitals in London, where the inmates were expected to contribute towards the cost of medicines and bandages whilst their nurses were the widows of soldiers killed in earlier campaigns. Three members of Honywood's regiment of the Essex militia were discharged from the Savoy in December.[2] Some casualties from the battle may have been amongst those sent from Ely House to 'take the waters' at Bath in 1652.

As the survivors of the Scottish army fled (the highest estimate being around 4,000 of the horse), they were pursued by a brigade of cavalry under a relentless Harrison who 'lapped them up as an ox lappeth up pastur'.[3] One column under Colonel Sanders was detached to pursue any that might try to flee through Derbyshire and Yorkshire. Some of the Scots were ambushed by the outlying garrisons at Bewdley, Kidderminster and elsewhere. Baxter was woken up at Kidderminster by the sound of the fleeing horse on the cobbles. He described the scene when 'many hundreds of the flying army' were ambushed in the market-place by about thirty troopers sent the short distance from Bewdley: 'And till midnight the bullets flying towards my door and windows, and the sorrowful fugitives hasting by for their lives, did tell me the calamitousness of war.'[4] But the pursuit of the fleeing Scots was not simply left to the army, and local people, resentful of this new attempt to bring the country to civil war, were eager to show their loyalty to the victorious Commonwealth. Cromwell reported that 'the country riseth upon them everywhere' and Clarendon later wrote 'very many of those who ran away were every day knocked in the head by the country people, and used with barbarity'.[5] He believed that these civilians acted far more cruelly than the soldiers in the battle. Nineteenth-century tradition tells of villagers from Chaddesley Corbett intercepting and killing stragglers at a road junction north of Barrett Hill, burying the dead in a simple roadside grave.

Part of Cromwell's own regiment of foot (detached before the battle) was involved in rounding up such prisoners in Shropshire and Cheshire. One of the officers, Captain John Hodgson, recorded in his diary how his men had 'pleasant work' with 500–600 of the exhausted Scots after blocking a road between Whitchurch and Nantwich. The Scots were by now too weak to resist and Hodgson wrote, 'Our musketeers would have gone into the lane, and taken by the bridle the best-like person they saw, and brought him out, without a stroke, so low was the Scot brought.' The exhausted survivors then fell into another ambush as they tried an alternative route towards Nantwich.[6] Here, Colonel Lilburne's men blocked their further progress whilst 1,500 horse and dragoons from the Worcester army under Colonel Blundell attacked them in the rear. This was the final straw for many of the fugitives and they decided to surrender; they included some major prizes for the Parliamentary forces. Another officer in Cromwell's regiment, Oliver Edge, was riding alone near Nantwich when he was confronted by a party of 18–20 horse. After confirming that he was indeed an officer, these men insisted on surrendering to him, including the Earl of Derby, the Earl of Lauderdale and Lord Sinclair. Their hopes of making good their escape after leaving the King at Whiteladies House in Shropshire (see p. 142 below) had been dashed when they had stumbled into the midst of the hot pursuit of Lord Leviston (who had commanded the King's Lifeguard) and a party of horse. Lord Talbot was also in the party but he managed to escape back to his family seat at nearby Longford House (1½ miles south-west of Newport) where he hid for a few days in an outhouse before also being captured. (He survived the Restoration and was killed in 1668 in a duel with the Duke of Buckingham.) The prisoners were taken to Whitchurch, Shropshire, and then on to an inn at Bunbury in Cheshire on their way to Chester Castle.

Around 3,000 men of Leslie's cavalry managed to reach Cheshire and Lancashire before being captured. As around 1,000 of the horse passed through Sandbach in Cheshire, they were set upon by local people armed with clubs, staves and even the poles taken from market stalls.[7] Local legend also tells of troops hiding nearby in a hollow (now called 'Piper's Hollow') where they were ambushed and massacred. On still nights it is said that a ghostly piper can be heard playing a lament! One graphic description is contained in the account of a Scottish prisoner finally captured at Preston, Lancashire. He was with the main body of the escaping cavalry and had ridden all night after the battle to reach Newport (c. 38 miles away). He then evidently avoided the ambush that sealed the fate of the Earl of Derby and their party at Nantwich and the mêlée at Sandbach. He and his companions thought that they must have outridden their pursuers but they had not counted on the careful preparations made for dealing with such a retreat before the battle, or on the readiness of the local people to inform the military of the movements of the fugitives:

> Our enemies' posts flew faster than we, and these wanted not considerable forces in every place to front us, and we were so closely pursued, in the day by the army and garrison forces, and in the night by the country, that from the time we came out of Worcester, until the Friday evening that I was taken prisoner seven miles from Preston, neither I nor my horse ever rested. Our body consisted of 3,000; in the day we often faced the enemy, and beat their little parties but still those of us whose horses tired or were shot were lost,

unless they could run as fast as we rode. In the night we kept close together, yet some fell asleep on their horses, and if their horses tarried behind, we might hear by their cries what the bloody country people were doing with them.[8]

Meanwhile, in Worcester the victors hunted through the streets and into the houses looking for fugitives. Under the contemporary rules of war attending the storm of a town, they took the opportunity to loot whatever they could find, showing little mercy as 'Lords, knights and gentlemen were there plucked out of holes by the soldiers'. Stolen goods included the Civic Sword, and there was even an attempt to steal city records. Five shillings had to be paid to a soldier by Stephen Field to return some civic records to the Treasury. A new sword had to be purchased in 1652 at a cost of £5 8s 6d.[9] Wine glasses, bottles, butter pots and pewter dishes were all lost from the Deanery, although it is not certain whether by carousing Royalists or plundering Parliamentarians. Sir Thomas Urquart of Cromarty, one of the Royalist camp followers, was billeted in All Saints parish with William Spilsbury, 'a very honest sort of man' according to Urquart and a member of the Council. Urquart complained bitterly that his possessions were 'plundered, pillaged, pilfered, robbed and rifled' after the battle. He had brought with him four large trunks of clothes including scarlet cloaks and buff suits and also three trunks containing one hundred of his precious writings. These were all carefully stored in Spilsbury's attic but the house was ransacked, the clothes stolen and his manuscripts at first scattered and then used to wrap food, light tobacco pipes and, worst of all to Urquart, used for 'posterior purposes'. Only a few of his possessions were eventually recovered, having been found under a pile of twenty-seven corpses in a Worcester street. Urquart was imprisoned in the Tower and then Windsor Castle until his release in October.[10]

Virtually no debris from the battle has survived. Much of the discarded equipment would have been collected up as loot, or sent back to the armouries. No doubt the local populace would have gathered up anything else that remained for the metalwork to be melted down and reused for more peaceful purposes. The wooden and cloth artefacts have long since disintegrated.

The aftermath of such a violent assault could be a dangerous time and Colonel Stapleton, for one, decided not to enter the city until 'the soldiers' fury was over'. No record has survived of the fate of the camp followers abandoned by the fleeing troops and trapped in the city. Although not considered worthy of comment at the time it is not likely to have been pleasant. Dawn would have brought a terrible sight to the citizens as they came out of their homes after a night of terror. Sir Rowland Berkeley described the scene of dead bodies lying from Powick Bridge to the town and in almost every street of the city.[11] Corpses lay within houses, in the College and Cathedral, the cloisters and in Cathedral Green, and on the east side of the city, a mile beyond Sidbury. The rotting bodies of men and horses were left so that 'there was such a nastiness that a man could hardly abide the town'.[12] It may be for that reason that Cromwell seems to have quickly decided to re-establish his headquarters at Evesham before returning in triumph to London. The captives were speedily divided according to rank, with the common soldiers being driven into the Cathedral. Others were held in the town hall (Guildh

Many of the wounded from the battle are likely to have died subsequently. Amputation of limbs was considered easier than trying to deal with the problems of infection from dirty clothing driven into the wound by the impact of shot. Despite the difficulties, some surgeons did perform complicated surgery – including brain surgery. (Stephen Rigby)

which had later to be disinfected at a cost of '2s – Paid for stonpitch and rosen to perfume the hall after the Scots'.[13] The official figures list over 10,000 men as having been captured, either in Worcester or on their abortive flight back to Scotland (Appendix 1.4). Many of those would have been wounded; amongst the nine captured Royalist surgeons under the surgeon-general, Alexander Pennycuik of Edinburgh, who would treat them in their cramped and filthy prisons were Peter Barwick, James Davies (surgeon to the Lifeguards) and Richard Wiseman. Wiseman (c. 1622–76) managed to escape from Worcester, leaving his assistant, William Clarke, to complete the treatment of his patients, but was captured in flight and imprisoned for many months at Chester. He used his experiences as an army surgeon in the Civil War to write a major treatise in 1676, *Of Wound, of Gun-shot Wounds, of Fractures and Luxations*, using examples from the battle of Worcester amongst his case studies.

The heavy, low velocity musket balls flying through the air with a corkscrew motion could inflict horrific wounds. They shattered bone rather than breaking it cleanly and could distort on impact, creating large gaping wounds as they exited. Injuries were made worse by the fact that they would tend to drive the filthy clothing of the injured deep into the wound, so increasing the risk of infection and death. One of Wiseman's main contentions in his treatise was the time-consuming necessity of carefully exploring the wound to remove such debris. Despite the difficulties, the surgeons attempted major surgery. Wiseman conducted brain surgery on one soldier shot in the head during a skirmish a few days before the battle – he trepanned the skull to extract the musket ball and cut away part of the damaged brain. The patient survived the operation and recovered consciousness, although Wiseman did not know how long he lived.[14] Even non-fatal wounds resulted in a high percentage of permanent maiming. Amputations were common as being simpler to undertake than dealing with an infected wound; Wiseman preferred to undertake them in the heat of battle, whilst the patient was still in shock and not so sensible of the pain. Operations were carried out whilst the patients were conscious, with alcohol being the principal means of easing the suffering. During the amputation of the arm of one Scottish soldier who had been shot in the elbow, Wiseman 'endeavoured to encourage the soldier to endure it'. The patient cried, 'Give me a drink, and I will die.' Unfortunately, this operation was not a success.[15]

There would have been little ceremony spared for the dead, stripped of their clothes and possessions. The late summer weather was hot and there was an urgent necessity to bury the corpses before they became a serious health hazard for the town. Some were carted away on a litter provided by St Michael's Bedwardine parish at a cost of 6d. Many of the Scots were buried in the parish (which included the Cathedral) at a cost of £2 9s 4d.[16] Some of the dead were buried in the Cathedral churchyard; others were buried in large pits on Powick Ham. A skeleton was also found in the city ditch beside Nash's Passage in 1975 which was thought at the time to be possibly from the Civil War.[17] Nevertheless, there is a marked lack of references to the burial of the dead in the local records, whose compilation was greatly disrupted throughout the period of the Civil Wars. The audit of city accounts for 1651, for example, was not actually undertaken until 1655.

The civilians of Worcester and those of the immediate surrounds of 4 to 5 miles suffered also. Nicholas Lechmere of Hanley Castle wrote in his diary, 'The city of Worcester was taken by storm and all the wealth in it became booty to the soldier.' Sir Rowland Berkeley of Cotheridge wrote of 'all houses being ransacked from top to bottom, the very persons of men and women not excepted' and the ruin of many families.[18] Even Cromwell was forced to write to Parliament that supporters in the town suffered alongside the Royalists: 'The town being entered by storm, some honest men, promiscuously and without distinction, suffered by your Soldier – which could not at that time possibly be prevented, in the fury and heat of the battle.' In all, the losses of 266 'well-affected' citizens was put at £18,708 19s 7d.[19] To help remedy the losses incurred, the Grand Inquest agreed at the Quarter Sessions of 30 September 1651 that £500 should be raised from the county to set the poorer victims in the city to work and repair the damage that had been caused. This money was to be kept under the control of the prominent Parliamentarians Colonel James, Gervase Buck, William Collins, Edward Elvins, Henry Ford and Simon Moore and was to be clearly directed towards their supporters so that 'the poor caveliers had no share to releeve them'.[20] Nevertheless, the parish of St Michael's Bedwardine claimed, in January 1652, that they should be entitled to one-tenth of this money because of the burden that they had suffered first in quartering the Scots and then in burying them. The city later estimated the total cost of plundering after the battle at £80,000 and some of the debts were not repaid until 1675. There was evidently considerable sympathy around the country for the plight of the inhabitants. In March 1652, the sum of £91 was raised by the citizens and Common Council of Gloucester 'for the relief of the poor inhabitants of Worcester that were plundered when the Scotts army was beaten out of Worcester'.[21]

For Parliament, the relief of victory was obvious. A reward of £30 each was given to the two men (Constantine Heath and Richard Caldwell) who had first brought the news of the victory to the government and messengers were dispatched all over the country to spread the glad tidings and ensure that no pockets of Royalist sympathisers would now dare to rise. Cromwell's own entry to the capital on 12 September became a triumphal procession. He was met by members of the Council of State, Members of Parliament, the mayor, sheriff and aldermen of London, the city militia and a guard of horse and foot. 'Many thousands others of quality' added to the parade, with the route to Whitehall lined with cheering crowds. The battle was also commemorated on 16 September with the launch of a new 60-gun frigate named *Worcester*.[22]

The government were, however, less willing or able to settle some of the costs of the campaign. The Cheshire brigade of militia were not paid the £1,218 owed for their two months' service until December 1656.[23] Recognizing the problem of having so many men in service, the government had tried to demobilize the militia as quickly as possible. On the day after the battle they were assembled prior to being sent back to their homes. The army chaplain Hugh Peters (1598–1660, later executed as a regicide) gave them the following exhortation to be humble and praise God for the victory, and on a more practical note, admonished them to respect the army and government. They were:

1. To think better of God than ever they had done, and go home with their faces *shining*, having spoken with Him on the *Mount*.
2. To think aright of our army, whom they saw so willing to do their work.
3. To study themselves, as unworthy and unlikely to be preserved, and yet made the monuments of mercy; not to go home boasting, but humble and wondering.
4. To mind the enemy, who was very strong and cruel.
5. To think well of the *present government*, who was so watchful for the whole.

They were finally sent home with a rousing Shakespearean call that 'when their wives and children should ask them where they had been and what news, they should say they had been at Worcester, where England's sorrows began, and where they were happily ended'.[24] By 14 September the Essex militia were back in their homes and were later rewarded with gratuities by their grateful County Committee.[25] The victory was, therefore, immediately recognized as being on such a scale from which it was inconceivable that the Royalists could recover.

Amidst all the euphoria in the immediate aftermath of the battle there was clear concern from the government to ensure that the guilty parties should answer for their treason. The surrender of Worcester to the King was not to be forgotten. The mayor and sheriff were arrested and taken to Warwick and thence to the Tower of London. The other aldermen were bailed to answer for their actions at a later date. There was then a search for other collaborators. On 11 September a warrant was issued to Salwarpe, outside Droitwich, to apprehend people assisting in the 'Scottish invasion', but this produced few results. Local society closed ranks and few seemed prepared to give evidence against those accused of supporting the King. There are also some instances where prosecutions were abandoned because it was suspected that the evidence had been manufactured to settle old scores.

The most prominent of the gentry that were found guilty of supporting the Crown faced a heavy financial penalty – not least because this was seen as one way of financing the war. The total losses of Sir John Packington of Westwood, for example, were estimated as £20,348. In May 1654, the proceeds from the sale of timber from the estates of Thomas Hornyold at Hanley and Blackmore was used to pay £600 compensation to Edward Elvins, that long-standing supporter of the Parliamentary cause who had fled on the approach of the Scots and returned with Cromwell's army. He had been persuaded to serve temporarily as governor and again on the city council 'to the hazard of his life among the sick Scots'.[26] This was a fortuitous appointment. Elvins was instrumental in lobbying the government for the preservation of the Cathedral which was close to ruin.

None the less, the majority of those listed in the muster on Pitchcroft seem to have escaped any real punishment. Robert Blount and Thomas Hornyold, as well as Thomas Hunt of Chaddesley Corbett and Richard Moore of Powick, all escaped charges of treason. Walter Blount, however, whose estates had already been sequestered in December 1650 as a 'papist delinquent', was reduced to near bankruptcy and was forced to sell a number of his estates in 1653. Colonel Birch also seems to have escaped punishment as he left the King before the actual battle. His somewhat weak excuse for this after the Restoration was that he did not think that there would actually be a battle! He was arrested and imprisoned in March 1654 on suspicion of again aiding the Royalists.

The national government was more ruthless than the local authorities in exacting revenge. On 19 September an order was sent to the Committee for Compounding in Shropshire (and no doubt to other counties) that 'As to prisoners of war, you need make no scruple in securing their estates.'[27] In London there was a blanket seizure of property belonging to Worcester citizens. The Worcestershire Committee for Compounding then had to reply as to which of those could be classed as loyal before their property could be released.[28] The Committee for London seized 79 estates in September, whilst that of Middlesex seized another 80 from Worcester and Worcestershire clothiers.[29] Most of these estates soon seem to have been released on the lack of evidence for any active participation in the invasion, including the property of Edward Heming (father of Walter Heming) who had actually gone to London one month before the arrival of the Scots and only returned a fortnight after they had been defeated. Such punitive measures caused great hardship. One London parish was forced to provide poor relief of 1s in 1652 to Mr Gosling and his wife who were 'undone at Worcester'.[30] Cases were still proceeding in September 1653 and the County Committee, anxious to reduce their workload, wrote to the Committee for the Advancement of Money as to whether they should still proceed with cases of men merely accused of being associated with the Scots but not actually accused of being under arms. The Committee insisted that they needed to examine each case on its merits.

Perhaps not surprisingly, rumours soon circulated as to the existence of a secret Royalist pay chest hidden during the battle. One Thomas Williams from Worcester was rumoured to be in possession of a small trunk of gold given to him by Charles II, which must have been thought to be of a considerable size as a reward of £1,000 was offered for its recovery. Williams was summoned before the Council of State in June 1652 but, no doubt to the chagrin of the Council, they had to discharge him in August on lack of any evidence to support the rumour.[31]

By 2 October the government was confident enough of the compliant state of Worcestershire to allow the notorious Royalist Samuel Sandys to return. The imprisoned mayor, Thomas Lysons, and sheriff James Bridges were examined in December 1651 as to what assistance they had actually provided to the Royalists; they were discharged from the Tower of London on 19 January 1652.[32]

The city must have been stunned by this last, furious stage in the Civil Wars – all the more so because of its still continuing efforts to rebuild the damage of the First Civil War. The first priority of the government was to ensure that Worcester could never be held against them again. The former garrison commander, Colonel John James, was appointed governor of the city and immediate orders were given (16 September) to demolish the city walls of Worcester and fill in the city ditches; workers were drafted in from the countryside, including Salwarpe, with spades, mattocks and shovels, but the work took a considerable time. As usual, once the initial interest had subsided, it became harder and harder to find workers, and archaeological evidence suggests that the ditch on the Butts was not finally backfilled until the late seventeenth century. This activity was not without incident: two men were killed and a third was maimed in an accident whilst

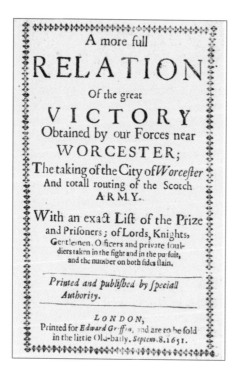

A more full

RELATION

Of the great

VICTORY

Obtained by our Forces near
WORCESTER;
The taking of the City of *Worcester*
And totall routing of the Scotch
ARMY.

With an exact List of the Prize
and Prisoners; of Lords, Knights,
Gentlemen, Officers and private souldiers taken in the fight and in the pursuit,
and the number on both sides slain.

Printed and published by speciall
Authority.

LONDON,
Printed for *Edward Griffin*, and are to be sold
in the little Old-baily. *Septem*.8.1651.

Cover of Parliamentary pamphlet describing
the battle. (Courtesy Worcester Record Office)

demolishing part of the city walls. In the Quarter Sessions of 30 September 1651 it was agreed that a pension of 30*s* per annum should be paid to the widows, Anne Jelly and Alice Swinfield, and also to William Crew.[33] The cannon from the city (along with those from Gloucester, Bristol, Chester, Liverpool and Beaumaris) were removed to the Tower of London in March 1653.[34]

There were soon renewed attempts to restore the damage of the war, although local government was greatly disrupted – there was a purge of suspected Royalist sympathisers and the Chamber did not meet for the first half of 1652. However, new building work on the Tything had begun by 1654 and the rebuilding of the street was complete by 1664. Other efforts took much longer. The damage to the Cathedral, 'much ruined by the late wars' according to John Evelyn in 1654, was estimated in November 1660 to amount to £16,354.[35] By then, the roofs of the Cathedral and cloisters had been stripped of lead and some of the roofing timbers destroyed. The vestries and even the north triforium of the nave had been turned into lodgings and the choir fittings destroyed. The damage caused by the 'late power' was estimated at only £8,204, and the rest was caused by theft and vandalism. The task of rebuilding the city housing stock was enormous: St Nicholas's parish only recovered its pre-war population figure in 1670. Some former building plots, especially in the suburbs that had been largely destroyed in 1643–6 and around Sidbury Gate, remained as waste ground into the 1680s; squatter cottages were eventually built over the demolished cottages in the Sidbury suburb – an area that had seen some of the most bitter fighting in 1651.

NINE

The Fate of the Prisoners

Most of the survivors of the Scottish army were taken prisoner in the battle or in the chase back to Scotland. The human cost of the battle was felt far from Worcester and, for Scotland, this was a national disaster. Thousands of menfolk from the Camerons, MacLeods, MacGregors, Mackinnons, MacNabs and the other clans at the battle failed to return to their homes – they were killed in battle, died in custody, were banished or were transported. The MacLeods lost between 50 and 80 per cent of their total strength of 1,000 men. Sir Robert of Opisdale (clan Munro) had five sons at the battle, two of whom were killed; William was transported to Massachusetts, and Donald and Hector may have been transported to Barbados.[1] Those men who eventually returned were usually impoverished and many were forced to turn to banditry. In January 1656 Daniel Clerk, a former prisoner from the battle, had to petition to be given an allowance from his sequestered estate in Scotland in order to subsist and to pay off his debts.[2] There could be even greater long-term complications. In 1666, a woman of the clan Gunn had to produce witnesses that her husband (a Robson) had been killed in the battle in order to be allowed to remarry.

After the first flush of relief at the scale of the victory, with 100 captured colours sent in triumph to London, the government soon began to worry about how to deal with the number of expected prisoners. Estimates vary, although the official total was 10,000. In addition, many of the men were accompanied by their wives, some of whom followed them to prison, while the rest were left to fend for themselves as best they could as they tried to return home. Of the general officers, only the Duke of Buckingham escaped capture. His party escaped the ambush at Newport, separated from the rest, and rode some 7 miles north to Blore Pipe where they abandoned their horses and reached Blore Park on foot. There, Buckingham exchanged clothes with a local labourer and was passed along a Royalist escape route to the house of Lady Villiers at Brooksby, Leicestershire. He eventually made his way to London where he reputedly disguised himself as an entertainer before escaping to the continent.

Leslie and Middleton fled with the horse but were captured shortly afterwards near Rochdale, Lancashire, and were imprisoned with many of the cavalry at Chester. As we have seen, the Earls of Derby and Lauderdale surrendered near Nantwich and the Earl of Cleveland was captured at Woodcote in Shropshire. Montgomery, with eighty men, was captured at Halifax.

*Prisoners were obliged
to scavenge pigswill to
feed themselves on the
march to prison.
(Stephen Rigby)*

Also captured in the battle were 10 colonels of horse and 13 of foot, 9 lieutenant-colonels of horse and 8 of foot, 8 majors of horse and 13 of foot, 37 captains of horse and 72 of foot, 84 lieutenants of foot and 76 cornets of horse (see Appendix 1.4). One captive, also taken near Rochdale, was the Dutch mercenary Major General Jonas Van Druschke who had commanded a cavalry brigade at Worcester but originally had been a Parliamentary engineer officer and a colonel under William Waller, transferring to the Scottish army at the end of 1645. Van Druschke had also been captured at Warrington in 1648 whilst fighting for the Royalists. After his release following the battle of Worcester he went on to serve the Tsar of Russia.

The prisoners were scattered in miserable prisons across the country – Shrewsbury, Stafford, Chester, Ludlow, Bristol and as far away as Newcastle and York. Many of the seriously wounded remained in Worcester where it would have been the responsibility of the local community to care for them. A great many of these probably died. Some of the prisoners were taken to Nottingham where local Presbyterians managed to have a number released and sent home with both new clothes and money.[3] Other individuals were immediately disposed of as 'gifts' to supporters. Cromwell made a present of two Scottish prisoners as servants to the members of the Parliamentary committee who came to greet him after the battle at Aylesbury. (Whitelock immediately sent his two prisoners back to Scotland.) The main body, however, were to be sent to London. Dunbar had already given the government an unwelcome experience of dealing with such large numbers of Scottish prisoners: those captured following the battle of Dunbar had been described by Harrison as 'unruly, sluttish and nasty'.[4] On 6 September the Council of State wrote to Cromwell at Evesham urging him not to be 'too speedy' in sending the prisoners across to London whilst they desperately sought to find enough accommodation and decided on a long-term policy to deal with them.

By 8 September the Council of State was planning to use the Tiltyard in Greenwich and the East India Company house and dockyard at Blackwall as temporary prisons. The next day, they viewed the artillery ground in Tothill Field, Westminster and prepared to turn that too into a prison camp. Chelsea College of Theology (later the Chelsea Hospital) and prison ships were also used. Initially, 4,000 prisoners were taken to London (driven like cattle, according to Clarendon) where they aroused some sympathy, as money and bread were thrown to them as they were marched by. In hiding at Moseley Hall on the evening of Tuesday 9 September, Charles II had witnessed the fate of highlanders from his own regiment who were probably escapees from a prison convoy. Father Huddleston described them as 'all of them stript, many of them cutt, some without stockings or shoes and scarce so much left upon them as to cover their nakedness, eating peas and handfuls of straw in their hands which they had pulled upon the fields as they passed'. They were also forced to eat 'roots and raw coleworts cast out of gardens for hoggs'.[5] They had come to the door of Moseley Hall, where Alice Whitgreave (mother of the owner, Thomas Whitgreave) offered them food and dressed some of the wounds as best she could. Security on the route of march had proved to be a major problem and some had escaped, due to the 'slender guard'. One escapee was Sir James Turner who cut his way out of the roof of a house in which he had been imprisoned overnight. He met up with some other fugitives who were, it seems, more interested in drinking ale at every inn they passed rather than in making a rapid escape. Turner ruefully explained that they made him pay for all the drink but at least 'I thank God they would drink no wine'. He reached London in a sorry condition whereby 'no man could ever have conceived that I had been an officer in any army in the world' and eventually escaped to the continent.[6]

Waiting for news of the soldiers was naturally an agony for the families involved. Lady Fanshawe of Hertfordshire wrote of the fate of her husband, Sir Richard, who was the King's secretary. For three days she did not know if he was dead or alive. 'I neither eat nor slept, but trembled at every motion I heard, expecting the fatal news.' Eventually, she discovered that he had been taken prisoner through the publication of a news-sheet on 5 September (Appendix 1.4). She saw him as he was marched into London with a column of hundreds of English and Scottish prisoners who 'march all naked on foot'. Stripped of all possessions, on the way to London Fanshawe had been reduced to accepting two women's shifts from Lady Denham at Bostal House in order to clothe himself. He was kept in solitary confinement in Whitehall until 'he grew so ill in health by the cold and hard marches he had undergone, and being pent up in a room close and small, that the scurvy brought him almost to death's door'. Lady Anne loyally stood below his window each morning at 4 a.m., rain or shine, in order to comfort him. Eventually he was released on bail in November, along with many other prisoners from the battle, but he was not given his full freedom until 1658.[7]

Lady Fanshawe (1625–80). Her husband, the King's Secretary, was taken prisoner at Worcester. (Engraving published in Memoirs of Lady Fanshawe, *1830)*

Maintaining the prisoners was a major expense for the government, despite the meagre rations that were allowed. A daily allowance of originally only 2¼d for biscuit and cheese was made for the common soldiers, with a higher rate for officers. Consequently, there were a number of incidents of soldiers found masquerading as officers. By 16 September it was costing £56 5s per day to feed them, which suggests that there were around five to six thousand prisoners in the capital. On 16 October, concern was raised that the prisoners held in the Tower would starve unless better provision was made for their care. Indeed, according to Clarendon, many of the prisoners in the capital did die of starvation or from disease. A fever also spread through the prisoners held at Shrewsbury.[8] On 16 September, surgeons were appointed to look after the sick and wounded at Tothill artillery ground; a shed was built to house them, but this was in a marshy area and prone to attacks of the plague even in the best of times. Certainly, by 6 November, there was such infection amongst the English prisoners at St James's House that disease had also spread to the garrison set to guard them. The costs mounted, and on 24 December Major Carr and James Keith were paroled to return to Scotland, in order to collect donations for the upkeep of their fellow prisoners in Chelsea College.

The Council of State was initially in no mood to show mercy to the defeated army. Cromwell was ordered to identify any Scottish soldier that had broken his parole from the Second Civil War not to fight against Parliament again. Excuses were eagerly sought to justify vengeance. The Council wished to see 'the narrative of the barbarous cruelties and murders committed by the Scottish people upon such of the nation as were taken, that they may consider whether it may not be fit to retaliate upon some of the Scots now prisoners here'. In the end the greatest vengeance was reserved for the English prisoners. The first to be captured had been the 400 men of the Earl of Derby taken at Wigan. On 2 September orders had been given to court martial all officers and every tenth common soldier; they would face execution in the hope that this would dissuade any further Royalist support. The order was repeated after the battle of Worcester. At least five prisoners in Cheshire were executed immediately after the battle, and the Earl of Derby was later beheaded. His two lieutenants, Fetherstonhaugh and Benbow, were also executed. It seems unlikely that all the sentences on the rest were actually carried out, as the usual practice in such instances would be for the condemned men to draw lots for who would actually be executed. The English prisoners from the battle of Worcester sent to London were held at St James's House and the Mews. On 16 October, twenty of their number were also selected for court martial but again there is no evidence that the sentences were actually carried out (they were still alive on 6 November). Attitudes softened to some degree after it was clear that the threat of rebellion had been truly laid to rest. In December it was eventually decided that the rest of the English prisoners were to be conscripted for military service in Ireland. Thus it was that many of the Royalists ended up fighting on behalf of the Commonwealth. This was not so strange, as it had been a frequent practice throughout the Civil War for common soldiers to swap sides when captured rather than face imprisonment.[9]

After the initial fury had abated, and in the context of the times, Parliament believed that it was treating the prisoners leniently. In pious tone, Cromwell wrote on 2 October that he thought that many of the Scots were godly but misguided, driven 'through weakness and the subtlety of Satan, involved in interests against the Lord and His people'. He consequently believed that the prisoners had been treated with 'tenderness'.[10] Indeed, few of the prisoners had actually faced the death penalty, and there is no evidence that Cromwell ever did single out any Scot for punishment as initially requested by the Council of State, but their fate was not to be an easy one.

Of the generals, only the Earl of Derby was executed. Hamilton had died of his wounds on 8 September and was buried in Worcester Cathedral, permission being refused for his body to be carried home. Wemyss, Keith and other colonels were imprisoned at Windsor Castle until the Restoration. The Tower of London proved less secure following efforts to make the prisoners more comfortable in December 1651: Dalziel escaped from there in 1652, took part in the Scottish rebellion of 1654 and then joined the Russian army. He returned after the Restoration and became Commander-in-Chief in Scotland from 1666 to 1679. Massey recovered from his wounds and also eventually escaped from the Tower of London, spending the next few years in a succession of Royalist plots. He returned to Gloucester as its MP at the Restoration and was later appointed governor of Jamaica. Middleton also escaped from the Tower and returned to the King in exile, subsequently trying to organize further Scottish resistance in 1652. Rothes was released from the Tower in 1658, but Pitscottie and Leslie (who had turned to drink) remained there until the Restoration. Leslie was then made Baron Newark and pensioned off into private life – he died in 1682. Lauderdale also spent the next nine years in prison. He later described his conditions as being:

> transported divers times from prison to prison, and with much patience, cheerfulness, and courage, past and endured in his person and estate all the degrees, kinds, and extremities of misery which could be expected from a cruel and implacable enemy to loyalty and faithfulness, and death itself in resolution and expectation which was unavoidable would have followed if God had not wonderfully restored the King.[11]

At the Restoration he returned to Scotland to enforce the restoration of the Episcopal Church. He became regarded as virtual dictator of Scotland and was finally removed by a Covenanter revolt in 1679. Drummond also escaped and entered the service of the Tsar before returning to the Restoration army in Scotland.

Apart from such high-ranking officers, holding the captives in prisons was seen as being only a temporary expedient and more permanent options continued to be sought to reduce their numbers as quickly as was possible. On 25 September, plans were laid to send individuals as servants to Members of Parliament and other loyal supporters. Something on a wider scale was, however, required and in the next week a considerable number of officers below the rank of captain were simply exiled; many of them probably ended up as mercenaries on the continent. Higher-ranking officers were also banished. This was to be the fate of Lord Spynie, Lord Ogilvy, Lord Sinclair and the Earl of Crawford in September 1654.[12] Those left behind had to manage as best they could. On 4 September 1655 Elizabeth, the wife of Colonel William Borthwick, had to petition for a pass to allow her banished husband to return to Scotland to settle some family business.[13]

TRANSPORTATION

The first solution in dealing with the bulk of the common Scottish prisoners was to transport them to the colonies as indentured servants for a period of seven years or more. In effect, they were kept as slaves, albeit only for a fixed period. The practice of the transportation of prisoners to the plantations in the southern colonies and the West Indies was now well established. Following the rising at St Fagan's in 1647, 240 unmarried Welsh prisoners had been transported to Barbados. Many Scots captured at the battle of Dunbar had also been transported. Prisoners from that battle, and possibly including some from Worcester, were referred to in a Council of State order of 10 September for the transportation of 1,610 prisoners to Virginia 'on the assurance that they will have Christian usage'.[14] Alexander and John Magruder (MacGregor) were part of one early transport shipped to Virginia via Barbados. They were some of the fortunate ones, as Alexander bought his freedom and settled in Maryland in 1652.[15] On 21 October, an order was also given for the transportation of prisoners to Bermuda.[16] They were in a poor condition for such journeys, to the great concern of the shipping merchants who saw them only as a commercial commodity. On 17 October, there was a complaint from John Allen and his partners that many of the Scottish prisoners had died before they could be shipped out and they therefore requested replacements.[17]

There were, however, worries at this particular time about sending prisoners to the traditional slave colonies of Virginia and the West Indies, which were in the midst of rebellion. A transport of 900 Scottish prisoners in 1650 to Virginia had been delayed 'till assurance be given of their not being carried where they may be dangerous'. Problems in the colony continued and on 26 September 1651 an order was given to appoint commissioners for 'reducing Virginia to obedience'.[18] Because of the time-lag in news reaching the colonies it was important for Parliament to stress the totality of their victory at Worcester and so dissuade any further Royalist uprising. Thus, on 30 September, 1,000 copies of the account of the battle of Worcester were ordered to be sent to Virginia. Virginia only formally surrendered to Parliament in March 1652. The problems in the West Indies were graver, as Barbados was in the midst of a much more serious armed rebellion which ended in January 1652.

As a consequence of such problems, the government also started to ship forced labour out to New England. At least one shipload of a consignment of 1,500 men also went to the gold mines of Guinea.[19] A formal committee to organize the transportation of prisoners from Worcester was appointed on 16 September. It was then agreed that men of the rank of lieutenant or cornet of horse and below could be transported to the plantations of Virginia and New England for terms of seven years or more.

Prisoners on a Virginia tobacco plantation. They were transported here for periods of seven years, although a few returned to Scotland. (Stephen Rigby)

One major consignment of prisoners from Worcester to the colonies was set to leave from Bristol. On 16 September, it was ordered that 1,000 prisoners under the rank of captain or cornet of horse were to be gathered from prisons in Chester, Shrewsbury, Stafford, Ludlow and Worcester to be taken to Bristol for transportation to New England. In the meantime, they were to be maintained at a cost of 2½d per day. However, on 28 November it was reported to the Council of State that some of the merchants involved had broken their contract and some of these prisoners may not actually have been transported. As a consequence of the continued overcrowding, disease had spread through the remaining prisoners in the city, and by 2 December they had been dispersed to other prisons throughout the Bristol area.[20] By now the cost of maintaining them had risen to 4d per day for common soldiers and 8½d per day for officers.[21] These sums could not be maintained indefinitely and the survivors probably joined the later release of prisoners back to Scotland. As a small comfort for the transportees, Scottish ministers were to be transported free by the merchants – one per 200 men – and were to be allowed their freedom when they arrived.

Another group of 300 prisoners set sail on 8 November 1651 from London on the *John and Sara* under the command of Captain John Greene, bound for Charles Town, New England. They arrived there some time before 24 February 1652.[22] They included men of the Grant, MacKannel, MacLean, Robinson, Ross, Simpson and Stewart clans. Twenty-eight of them died on board; the survivors were destined for the saw mills of Durham and Newmarket in New Hampshire, and the ironworks of Lynn. The prisoners were first marched to Lynn; the journey lasted two days and more men died en route. Thus it was that a charge was made for a winding sheet for 'Davison the Scott'. The prisoners fared better than most and the account book of the Lynn ironworks offers a flavour of the efforts made to care for them, as befitted a good investment. A new timber-framed building was provided for them, with £35 being spent on 'framing the Scotts house' – this was probably on the scale of a large barn. They had to be re-clothed, providing 65 pairs of shoes, 92 pairs of stockings and 72 shirts for this purpose. Medical needs were also taken care of, with Goody Burt of Lynn being paid to minister to the sick. Conditions were cramped by modern standards and the Scots had to sleep three to a bed. As a luxury, 200 lb of tobacco was also bought for them at a cost of £13 17s 4d.[23] There was less sympathy for these men in London, where the owners of the ironworks expressed great concern at the higher than expected costs of maintaining the prisoners. The owner, John Becx, wrote urgently to the manager to complain: 'We wrott you that we desired the Scotts should be dietted by some ther in the County by those that would have [supplied the] best and cheapest and not to have it done by you at such a high Rate the Company not being willing to allow above 3s 6d per week and you being 5s.'[24]

One consequence of the new easy availability of such 'slaves' was that the price of human labour plummeted. A transportee could now be bought in London for as little as £1. An account of two later Royalist prisoners (Marcellus Rivers and Oxenbridge Foyle) shipped to Barbados in 1656 gives an idea of the conditions that the Worcester prisoners may have suffered on the voyage to the New World.

In that case the prisoners were kept below deck in a vermin-ridden hold for the whole of the five-week voyage. A gun port had been made in one of the bulkheads and a cannon loaded with case shot was trained on them in case of trouble. Once they had arrived in the colonies, the treatment of the transportees varied greatly. It seems to have been particularly harsh in the West Indies. One other transportee to Barbados was the German mercenary Heinrich von Uchteritz, who described the 'miserable life' of the prisoners in working a twelve-hour day mucking out animals, cleaning slave quarters or working on the plantations in the searing heat. He was more fortunate than many in being ransomed after only eighteen weeks by some passing German merchants for the equivalent price of 800 lb of sugar.[25] Rivers and Foyle also described an 'insupportable captivity . . . grinding at the mills, attending furnaces, or digging in this scorching island, having nothing to feed on – notwithstanding their hard labour – but potato roots, nor to drink but water with such roots mashed in it . . . and sleep in styes worse than hogs in England'.[26]

By contrast, in New England, the Revd John Cotton of Boston, Massachusetts (a former Lincolnshire cleric) wrote on 28 May 1651 to Cromwell concerning the fate of 150 Scottish prisoners transported there after the battle of Dunbar. He said 'we have been desirous (as we could) to make their yoke easy. Such as were sick of the scurvy or other diseases have not wanted physick and chyrurgery. They have not been sold for slaves to perpetual servitude, but for 6 or 7 or 8 years, as we do our owne.'[27] Here, they were expected to work three days for the master and four for themselves, and each group of four prisoners was provided with a house. Help was also provided for when they were released. In 1657 a 'Scottish Charitable Society' was founded in Boston 'for the relief of Scotchmen' after their term of transportation was completed.[28] Some men prospered: by 1665, the Scottish minister of Ware parish in Virginia, Alexander Moray, who had himself served in the army at Worcester, could write that many of the former prisoners 'are now herein great masters of many servants themselves'.[29]

FEN DRAINAGE

From October, a large number of the Scots were transferred to a scheme to drain the fens of Norfolk and Cambridgeshire. This bleak landscape, flat and windswept, would have seemed almost as foreign as the tobacco plantations of Virginia. The fens were described by Samuel Pepys in 1663 as a 'heathened place', where horses sank up to their bellies and where he was 'bit cruelly by gnats'.[30] Malaria was indeed endemic in the fens until the twentieth century.

The scheme was the construction of the New Bedford River, designed by the Dutch engineer Cornelius Vermuyden on behalf of the Company of Adventurers.[31] The artificial watercourse was 30 m wide and 24 km long, running south to north from the River Ouse at Earith (Cambridgeshire) to the Denver Sluice outside Downham Market (Norfolk), and it completed the construction of 'The Washland' between it and the Old Bedford River, built in 1631. The scheme had already aroused considerable local opposition and had run into severe financial difficulties. There was a mutiny of workmen in 1649 and in 1651 a

Over 1,000 Scottish prisoners were set to work on the fenland drainage schemes in Cambridgeshire and Norfolk. They helped construct the 30 m wide and 15 mile long New Bedford River. (Stephen Rigby)

petition of around 500 men claimed that they were owed £5,000 in unpaid wages.[32] It had become increasingly difficult to recruit local labour and therefore the prospect of a cheap supply of forced labour seemed very attractive to the Company of Adventurers. After making an inspection of some of the prisoners at Tothill on 1 October, the Company therefore applied to the government to make use of the Scots. In doing so, they were able to use the influence of their patron Lord Chief Justice Oliver St John, a friend of Cromwell. The intention was to use them first of all in marking out the boundary of the scheme, and then to complete the works on the north side of the Bedford Level before being employed on the south side.[33]

The Council of State authorized, in principle, the transfer of 1,000 men to the scheme on 1 October. More negotiations followed. On 9 October they agreed that common soldiers held both on Tothill Fields and at York could be transferred to this scheme. There was a proviso that prisoners would face the death penalty if they strayed more than 5 miles from their place of work. On 14 October, authority for the scheme was extended to soldiers held at Newcastle and Durham. However, the terms were not finally agreed by the Company until 15 October.[34] Delay had been caused by negotiation over penalties for any escapes; it was realized that some escapes would be inevitable, but to limit this the government insisted on a clause in the agreement that the Company would pay £5 for every man who escaped north of the River Trent or who 'shall act in any things prejudicial to the state', over and above a level of 10 per cent of the total number of prisoners. The Company had to provide monthly returns of losses through death or escape. Reluctantly accepting these terms, the Company proposed to appoint a provost marshal (John Johnston) and an overseer-in-chief (John Kelsey, at a salary of 10s 6d per week) to organize the guard of the prisoners. The prisoners were also to be dressed in distinctive 'habites' or smocks made of white kersey (a woollen cloth with a twill weave), with caps of a different colour. This was so that they could be distinguished from the English workmen and to make flight more difficult.[35]

On 15 October, Thomas Bunbury and Hugh Farnham from the Company were instructed to receive 166 prisoners at Earith from a convoy under Corporal Foster.[36] A 2 ha Civil War fort survives at Earith between the Old and New Bedford rivers. Although probably built during the First Civil War to control the crossing over the River Ouse and Old Bedford River, this fort seems likely to have been the headquarters of the operation (unfortunately there is no documentary or archaeological evidence to confirm this). The men had been transported from London at a cost of 4d per man per day. After the event, this was reckoned to have been too small an allowance so it may be presumed that the prisoners arrived in a sorry state. For their efforts, on 22 October Corporal Foster and his fellow guards from the convoy were awarded a gratuity of 40s. The Company soon began to scour the other prisons, as permitted by the Council of State. On 16 October, Thomas Bunbury was sent to York to establish how many of the prisoners were 'hayle and sound' and also 'without wives' (a confirmation of the presence of Scottish camp followers), who would have been an unnecessary drain on the Company's resources. Prudence was everything: on 14 November a warning was given to ensure that the transport was conducted as cheaply as could be managed.

With the idea that the state would carry as much of the expense as possible, the intention was to take responsibility for them only when the convoy of prisoners reached Peterborough. Some additional costs were, however, unavoidable and the Company was reconciled to having at least to pay for new shoes and stockings for these prisoners: shoes of sizes 12–14 (modern sizes 9–10½) had already been supplied to the other prisoners on 22 October.[37]

As costs continued to mount, one means of raising the revenue to pay for their upkeep was to subcontract them to local farmers to have their land 'hassacked' at the rate of 6s per acre.[38] Problems of security continued, and on 19 November Parliament ordered that any Scot who tried to escape was to be put to death without mercy. The Company circulated 500 copies of the order throughout the fens. None the less, the escapes continued, aided by the local inhabitants who, aside from any sympathy that they might have felt for the prisoners, also saw this as a means of disrupting the drainage scheme itself.[39] On 31 December, the Company agreed to ship a further 500 prisoners from Durham to the port of King's Lynn for the drainage works. By 9 January, in the midst of winter, many of the prisoners were described as being destitute; 256 shirts, 128 suits (coat and breeches) and stockings were ordered for them.[40] As a means of spreading the cost, it was decided on 23 February to divide up the prisoners according to lots between the members of the Company.[41] Most of the prisoners had returned home by 1653. Their numbers were then replaced by prisoners from the Dutch War, but some of the Scots actually settled permanently in the fenland.

FINAL RELEASE

Once such means had been explored, the only option in dealing with the remaining prisoners was simply to release them. The only safeguard was to oblige them to sign an 'engagement' never again to take up arms against the Commonwealth, despite reports coming back to London in November that some of the prisoners who had already been released were causing disturbances in Scotland. On 17 December, an order was granted allowing the very sick to be sent home, supplied with money and clothing but also with a time limit by which they had to complete their journey north of the border. The remaining English prisoners at St James's House and the Mews were also released. Prisoners held at Newcastle, York, Durham, Shrewsbury and Gloucester were released throughout the first half of 1652, although some were still being held in Chester as late as August 1652.[42] Some prisoners were still being transported to Massachusetts as late as 1653.[43]

Many of the Scottish soldiers returned penniless and proved to be a heavy burden on their communities – some turned to banditry and joined the robber bands of 'moss troopers'. Robert Bell, a survivor from Worcester, was later sentenced to hang for robbing an English soldier of £10.[44] The sequestration of estates brought financial ruin to many of the Scottish gentry who had been involved in the campaign. Many estates were left empty and the dispossessed therefore had little to lose in supporting the rising of 1654. Former English Royalists at the battle also took to highway robbery, including the most famous highwayman of his time, James Hind, though he was reputed to have only robbed Parliamentarians. Hind was finally caught in 1652 and hanged in Oxford along with two other fallen Royalists.

The treatment meted out to the Scottish prisoners was not unique to the Commonwealth side. King Charles II later had no compunction in transporting Scottish prisoners to Virginia after the rising of 1678. Charles had become quickly disillusioned with his new Scottish allies. Later in Paris (and much against the advice of his wife), he bitterly complained in public against them 'for using him servilely, heaping indignities upon him'. He claimed that of the 12,000 Scots, only 5,000 had fought as they should.[45] Significantly, soon after the Restoration (22 May 1661) the Covenant was ordered to be burnt by the common hangman throughout London.

Equally, many of the Scots felt that their sacrifice was never rewarded by their King, and this was given as one reason why the MacLeods did not support the Jacobite cause. Although the highlanders came to be regarded as natural supporters of the Stuarts in times of war, the monarchy was not so ready to show support in return when there was no such pressing need.

TEN

The King's Escape

The only failure of the battle of Worcester was that King Charles was not killed or captured. Even this might have caused problems, however. The death of a king in battle would have made him a new martyr, whilst capture would have meant another trial. The escape of the King has become an enduring romance of English history. The King himself frequently told the story, and his reminiscences were published from accounts told both on the voyage back to England in 1660, and twenty-nine years later in a dictation to Pepys.[1] Other accounts from those involved were published immediately after the Restoration in 1660 in Thomas Blount's *Boscobel*.[2] The story has inspired many legends (including the fathering of a child by the daughter of a local blacksmith) and many claimed credit for participating in it.

Charles was in hiding for six weeks, with a price of £1,000 on his head. His escape would not be easy. Charles had distinctive looks: he was about 6 ft 2 in tall which made him a giant of his time, and with a swarthy complexion from Italian blood in the French royal family (leading to the nickname 'Black Boy' after the inn sign). As a consequence, the Parliamentary 'wanted' posters sought 'a tall black man, over two yards high'. He had a mass of black hair and heavy black eyebrows, with a curling mouth that was described as large and ugly. Hiding such a figure was going to be a difficult task and it is remarkable how few people did actually recognize him whilst on the run. Simply to find shoes that were large enough was to prove a major problem. More than this, however, Charles had to cope with impersonating someone from a class that was foreign to him. He had to learn to walk without his regal gait, to be subservient and to handle the day-to-day tasks that would be expected of his guise – turning a spit, helping a lady mount a horse. Nevertheless, at times, as when conversing with Parliamentarian smiths and swapping curses on his own name, he seems actually to have relished this role.

His first inclination was to try to reach London, although this was against the advice of his companions. But, in any case, Charles had first to break out of the crush of his cavalry who were also trying to escape. After a hurried meeting to discuss tactics at Barbourne Bridge, just outside Worcester, the royal party, including the Duke of Buckingham, the Earl of Derby, the Earl of Lauderdale, Lord Wilmot, Colonel Blague and Lord Talbot, rode through Ombersley to Hartlebury, guided by a local man, Richard Walker. The latter had been a member of Lord Talbot's troop of horse and a 'scout-master' (in charge of reconnaissance

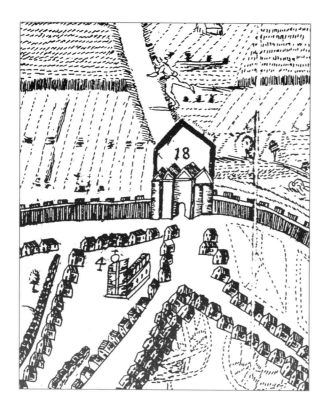

*St Martin's Gate in 1651,
from the Vaughan Map of
1660. King Charles escaped
from here at the end of the
battle of Worcester.*

and also of running spies). But the large number of men surrounding the King were too obvious a target for any pursuers. It was therefore decided to separate from the main body of fugitives at the turn off from the main road east towards Stourbridge. Charles later explained: 'We slipped away out of the high road that goes to Lancashire, and kept on the right hand, letting all the beaten men go along the front road.'[3] The rest of the fugitives continued to reverse the route that they had taken to Worcester just two weeks before. This had been foreseen by Cromwell, and as they rode on to Kidderminster and beyond many were ambushed and killed or captured.

Instead, the King, accompanied by the Duke of Buckingham, Lord Wilmot (later Lord Rochester) and initially around sixty others, chose to ride through the night via Chaddesley Corbett and Hagley to Stourbridge and then into Shropshire. In a somewhat bizarre aristocratic concept of what constituted an unobtrusive disguise, the party decided to speak French as they passed through Stourbridge! On the advice of the Earl of Derby, they were heading for the remote Boscobel House, then a hunting lodge deep within Brewood Forest. The landscape is very different today, but in the seventeenth century it was heavily wooded and the ideal type of ground in which to hide a fugitive. Boscobel was owned by the Roman Catholic Giffard family and had been used as a temporary refuge by the earl as he travelled south from his disastrous battle at Wigan. The

King would then be in the hands of a well-organized Catholic underground movement based around a network of friends and servants of the Giffards. The personal contacts of the Giffard family were to prove crucial in the fate of the King during the first few days of flight. Fortunately, Charles Giffard was himself part of the royal party, and they were led there by one of Giffard's servants, Francis Yates (later executed for refusing to inform on the rest of the party). There was, however, a change of plan as to the final destination. Too many men within the larger escape party from Worcester could guess the plan, and Charles may also have been concerned that Boscobel's earlier role as a Royalist hideout had been discovered. Thus it was that at around 3 a.m. on 4 September they arrived instead at the isolated Whiteladies House, half a mile from Boscobel House itself, and 26 miles from Worcester. Whiteladies House was also owned by the Giffards and was occupied at the time by a mixed household including Charles Giffard and his wife, George Giffard and his wife, Mrs Anne Andrews, a priest (Father Walker) and their woodman and servant John Penderel. The five Penderel brothers were to play a major role in the King's survival at this stage and were handsomely rewarded after the Restoration. Apart from John, there was George who was another servant at Whiteladies; William (the eldest) was a farmer and housekeeper at nearby Boscobel House with his wife; Richard lived

Boscobel House, Shropshire. King Charles hid here on 6 September.

with their widowed mother at Hobbal Grange and Humphrey was a miller close to Whiteladies. They were Catholics, and George and John had already shown their loyalty in joining the Royalist army during the First Civil War. A sixth brother, Thomas, is described in some sources as variously having been killed at Edgehill and Stow-on-the-Wold, but actually seems to have been in Barbados at the time.

Even within the forest the escape party with their horses was far too large to be inconspicuous and continued to put the King at risk of discovery from the local militia and cavalry that were pursuing the fugitives. Fortunately for Charles, most of his companions now decided to rejoin Leslie's cavalry, who were reported to be only a few miles away at Tong Castle. Cromwell's relentless troopers were, however, on their scent and many were captured by a troop of horse soon afterwards, only a matter of six miles away from the King near Newport, and too close for comfort. This confirmed King Charles's opinion that he was right not to remain with men who had run away once.[4] The rest of his escape party was then involved in a running fight northwards to Nantwich where they were caught in an ambush. Charles Giffard was one of those said to have been captured there with the Earl of Derby, though Giffard later managed to escape from the inn in Bunbury where he and the others were being temporarily held.

A disguise for the King was needed. He had his hair cut short and was provided with less conspicuous countryman's clothing. This consisted of a coarse hemp 'hoggen' shirt that quickly gave the King sores, green doublet, grey breeches and a leather doublet. The shoes were worn out and had to be slit to allow his large feet to fit, giving him blisters. (His own clothes were thrown into a privy.) To complete the disguise, his face was dirtied with soot. He spent the next day in hiding in the nearby wood known as Spring Coppice along with Richard Penderel. It must have been a particularly miserable time for the King. He had lost his chance to win back his throne and was now cold and hungry, lying in a wood in the pouring rain, wearing a coarse itchy shirt and his feet hurting from ill-fitting shoes. The day also gave him an opportunity to decide his next move. Large bodies of militia under Colonel Ashenhust were patrolling the roads from their headquarters at Cotsal, only three miles away, and capture must have seemed only a matter of time. The King now decided that, with Richard Penderel's help, he would try to reach Wales with its strong tradition of Royalist support. His disguise was to be that of a woodcutter called William Jones who was looking for work in the area. That evening they set off by foot to try to reach the house, nine miles away, of yet another Roman Catholic, the 69-year-old Francis Woolf (d. 1666), at Madeley. This was only 1½ miles from a crossing over the River Severn but the area was swarming with troops, and they had a nasty scare 3 miles from their destination when they were heard by the miller from Evelith Mill who chased them away. They feared the worst and expected soldiers to quickly appear, but ironically, the miller later claimed that he was only trying to protect other Royalist fugitives hiding at the mill. The final straw was the discovery that the river crossing was guarded by two companies of militia, and that all boats had also been seized.

The 'Royal Oak' at Boscobel. The present tree probably grew from an acorn from the original. The latter soon fell prey to souvenir-hunters after the Restoration, who stripped it of leaves and branches. In the seventeenth century this was all dense woodland.

As a consequence, concluding that the attempt to reach Wales was hopeless and after having spent the day in Mr Woolf's hayloft, the next night the disappointed fugitives turned back to Boscobel House, arriving there around 3 a.m. Here they met up with another of the officers from Lord Talbot's troop, a local man, Colonel Carlis – one of the last men to escape Worcester. It was obvious that the houses of such well-known Catholics were likely to be searched and so, after a breakfast of bread and cheese, with a posset of thin milk and small beer, the two men were once again sent out into the woods to hide. It was here, on 6 September, that occurred the most famous episode of the escape. Charles and Carlis were forced to hide for the whole day, supplied with bread, cheese and small beer, in an oak tree in Boscobel Wood. The tree had been well chosen by the woodsmen.

Although close enough to the house (137 m) to allow a watch to be kept on it, the tree had been pollarded three or four years previously and the centre had therefore grown thick and bushy with new growth. Militia searched close by but did not pass by the tree itself and the King was at last able to get some sleep, resting on the arm of Carlis. There was now a reward of £1,000 posted for the King's capture and Charles momentarily doubted that anyone could resist such a bounty. But he was in safe and loyal hands with the five Penderel brothers. William Penderel furthered the King's disguise by shaving him and cutting his hair 'as short at the top as the scissors would do it, but leaving some about the ears, according to the country mode'.[5] That night King Charles slept in a 'secret place' within the house. Traditionally, this is the small chamber, 1.2 × 1 m and only 1.2 m high, built under the floorboards of the attic. The King must therefore have had an extremely cramped and uncomfortable night. The attic is what is described as the 'gallery' where the King paced, at prayer and no doubt anxiously pondering his likely fate. John Penderel described him as being 'much dejected, having no hopes or prospect of redress'.

On the evening of Sunday 7 September the Penderels took the King to be reunited with Lord Wilmot. Wilmot had been moved on to Moseley Hall, near Wolverhampton, and only six miles south-east of Boscobel. Like Boscobel it was a remote place, deep in the woods. The hall was owned by another Catholic,

CHARLES ATTENDED BY THE PENDEREL BROTHERS ON HIS WAY TO MOSELEY HALL

On the evening of 7 September, the Penderel brothers took the King to Moseley Hall in an impressive, if conspicuous, convoy. (Engraving published in Blount's Boscobel, *1660)*

Thomas Whitgreave (1614–1702), who had served in the First Civil War as a cornet under Thomas Giffard. Apart from Wilmot, Whitgreave was already sheltering a 23-year-old priest, Father Huddleston, who acted as a tutor to the children of the household. The escort of William, John, Richard, Humphrey and George Penderel together with their brother-in-law Francis Yates (not to be confused with the guide of the same name) made an impressive, if conspicuous, convoy. Each carried a pike or billhook and some had pistols. Two marched in front, one on each side and two behind. The King rode to within two miles of the house, although he complained that the horse was 'the heaviest dull jade he ever rode on'.[6] Wilmot had made contact with the 42-year-old Colonel John Lane of nearby Bentley Hall, five miles to the south-east. His younger brother Richard had been in the Royalist army at Worcester and no doubt the colonel was eager for news. In fact, Richard was safe amongst the prisoners. This meeting led to an important piece of luck. The colonel's sister, Jane, had a pass from the governor of Stafford, Captain Stone, to take herself and a manservant to Bristol in order to be with a friend, Ellen Norton, who was expecting a child. The new plan was for King Charles to impersonate this servant and to try to find a ship at Bristol or on the south coast. Wilmot would travel independently in order to arrange contacts with local Royalists. Colonel Carlis agreed to separate and make his own escape as he was too well known in the region.

The young Father Huddleston described his first sight of the King as the latter approached the back door of Moseley Hall. He wore:

a very greasy old gray steeple-crowned hat, with the brims turned up, without lining or hatband, the sweat appearing two inches deep through it, round the band place; a green cloth jump coat, threadbare, even to the threads being worn white, and breeches of the same, with long knees down to the garter; with an old sweaty leathern doublet, a pair of white flannel stockings next to his legs, which the King said were his boot stockings, their tops being cut off to prevent their being discovered, and upon them a pair of old green yarn stockings, all worn and darned at the knees, with their feet cut off . . . his shoes were old, all slashed for the ease of his feet, and full of gravel, with little rolls of paper between his toes . . . he had an old coarse shirt, patched both at the neck and the hands, of that very coarse sort which, in that country, go by the name of hogging shirts.[7]

The shoes and stockings were apparently not even matching pairs. The tops of the boot stockings had been cut off because they were embroidered and were therefore too obviously rich for the rest of the ensemble. Lord Wilmot must have been appalled by the spectacle. He was the quintessential cavalier, aged thirty-eight and full of bravado to the point of indiscretion. Throughout the adventures of the royal escape he refused to be parted from his horse and his only concession to a disguise was to carry a hawk on his arm and pretend to be a gentleman out hunting![8] He did, nevertheless, play a major role in organizing the escape route, with the aid of his former comrades in the First Civil War, although sadly he was not able to see the final triumph of the Restoration, as he died in 1658.

Parliamentary troops were now close on the heels of the King. A prisoner taken in Cheshire had told his captors that the royal party had ridden to Whiteladies House and this was consequently searched from top to bottom. In answer to some rough questioning, George Giffard claimed that a party of Royalists had certainly ridden through, but he had not known if the King was amongst them. Even worse, an attempt was also made to search Moseley while the King was hidden in a priest hole (traditionally that on the first floor, below a wardrobe), but this was cunningly foiled by Whitgreave who made a great show of leaving doors open to prove that he had nothing to hide.[9] The King remained there in hiding until Tuesday night. His presence could not be kept a complete secret from the servants. Those that were not Catholics were sent out of the house on errands or kept busy below stairs, but one Catholic kitchen maid was confided in to the extent of being told that there was a visitor who was a relative of her priest, Father Huddleston, and who had been at the Worcester battle. At midnight on 9 September, Colonel Lane collected Charles to take him to Bentley Hall and the next morning Charles began his hazardous trek to the south coast with Jane Lane. They were also accompanied by her cousin Henry Lascelles who had served as a cornet to Colonel Lane in the First Civil War. The King's role was as the son of one of Jane Lane's tenant farmers, acting as her attendant for the journey. He was disguised in the grey Sunday best suit of a poor farmer, under the name of Will Jackson. The King described the next stage of the journey:

> We took our journey towards Bristol, resolving to lie at a place called Long Marson [Long Marston], in the Vale of Evesham. We had not gone two hours on our way before the mare I rode cast a shoe, so we were forced to ride to get another shoe at a scattering village, whose name began with something like 'Long ——', and as I was holding my horse's foot I asked the smith the news. He told there was no news that he knew of, since the good news of the beating of the rogues, the Scots. I asked him whether there were none of the English taken that joined with the Scots. He answered that he did not hear that rogue, Charles Stuart, was taken, but some of the others, he said, were taken, but not Charles Stuart. I told him if that rogue were taken he deserved to be hanged more than all the rest for bringing in the Scots, upon which he said I spoke like an honest man, and so we parted.

Local tradition places this incident with a Parliamentarian blacksmith at Bromsgrove, although there is no real proof of this. It depends on the equation of Bromsgrove with the 'scattering village' beginning with 'Long ——' although at the time this was a town with a population of around 2,000 people and clearly named on maps of the period. Longborough has been suggested as an alternative.[10] Later stories also claim that they spent a day on this journey in the woods behind the home of the mother of Anne Tomlinson at Bously Lodge in Alvechurch parish.[11] From there they went to Stratford where they had to manoeuvre past a troop of Parliamentary horse and then spent a night with friends of Jane Lane (John and Amy Tomb) at Long Marston. There he had to act out his role of a clumsy gentleman servant in the kitchen, having failed to work the spit properly. They spent the night of Thursday 11 September at the Crown Inn, Cirencester. The King and Henry Lascelles shared a room but, as befitted his role as servant, 'Will Jackson' was only given a truckle-bed, pulled out from beneath the four-poster bed. When left alone, Henry generously swapped beds with his sovereign.

From Cirencester the party passed through Bristol and arrived at their official destination, the Norton household at Abbots Leigh (a few miles to the west of Bristol and overlooking the Bristol Channel) on the Friday. Here occurred another famous encounter as the King met a soldier from his own regiment who failed to recognize him and indeed said that the King was at least three fingers taller. The butler at the house, John Pope (a former servant at the court who had served at Lichfield in Colonel Bagot's regiment), did, however, recognize him but remained loyal and was sent out to discover details of any suitable shipping that was leaving Bristol. Unfortunately there were none available and so, after a brief rendezvous with Lord Wilmot, who had also made his way south (after hiding with Sir John Winter in Gloucestershire), the King set off on Tuesday 16 September towards the south coast. They were now heading for the home of Colonel Wyndham at Trent Manor (approximately forty miles south of Abbots Leigh on the Somerset/Dorset border near Sherbourne) who had been the governor of Dunster Castle during the First Civil War. Fearing that the coast itself would be heavily guarded, it was hoped that this would serve as a safer base whilst looking for a ship. Here Charles said his farewells to Jane Lane and Henry Lascelles, who headed back home. In case their role in the escape became known, John and Jane Lane then made their own escape to France.

While at Trent, Charles was obliged to listen to the sounds of celebration from the nearby village as the occupants entertained a trooper who claimed to have personally killed the King at the battle of Worcester and had taken his buff coat. Along with much drinking, the church bells were rung, guns fired and bonfires lit. According to the then nineteen-year-old Lady Anne Wyndham, writing in 1681, such popular expressions of disloyalty did not engender public anger or bitterness within the King but merely pity: 'Alas, poor people!' he sighed.[12] His more private thoughts were not, however, recorded. Unfortunately for the King, there was a great shortage of vessels in the area as many had been pressed into service to carry the army to Jersey (which still held out for the King). This also meant that there were large bodies of troops in the area. Fortunately, the government seemed to have little idea of where the King actually might be and, as the incident at Trent demonstrates, rumours abounded. Reports were published that the King was on his way to Scotland, the Isle of Man or even had taken up with a highwayman near Coventry.[13]

The first attempt to board a ship was made on a coal-ship at Charmouth. On this occasion the story told to the owner, Captain Ellesdon, was simply that some escapees from the battle of Worcester needed passage to France. Ellesdon was known to have organized similar escapes before. In this case, however, the proceedings turned into a fiasco as the wife of the ship's captain, Stephen Lim discovered what was afoot and locked her husband in the bedroom to prevent him from getting involved in such a dangerous venture.[14] The preparations had meant taking a room in the Queen's Arms at Charmouth, and the suspicions of the ostler, Henry Hall, who was a member of the local militia, had been aroused by the comings and goings of his guests waiting for the arrival of the King. In particular, they kept their horses saddled all night ready for a rapid departure. He was not satisfied by the story told to the innkeeper's wife, Margaret Wade, that the party were simply planning an elopement between two ill-starred lovers (acted out by the King and the niece of Lady Anne Wyndham, Juliana Coningsby). His suspicions that these were actually senior Royalists planning an escape then seemed to be confirmed when he was told by the local smith that Lord Wilmot's horse had been shoed in three different counties, including Worcestershire. The ostler passed on his suspicions to the local parson (Benjamin Westley, the great-grandfather of Samuel Wesley), who guessed that this might be the royal escape party. Fortunately, it was only then that Hall decided to inform his commanding officer in the militia. The local military were mobilized and searched the inns and the houses of several known Royalists in the area, convinced that the King was trying to escape dressed as a woman.

The delay in taking any form of action on these suspicions had already allowed the royal party to flee Charmouth, not knowing the reason behind the non-appearance of Limbrey's ship. They first went to Bridport and then on to Broadwindsor in Dorset. All the time they had to pass through troops mobilizing for the invasion of Jersey, and had a party of a dozen troopers close on their heels. Drama turned almost to farce at the George Inn in Broadwindsor. After taking rooms there on the top floor, the rest of the inn was commandeered by around forty soldiers who were passing through to the coast ready for embarkation. The King was trapped and could easily have been discovered by a cursory search. The soldiers were, however, accompanied by some of their families and camp followers who included a pregnant woman. The latter promptly proceeded to go into labour. The noise of the labour pains was accompanied by fierce arguments between the soldiers and the officers of the parish as to who would be responsible for maintaining the mother and child when the soldiers moved on. This was all sufficient distraction to ensure that Charles spent the night, if not in peace, then at least in relative safety.[15] Meanwhile, Ellesdon had gone to the house of Sir Hugh Wyndham (uncle of Francis Wyndham) at Pilisdon House, Devon, looking for the King. It appears that he had been followed by soldiers from Charmouth, as the house was raided soon afterwards. The troopers treated the household roughly and 'did not spare the young ladies'.[16]

Disappointed at this failure to find a ship, the King returned inland to Trent. The area was, however, clearly becoming unsafe, as the preparations for Colonel Heane's expedition to Jersey offered little chance of success of finding a vessel (the fleet of around eighty vessels finally sailed on 17 October from Weymouth). New arrangements for a ship collapsed when it was actually pressed into the navy. Charles had now been a fugitive at Trent for nineteen days, too long for safety. During this time he had been obliged to spend most of his time in his room, which had a secret chamber attached. One way of passing the time was to bore holes in some gold pieces (possibly part of £100 in gold sent to him by Colonel Strangeways to offset the fact that he could not, or would not, offer help in finding a ship) to turn into keepsakes for those who had helped him.[17] On Monday 6 October (or 3 October according to *Boscobel*) he was moved by 'private ways' further inland to Heale House, on the River Avon near Salisbury, home of the widow Katherine Hyde (a cousin of Clarendon). He stayed there for four or five nights while Wilmot sought contacts with local known Royalists. It was difficult for an over-awed Katherine to maintain the alias of the King in front of her servants. One night at supper, he was seated at the lower end of the dining table as befitted his assumed position, but she could not resist giving him two larks to eat when everyone else was only given one![18] Meanwhile, Wilmot's enquiries had led him to Colonel George Gunter from Racton, near Chichester, and together they scoured the Sussex coast for a ship. Eventually, Gunter decided to risk approaching a slight acquaintance, Francis Mansell, who was a Chichester merchant trading with France and might therefore have some useful shipping contacts. He claimed to want passage for two friends who had been involved in a duel. Mansell agreed to help and went with Gunter to Brighton where, after another hiccup in planning, they made contact with Nicholas Tettersell, the master of the 34 ton coal-ship *Surprise*. After a long negotiation, Tettersell agreed to carry the 'duellists' and Gunter was finally able to report a successful outcome to Wilmot.

The King left Heale House at 2 a.m. on Sunday 12 October by a back way and started his ride eastwards towards the Sussex coast, resting overnight at Thomas Symons's house at Hambledon (Symons was the brother-in-law of Colonel Gunter). Thomas Symons was not at home when they arrived but came in later after a day of hard drinking in the local inns. In a state of drunken confusion, he at first mistook the King, with his short haircut and in the dress of a 'meaner sort of country gentleman', for a Roundhead colonel.[19] Thomas was rewarded at the Restoration with the appropriate gift of a drinking cup. On the way they had another close encounter with Parliamentary troops, this time those of Colonel Morley who were guarding Bramber Bridge, but they finally reached Brighton where the party, now consisting only of the King, Wilmot and Gunter, took a room at the George Inn on West Street. (This was later renamed the King's Head.) The cheerful tone of the evening disintegrated as Tettersell came to realize who one of his 'duellists' actually was. There was an argument with Gunter over re-negotiating a new price for the passage and the King must have feared that the arrangement was going to collapse. King Charles smoothed the situation, however, and around 4 a.m. on Wednesday 15 October he and Wilmot finally boarded the ship at anchor in Shoreham Creek. They set sail at around 8 a.m. and were put ashore at dawn the next morning via a small cock-boat just outside Fécamp harbour in Normandy. The King was now a sorry sight. When he arrived in Paris the Venetian ambassador reported how 'his dress was more calculated to move laughter than respect, and his aspect is so changed that those who were nearest believed him to be one of the lower servants'.[20] One may wonder which reaction Charles hated more – the ridicule or the pity. Charles was to spend the next nine years in exile. In 1681 Thomas Blount summed up the emotion of the flight:

From the 3 of September at Worcester to the 15 of October at Brighthemston being one and forty dayes. He passed through more dangers than he travailed miles, of which yet he travers'd in that time only neer three hundred (not to speak of his dangers at Sea, both at his comming into Scotland, and his going out of England nor of his long march from Scotland to Worcester) some-times on foot with uneasy shooes; at other times on horseback, encumbered with a portmanteau and which was worse, at another time, on the gall-back'd slow paced Millers horse; sometimes acting one disguise in course linnen and a leather doublet; sometimes another, of almost as bad a complection; one day he is forced to sculke in a barn at Madely; another day sits with Colonel Carlos in a tree, with his feet extremely surbated and at night glad to lodge with William Penderel in a secret place at Boscobel which never was intended for the dormitory of a King.

Sometimes he was forced to shift with coarse fare for a belly-full; another time in a wood, glad to relieve the necessities of nature with a messe of milk served up in an homely dish by good-wife Yates a poor country woman. Then again for a variety of tribulation, when he thought himself almost out of danger, he directly meets some of those rebels, who so greedily sought his bloud, yet by God's great providence, had not the power to discover him; and (which is more than has yet been mentioned) he sent at another time to some subjects for relief and assistance in his great necessity who out of a pusillanimous fear of the bloudy Arch-rebel then reigning, durst not own Him.

Besides all this twas not the least of his afflictions daily to hear the Earl of Derby and other his most loyal subjects, some murdered some imprisoned and others sequestred in heaps, by the same bloudy usurper, only for performing their duty to their lawful King. In a word there was no kind of misery (but death itself) of which His Majesty in this horrid persecution, did not in some measure, both in body, mind and estate, bear a very great share.[21]

ELEVEN

Later Events

IMPACT OF THE BATTLE

The news of the scale of defeat at Worcester was completely demoralizing for the remaining English Royalists. At first, Royalist circles simply refused to believe the enormity of their defeat. One rumour even claimed that it was the Scots who had won a victory over Lambert, with King Charles having taken the main army west to Hereford. Such stories circulated even longer on the continent. Thomas Killigrew, the 'Resident of England' at the court of the Doge in Venice, proudly reported on 2 October that the Royalist army had firstly killed 4,000 of Cromwell's men at Warrington and then had entered Worcester with 20,000 horse and 16,000 foot; the citizens were reported to have massacred a Parliamentary garrison of 4,000 men. One can only imagine Killigrew's embarrassment and despair when letters arrived the very next day from the Venetian ambassador in France with a more accurate account of the battle.[1] Such rumours are typical of the propaganda used by both sides during the Civil Wars. Bewildered, the only explanation that many could find for the scale of the defeat was treachery or cowardice. Much of the blame was placed on Leslie. As a result, some of those in exile, such as Sir Edward Nicholas, were now ready to give up the struggle and hoped that the scale of victory would allow Parliament to be magnanimous and allow them to return home without penalty (see Appendix 1.5, p. 169).

The destruction of the Scottish army had serious constitutional implications for Scotland. Organized military resistance to the Commonwealth had been crushed, and in 1652 the English government was able to impose a Declaration of Union with Scotland. The independent institutions of the latter – the Edinburgh Parliament, Committee of Estates and the General Assembly of the Church – were suppressed and the legal system was remodelled on English lines. This was overseen by an army of occupation paid for out of punitive taxation. Some of the survivors from the battle, especially from the Highlands, did fight on, although Argyle submitted (and was executed for treason after the Restoration). Chief 'Smooth John' MacNab was killed in 1653, still fighting the Commonwealth, and there was continued Highland support for the Royalist rising of 1654. At the same time, however, the tensions between lowlanders and highlanders, and between clans, continued. This greatly hampered any effective resistance to the English occupation.

The success of the Worcester campaign in removing the immediate threat of Royalist insurrection meant that the huge New Model Army could at last be reduced. By the time of the battle there were c. 50,000 men in the army as a whole. But in the autumn, five regiments of foot, thirty independent companies of horse and two regiments of horse, together with a number of garrisons, were disbanded. Many of the surviving troops could also now be released for service in Ireland. The army was also again free to think about politics and religion. The assembly of such a large part of the army and its generals at Worcester may even have provided a forum for the events that were to follow. Many considered that the Rump Parliament had failed the ideals that they had fought for. Some turned to the fanaticism of the Fifth Monarchist movement (which believed that a 1,000 year rule of Christ on earth was imminent), now led by General Harrison. Others followed the more secular faction led by General Lambert who wished to see the establishment of a small Council of State until a new Parliament could be elected. The immediate consequence of the success at Worcester was that senior officers could return to government. Cromwell held the various factions in check until he too finally lost patience with what were now regarded as purely self-seeking Members of Parliament. Thus it was that in April 1653 the army marched into Parliament to expel the Rump. Instead, an assembly of 140 men nominated by the Council of Officers was gathered that later took up the name of the 'Barebones Parliament' (after 'Praise-God Barbon', a London leather merchant and Baptist lay preacher). The members for Worcestershire were Colonel James and Richard Salway, but no other members were returned for the towns in the county. Factionalism continued to plague the new assembly and in December 1653 a plot was engineered for the moderates within it to resign their authority into the hands of Cromwell. The latter was then solemnly installed as Lord Protector, but this was not enough to create a stable government.

LATER EVENTS

In this atmosphere of continuing instability a watchful eye continued to be maintained on Worcestershire's loyalties as rumours of further plots circulated throughout the country during 1654–5. The names of the same small group of active Royalist gentry in the county come up time and time again but there is no evidence that they attracted any wider support. There were reports that Samuel Sandys of Ombersley had held a secret meeting on the London waterfront in the autumn of 1654 with Sir Henry Lyttleton, Sir John Packington and the Royalist agent Major Henry Norwood. It is likely that as a consequence of this meeting, Lyttelton and Packington were arrested in December on charges of receiving arms from Norwood and were thrown into the Tower of London. Norwood had supplied 40 pairs of pistols, 29 saddles and 20 carbines to Lyttleton and had also sent crates of arms to Packington and other Midlands Royalists labelled 'bottles of wine'.[2] In January 1655 Francis Carter of Kidderminster reported a local man, Thomas Thompson, as a Royalist agent. Thompson was summoned in turn before the Kidderminster bailiffs, Worcester JPs and finally the Council of State where he turned informer. Amongst the fourteen names that he gave as conspirators with Royalist exiles in Amsterdam were Sir Rowland Berkeley, Sir John Packington and Sir Henry Lyttleton. It is not clear how real this plot was, but Carter was awarded £20 for his information.[3] Packington was released from prison in September 1655 on a bond of £5,000 to appear on summons and to be of good behaviour.[4] Lyttleton, however (then high sheriff of the county), remained imprisoned in the Tower of London for two years until, in July 1656, he was transferred to St James's House where he had more freedom 'and refreshment'. He survived to become MP for Lichfield in 1678–9 and died in 1693.

In March 1655, a series of ineffective Royalist conspiracies culminated in the Penruddock Rising in Salisbury. This was quickly quashed and Cromwell wrote to Nicholas Lechmere (the militia commissioner who had been MP for Worcester in 1654), John Walsh (sergeant-at-law) and the Justices of the Peace of the county warning them to keep a watch on strangers in the county who might 'kindle fires' of dissent.[5] Rumours continued to abound; local Royalists under the leadership of Samuel Sandys and Lord Windsor did, at the least, continue to maintain links with exiled Royalists even if claims of actual conspiracies may have been exaggerated. The government was determined to keep a tight control on the county in order to prevent such contacts developing into a real threat. Troops were sent into Worcester from Hereford in order to guard against possible trouble at the horse fair. A number of the familiar Royalist names were also detained in June 1655 for a time as a precaution against future revolt. They included Samuel Sandys, the now 68-year-old Sir Ralph Clare of Caldwell, Thomas Savage of Elmley Castle and Sir George Wyntour of Huddington. Restrictions were also put on the movements out of the county of other veterans of the Worcester battle such as Captain Sheldon from Broadway (who was arrested for going to London, albeit to sit on a jury, without permission). Such moves may well have deterred any serious plans that there may have been to raise the county in rebellion, and no mention was made of Worcester in the list made in October 1655 of towns where rebellion had been intended during the year.[6]

To guard against future attempts to organize rebellion, the country was divided into eleven military districts each under an experienced major general. Their principal task was to round up suspected Royalist activists; they were assisted by a newly raised mounted militia, which was to be funded out of a new 'decimation tax' consisting of a 10 per cent levy on all Royalist estates worth above £100 per annum. Seemingly in contravention of the 1652 Act of Oblivion, it was not simply those who had taken up arms in the recent risings that were to suffer but any that had supported the crown in the past. In both an effort to prevent the gathering of trouble-makers and also to support the 'godly' community, horse racing, bear-baiting, cockfights and plays were banned. Malignant clergy were also ejected. A comprehensive register of Royalist sympathizers was planned but was applied only patchily. In September 1655 Major General James Berry was sent into Worcestershire as part of a large district including Shropshire, Herefordshire and Wales. His headquarters were in Shrewsbury, with Captain Talbot Badger of the militia acting as his deputy in Worcestershire. Berry had begun his military career as captain-lieutenant in Cromwell's regiment of horse and was promoted to command his own regiment of horse in 1651. He had been close friends with the Kidderminster clergyman

Richard Baxter before the war, but they had fallen out over politics and religion (Berry being more of a radical and an Independent) and Baxter later disdainfully referred to him as having merely been the clerk of an ironworks before he joined the army. (He had probably worked for Richard Foley of Stourbridge.) Baxter believed that Berry had been corrupted by Cromwell and described his time in power as 'modest and short; but hated and scorned by the gentry that had known his inferiority'. Whether they resented him or not, the gentry recognized his power and 'attended to him as submissively as if they had honoured him, so significant a thing is power and prosperity to worldly minds.'[7] The tactic worked. Berry was one of the most able of the major generals and was comparatively moderate in his exactions: he took only eleven bonds for good behaviour in Worcestershire as compared with Desborough's 316 in Gloucestershire and Worsley's 472 in Cheshire.[8] Nevertheless, his own inclination would have been to extend the decimation tax to all Royalists with estates worth over £50. He used his position well and in 1656 Berry was returned as one of the five MPs for Worcestershire.

Cromwell rejected the title of king in 1657 and died the following year, to be succeeded by his son Richard. According to legend, the devil then claimed his soul during a violent storm, supposedly as a result of a pact made at Worcester to ensure Cromwell's victory in return for his soul after seven years.[9] Jane Gallett of Tarrington (near Hereford), who died in 1749 aged over 105 years old, remembered 'Oliver's Wind' passing over on the day of his death – on the seventh anniversary of the battle of Worcester on 3 September 1658. The city officers remained on watch for three nights after the death of Cromwell to guard against any possible disturbances.

There was yet another attempt at a rising in the region during 1659, but this was again forestalled by the government. Sir George Booth was a Cheshire landowner who tried to raise his county and adjacent areas on 1 August, calling for a new Parliament. The revolt was only thinly supported, however. The Worcestershire militia was mobilized against the threat of rebellion. New foot was raised from Worcester in July, and three troops of horse were ordered to be raised from the county on 15 August to help counter the threat, along with a troop of dragoons under the command of Captain Boyleston (who had commanded the Parliamentary rearguard at Worcester in August 1651). The rising did not, however, directly affect the county.[10] Exaggerating slightly, the County Committee for Worcestershire proudly told the Committee for Compounding that locally only the Lyttleton family had joined the revolt. Sir Henry Lyttleton and his brother Constantine were both taken prisoner in the fighting but Charles and William managed to flee.[11] The Committee had already placed Colonel Samuel Sandys, Sir John Packington and other members of the Worcestershire gentry under preventative arrest. None the less, there were still some in Worcester who tried to raise support for the rising. The bookseller, Francis Rea, distributed Booth's Declaration in the city. The rebels were routed by Lambert at Hartford Green, near Northwich, on 19 August. Although the local militia was soon stood down, there was a mounting sense of unease in the county and indeed in the country as a whole. From 14 September Worcester was garrisoned by three companies of regular troops from Samuel Clark's regiment, newly returned from Flanders 'for the preservation of the peace'.[12] The Governor of Worcester in 1660, William Collins, wrote to the Commissioners for the Government of the Army on 4 January that his garrison had been on 'hard duty' for eight weeks because of 'highway robbers, being considerable parties, and supposed to be of the old enemy, they riding in the posture of soldiers'.[13] The reality was that the Protectorate of Richard Cromwell was already in its final death throes; the various intrigues of the Royalist 'Sealed Knot' were to prove to be irrelevant.

THE RESTORATION

The battle of Worcester, that 'crowning mercy' according to Oliver Cromwell, had marked the effective end of the attempt to settle the long-running conflict between King and Parliament by force.[14] The Restoration was now about to be achieved by popular consent. A groundswell of support for Charles II that was so noticeably lacking in 1651 was now sweeping the country in its desperate search for stability in traditional institutions. Richard Cromwell, a civilian, resigned as Protector in May 1659 and the purged Parliament was restored. As well as electing the governor, William Collins, as MP in 1659, Worcester had also elected Thomas Streete, unseating Edmund Gyles who was a relative by marriage of Oliver Cromwell. The enraged supporters of Gyles described Streete as 'a person who had been in arms, and a common swearer, [who] was chosen by the profane rabble and cavaliers'.[15] Streete was able to defend himself successfully against the charges and his brother testified in particular that he had advised having nothing to do with the Scots when they came to Worcester in 1651. But the winds of change were blowing close. In October, Lambert and the hardliners in the army attempted to expel Parliament once again. General Monck, in Scotland, condemned the action and began to march south with his army to restore Parliament. He arrived in February 1660 and enforced the readmittance of the expelled members of the Long Parliament.

Parliament now opened negotiations with the exiled Charles II. Lambert's last-ditch attempts to halt the process in April were defeated, and Charles finally landed at Dover on 25 May, arriving in London in time for his thirtieth birthday. On his return, the New Model Army that had sealed his downfall in 1651 formed the guard of honour. The diarist John Evelyn wrote that the Restoration was accomplished 'without one drop of blood shed, and by that very army which rebelled against him'.[16] In similar vein, Richard Baxter also marvelled at how 'an army that had conquered three such kingdoms and brought so many armies to destruction, cut off the king, pulled down the Parliament and set up and pulled down others at their pleasure' could acquiesce at the Restoration 'without one bloody nose'. For Baxter this was the supreme proof of the existence of a God.

Worcester also celebrated and no doubt was confident that the city would receive a reward for its self-proclaimed faithfulness. Many of the county gentry had only recently been released from prison in the aftermath of Booth's rising, and now there were parades with drum and trumpet, and much sword waving. Bonfires were lit in the street, so that 'At night the city seemed in a flame, all

At the Restoration, the King was escorted through the streets of London by the same New Model Army that had been the cause of his defeat at Worcester. (Stephen Rigby)

night four or five bonfires in every street; in some streets, 12.'[17] Worcester then tried to return to pre-war normality. Despite all of the damage, enough was repaired of the nave of the Cathedral to enable a service to be held on the anniversary of the battle on 3 September 1660, and an appeal was launched to raise funds to prevent what was seen as a real danger of the collapse of the building. The celebrations continued at the coronation in April 1661, when a total of 53 lb of gunpowder was provided to fire gun salutes; there was also a huge feast at the town hall costing £8 15s and including 12 quarts of claret, 11 of sack, 11 of white wine, 18 papers of sugar, 2 lb of tobacco and a gross of tobacco pipes. The mayor and council gave out wine and biscuits to the community. One cannot help but wonder, however, what some of the Parliamentarian stalwarts such as Sir Nicholas Lechmere thought of the proceedings. Did they feel that the struggles of the past eighteen years had been wasted? In truth, the monarchy would never be the same. There were certainly some in the city who remembered well the alliance of Charles with the Scottish Covenanters. A disgruntled Presbyterian posted the following rhyme around the city before the Coronation:

> This day it is said the King shall swear once more
> Just contrary to what he swore before,
> Great God, O can thy potent eyes behold
> This height of sin and can thy vengeance hold?
> Nip thou the Bud before the Bloom begins,
> And save our Sovereign from presumptuous sins.
> Let him remember Lord; in mercy grand
> That solemly he swore the Covenant.

The militia was mobilized to prevent any other disturbances by supporters of the 'good old cause' and a reward of £20 was later offered for the identification of the author.[18]

The human consequences of war were to stay with the people for a long time. By October 1662, £240 per annum was being paid by the county for the relief of maimed soldiers. There was a similar story in other counties. Robert Coller, a carpenter, was a former Parliamentary soldier from Kingstons Langley in Wiltshire. In 1659 he petitioned for a pension on the grounds that he had been shot in the thigh and wounded in the head whilst serving with Massey at Redmarley in Gloucestershire. He had then been wounded in the face at Rowton Heath and had finally fought at Worcester where his brother had been killed. He was awarded 20s with an annual pension of 40s.[19] In Essex, the role of the militia at the heart of the fighting was reflected in a large number of compensation claims. Christopher Ellin (one of those militia men treated at the Savoy Hospital in London) complained in 1652 that, because of the musket-ball wound to his arm, he could no longer work as a blacksmith and had a wife and child to support. His wounded comrade-in-arms, Thomas White, received a pension of 40s per annum.[20]

On the voyage back to England King Charles had regaled his fellow travellers with stories of his escape, no doubt embellished with time – stories that made

Samuel Pepys 'ready to weep'.[21] But the memory of those days was evidently still very bitter and he retained a sense of betrayal that the English had not, as had been promised, risen in any large numbers to support him. This made it possible later for a man such as Colonel Birch, who had in reality played no significant part in the campaign, to use his mere presence at Worcester as a weapon with which to irritate Royalist critics who had found reason to be elsewhere at the time. He referred to the battle in his final speech to Parliament in 1681 when he reminded his audience that 'I waited upon the King at Worcester and it cost me pretty dear'.[22]

King Charles chose never to return to either Scotland or to Worcester – rejecting an invitation from the Bishop of Worcester to celebrate the anniversary of the battle there in 1661 so that he could 'pay God his thanks upon the place where he received the great deliverance from his bloody and malicious enemies'.[23] Already the battle was being elevated in the Royalist mythology and the concept of divine intervention was being seen as responsible for the King's escape.

After the Restoration, the people of Worcester and surrounding areas tried to make capital of this last major Royalist stand of the Civil War. Some claims for sympathy may well have been genuine. In 1676, 10s was given by Hartlebury parish to Captain Underhill, 'a poor cavalier'. But paupers, such as Richard Hall of Kempsey in 1675, would invariably claim at the Quarter Sessions that they had been wounded in the battle, as an excuse for their condition. Walter Jones of Rock also conveniently claimed that a deed of assignment for one of his estates had been 'lost' when the Scots entered Worcester.[24] In 1661 one John Seamore, son of a Herefordshire glover, lay in Worcester gaol, described as a 'wandering cheater' and accused of trying to trick people out of money in the belief that he was a destitute ex-prisoner from the battle. It appears that he had been travelling through Derbyshire and Shropshire since 1656, using the name John Stanhope and claiming to be the son of Lady Jane Stanhope of Chesterfield. He said that he had been a tutor to the King and had commanded highlanders at the battle of Worcester. He then claimed to have been captured and transported to Barbados from where he had returned penniless and in need of support. Unfortunately for him, evidence was brought from Milsom on the Shropshire border that detailed his activities as a confidence trickster and Lord Stanhope disowned him, saying that there was no such person as Lady Jane Stanhope.[25] Perhaps the most enterprising attempt to curry favour was that of Thomas Cock. A medical student at the time of the battle of Worcester, he had been arrested in mistake for the King when the Parliamentary army stormed the city. Nine years later, Cock had still not managed to qualify and therefore petitioned the King to ensure that the University of Oxford granted him a degree as Doctor of Medicine.[26]

The legend of the loyal city was reinforced in the eighteenth century when historians took much of the pro-Royalist propaganda at face value as a useful weapon to counter continental republicanism. Charles II himself, however, was certainly not impressed by the professions of loyalty and gave no reward to the city. He presumably took the view that their opening of the gates to him in

August 1651 was simply a matter of pragmatism rather than a genuine expression of loyalty. This caused considerable disillusionment with the Stuart dynasty from the Royalist sympathizers in the city. A Worcester man, Lord Somers, played a leading role in the Glorious Revolution of 1688.

Instead, the thanks of Charles II was reserved for those who had risked their lives in assisting his escape. The son of the executed guide, Francis Yates, was given a pension of £20 per annum, his widow and eldest son £50 each and his youngest son £20; Charles Giffard was given a pension of £300 per annum, Francis Whitgreave £200, Colonel Lane £500 and Jane Lane £1,000 (plus £1,000 to buy a jewel). Francis Mansell received a pension of £200 per annum and Wyndham £600 per annum, £1,000 to buy a jewel and in 1670 the extraordinary sum of £10,800. By 1668, a large part of a budget of £33,524 4s 2d had to be set aside for pensions to those who could make some legitimate claim to have helped in the King's escape.[27] The Penderel family always retained a special place in the King's affections. Apart from pensions in perpetuity to the brothers, a number of additional payments were made to them and their dependants by both Charles II and James II from 1679 to 1688.[28] These helped to pay for apprenticeships and to set them up in new trades: in 1687, for example, James II helped to establish William Penderel as a goldsmith. The pensions were only commuted in 1922, by which time there were qualifying descendants all over the world; some payments are made to this day.

It was proposed to have an 'Order of the Knights of the Royal Oak' for supporters in the war and in the royal escape. A number of the county gentry might have expected to have been members of this. In the end, this did not materialize, first because the fees for entry were thought to be too high and also 'lest the Order might create heats and animosities, and open those wounds afresh which at that time were thought prudent should be healed'. These sentiments were repeated in a declaration from the loyal gentry of the county to General Monck at the Restoration. They assured him that they were 'willing to lay aside all animosity and return to mutual Christian love'.[29] The signatories include some of the best known Royalists of the period: the Earl of Shrewsbury, Sir John Packington, Sir William Russell, Sir Ralph Clare, Sir Rowland Berkeley, Colonel Samuel Sandys, Thomas Savage, Henry Townshend and William Sheldon. One notable absentee from the list is Sir Henry Lyttleton. He had been released from imprisonment in 1656 only to take part in Booth's rising in 1659 with his three brothers: he possibly still felt bitter towards his former enemies. The spirit of conciliation certainly worked in the case of that noted Parliamentarian Nicholas Lechmere, who had played such a key part in Worcestershire's affairs during the Commonwealth. Although he did not return to Parliament after the Restoration (having been Worcester's MP in 1658–9), he was made sergeant-at-law in 1669, was knighted in 1689 and served as a Judge of the Exchequer from 1689 to 1700 (he died in 1701).

The old order was, however, quickly restored in local government. By September 1660 most of the leading Parliamentarians had been removed from the city council and formerly expelled Royalists (such as Edward Solley, removed after the siege of 1646) were reinstated. The elections to Parliament in 1661 also saw familiar names returned to power. Samuel Sandys and Sir John Packington were elected from Worcestershire and Sir Rowland Berkeley and Thomas Streete from Worcester. One of the Evesham MPs was Samuel Sandys's uncle, William. Samuel Sandys himself died in 1685. His epitaph pays tribute to the loyalty that he showed the Royalist cause:

> Upon a pattem (reader) cast your eye
> Of suff'ring, yet unconquer'd loyaltie.
> None greater courage shewed to serve the crown
> And church when haughty rebells cry'd them down.
> To both he faithful was; life and estate
> 'Tis known he priz'd not at so great a rate,
> As to spare either for the public good;
> So little valu'd he his dearest blood.
> To's king and country he was always just,
> Nothing could tempt him to betray his trust.
> For prudence valour, and a gen'rous mind,
> Tho' equall'd, not excell'd among mankind.
> He was the clergy's friend, the poor's relief;
> Our heart's joy once, but now his death's our grief.
> Here now he lies, in hopes to rise again
> When Doomsday trumpet sounds, with Christ to reign.

Of the victorious Parliamentary generals involved in the battle, Richard Deane was killed at the battle of Solebay in 1653. Lord Grey and Thomas Pride also died before the Restoration. The King soon took revenge against his opponents at Worcester, many of whom had been regicides in signing the death warrant of his father. Of the principal characters, mercy was shown only to Charles Fleetwood who had not been involved at the King's trial and was allowed to retire to private life, and to Colonel Ingoldsby. The latter, although a regicide, claimed that he had acted under duress and had made an early peace with the King. Colonels William Goffe and Edward Whalley, who had both commanded regiments at Worcester, were also regicides and eventually made their way to sanctuary in Massachusetts. Relentlessly pursued by the Restoration government, they had to remain in hiding for the rest of their lives. The worst fate was reserved for Thomas Harrison. He had been cashiered by Cromwell in 1653 but, stubborn to the end, was now hanged, drawn and quartered for his role in signing the death warrant of Charles I. Colonel Hacker, who had been responsible for the actual execution of the King, was also executed. Robert Lilburne (d. 1665) and John Lambert (d. 1683) were both sentenced to life imprisonment for their role in trying to oppose the Restoration. Oliver Cromwell himself, although dead, was not left in peace; his body was exhumed, beheaded and left to hang on a gibbet. In Worcester, he is remembered by the devil's head pinned by his ears above the door of the rebuilt Guildhall, flanked by statues of Charles I and Charles II. Sadly, there is no memorial to the thousands of ordinary Scots who died so bravely for what turned out to be such an ill-timed and hopeless cause.

'For God and Parliament – The Lord of Hosts!' The Essex militia stormed Fort Royal in a ferocious charge. (Stephen Rigby)

Like most of the rest of the country, the inhabitants of Worcester were largely passive observers of events, although they could not escape the consequences of having a major battle fought out around their streets and homes. The majority of Royalist sympathizers in the county remained in their homes and it was left to a small number of gentry to take an active role. By contrast, the participation of the local militia on the side of Parliament reflected the national enthusiasm to destroy what was seen as an invading Scottish, rather than Royalist, army. The history of the battle did not simply end with the final surrender of the last Royalists in the Guildhall. The problems of dealing with such large numbers of prisoners, the transportation of many to the New World, and the effects of the loss of so many menfolk had immense personal consequences, particularly for the Scots. This in turn allowed a new constitutional settlement to be imposed on Scotland. As such it reinforces the fact that the term 'English Civil Wars' is a misnomer, as the wars affected not only England, but also Scotland, Wales and Ireland. In England, the comprehensive nature of the defeat crushed any possibility of an effective Royalist rising in the future and also provided a focus for the army in once again taking control of government. Subsequent events in the county illustrate the control that Cromwell was able to maintain throughout the country, as exemplified in the administration of the major generals. Finally, Worcester was able to share in the general reconciliation that came with the Restoration of 1660. Many of those sharing in the scenes of celebration in Worcester, Royalist and Parliamentarian alike, must have cast a thought back to that terrifying night of 3 September 1651 when the same streets echoed not to the sound of revelry but to the gunfire and screams of the last act of the Civil Wars.

APPENDIX 1

Contemporary Accounts of the Battle

A number of letters and reports were written at the time of the battle. These provide details of the fighting and are also important in giving a flavour of the participants' thoughts and emotions at the time. It should, however, be noted that some details contradict, as one might expect in the hurried circumstances. The following have been selected to illustrate the views of both Royalist and Parliamentarian, both participants and onlookers.

1. LETTER OF OLIVER CROMWELL TO SPEAKER OF THE HOUSE OF COMMONS: 10 P.M., 3 SEPTEMBER 1651

This account to Parliament by the weary Cromwell himself, hurriedly written in the very closing stages of the battle, may be compared with a letter of Robert Stapleton written at the same time.[1] One can perhaps imagine him dictating this letter both exhausted and elated, whilst in the background occasional shots and cries can be heard as his men begin rounding up the Scots who are desperately trying to avoid capture. In his letter he describes the fighting as among the most fierce that he had ever faced in his career. This would prove to be his final battle.

For the Right Honorable William Lenthall, Esquire, Speaker of the Parliament of the Commonwealth of England: These haste, haste, post haste for the special service of the State[2]

Sir,
Being so weary, and scarce able to write, yet I thought it my duty to let you know thus much; that upon this day, being the third of September (remarkable for a mercy vouchsafed to your forces on this day twelvemonth in *Scotland*), we built a bridge of boats over *Severn*, between it and *Thame*, about half a mile from *Worcester*; and another over *Tame*, within pistol-shot of the other Bridge. *Lieutenant-General Fleetwood* and *Major-General Deane* marched from *Upton* on the south-west side of *Severn* up to *Powick*, a town which was a pass the enemy kept. We passed over some horse and foot, and were in conjunction with the Lieutenant-General's forces. We beat the enemy from hedge to hedge till we beat them into *Worcester*.

The enemy then drew all his forces on the other side the Town, all but what he lost, and made a very considerable fight with us, for three hours space, but in the end we beat them totally, and pursued him up to his Royal Fort, which we took, and indeed have beaten his whole army. When we took the fort, we turned his own guns upon him. The enemy hath had great loss, and certainly is scattered, and run several ways. We are in pursuit of him, and have laid forces in several places, that we hope will gather him up. Indeed this hath been a very glorious mercy, and as stiff a contest for four or five hours as ever I have seen. Both your old forces and those new-raised, have behaved themselves with very great courage; and He that made them come out, made them willing to fight for you. The Lord God Almighty frame our hearts to real thankfulness for this, which is alone His doing. I hope I shall within a day or two give you a more perfect account.

In the mean time I hope you will pardon, Sir,

Your most humble servant,
O. CROMWELL. Near Worcester, Septemb. 3d, 1651,
(10 at night).

2. PARLIAMENTARY PAMPHLET, 5 SEPTEMBER 1651

Parliament ensured that news of the victory was disseminated as quickly as possible to discourage any further Royalist rising. This pamphlet, dated 5 September, was printed in London 'by special command and authority' of Parliament. It may have been written by Robert Stapleton and may be compared with an account in *Mercurius Politicus*, already published.[3] These are two of the most detailed accounts of troop dispositions during the battle.

A more Exact Relation of every particular of the fight at Worcester And ordering the battle on both sides of the river of Severne, from an emminent Officer of the Army[4]

Upon Wednesday morning between 5 and 6 of the clocke we began to march from Upton, and by reason of some hindrance in our march we reached not to *Tame* River till betwixt 2 and 3 in the afternoon: As soon as our boats came up, which was much about the same time, the Bridge was presently made over the Severn on the Generalls side, and another over the River Tame on our side, we were come as far as Poyick, half a mile on this side the Bridge wich our Van before the Enemy took the Alarm, which after they had taken, they drew downe both their Horse and their Foot from their Leaguer at St Jones, to oppose our passing over our bridges of boats: The Generall presently commanded over Col. *Ingoldsby*, and Col. *Fairfax* their Regiments, with part of his own Regiment, and the Life Guard, and Col. *Hackers* of Horse over the River, after these on our side were commanded over Col. *Goffes*, and Major Gen. *Deans* Regiments, all of which advanced toward the Enemy, who had lined their hedges thick with men, but it pleased the Lord after some sharp dispute, ours beat them from hedge to hedge. Col. *Blake*, Col. *Gibbons*, with Col. *Marshes* Regiment were commanded over as seconds to the former, and to attempt the Enemy in other places, where they had drawn down their men: My Lord *Gray's* was likewise order'd over and it pleased the Lord in half an hour or an hours dispute the enemy quitted their ground and fled away, only about Poyick Bridge (which they had broke down, having the advantage of hedges and ditches) they continued a sharp dispute with Col. *Haines* his Regiment, and Col. *Cobbet*, Col. *Matthews* being as reserve to them both, and it pleased the Lord that the Enemy likewise quitted the ground and runne away, some of Col. *Hains* his men wading over the River to advance upon them; about a mile beyond Poyick the Enemy had broken down another bridge upon the passe, unto which place we sent some dragoons, who with the assistance of some Horse made the Enemy quit that place, which gave a passage over for Lieut. Gen. *Fleetwoods* Regiment, Col. *Twistetons* and Col. *Kenricks*, who were commanded to pursue the Enemy, who as we had supposed made towards Hereford or Ludlow, but they wheeled off and run into Worcester, only some few who were taken. The ground where we fought was full of hedges that our horse had not much liberty to engage: but both Horse and Foot where they had opportunity (through the Lords presence strengthening of them) did very gallantly: After the Enemy had run away into Worcester, they drew out their whole army of Horse and Foote upon our Army on the other side, supposing that most of our Army had been advanced over the River, but the Lord made our Army there alike successfull as on the other side; being assisted by Major Gen. *Desboroughs* Regiment of Horse, and Col. *Cobbets* of Foot, on that side was part of the Generals Regiment, Major Gen. *Lamberts*, Commissary Gen. *Whalies*, Major Gen. *Harrisons* brigade, and Col. *Tomblins* with some of the Surrey and Essex Troops, those of Foot were Major Gen. *Lamberts*, Col. *Prides*, Col. *Coopers*, the Cheshire Brigade and the Essex Foot, all of these as the Lord gave them opportunity did behave themselves very gallantly, and beat the Enemy that came out, and those of them in the Royall Fort into the Town, and afterwards in the night time possessed themselves of the Towne, but as many Horse as could got away, though I suppose not three thousand in all escaped us: Col. *Barton* being commanded to Bewdley the day before with some Horse and Dragoones, did take many prisoners in their running away, it is said 1200. Yesterday morning by order from the Generall we commanded 1500 horse and dragoons to pursue after the Enemy (under the command of Col. *Blundell*) who fled in the same way they came hither, M.G. *Harrison* is likewise gon after them, and will we doubt not (through the Lords mercy) overtake most of them, Col. *Lilburn* will, we hope, put a stop unto them.

The King (it is said) went away with not above 12 horse, tis thought there is not 1000 horse of them together; In all the engagements that ever have beene, I think we have not seen a more immediate hand of God appearing than in this; I believe there was never more courage and resolution in an Army, yet lesse done by us as men; that which adds much to the mercy is that the presence of the Lord was so immediate with us, that we may say no flesh hath cause to boast, but we must say it is the Lord hath done all these things; and O that we may have hearts to walke suitable unto what the Lord hath done for us, that it may appear by our walking and actings, that we are the people that the Lord hath done all this for.

The number of those that are taken are said to be about 10000, and neer 3000 slain, but in neither can I be positive, of all that were slain on our side, I am perswaded that there is not 100: of Officers I hear but very few, Lieut. Col. *Mosely* and Capt. *Jones* of Colonel *Cobbets* Regiment were slain, Major General *Lamberts* horse was shot: the number of the Arms and Colours are so many, that as yet there can be no certain accompt given of them; the General did exceedingly hazard himself, riding up and downe in the midst of their shots, and went himself up to their Fort and offered them quarter, was then answered with nothing but shot, the major General likewise and all the other Officers, did doe in their several places very gallantly. In the persuit, Col. *Lilburns* and the Generals Regiment of Foot have taken the Earl of *Derby*, Earl of *Louderdale*, Earl of *Cleaveland*, and about 140 more persons of quality; they are still in persuit of the rest,

September 5. 1651.
neer Worcester.

3. A ROYALIST VIEW: A LETTER WRITTEN BY A SCOTTISH OFFICER IMPRISONED IN CHESTER AFTER THE BATTLE

A number of different versions of this letter survive and it was clearly heavily edited by the royal court. The letter was first published in France in December 1651. The present transcription follows the copy of the text that had come into the hands of Clarendon and was published in Hughes's edition of the *Boscobel Tracts* in 1830.[5] A slightly different version came to Pepys, published in 1967.[6] Another letter with a very similar opening and with the same date was inserted into the State Papers Domestic and is probably another version of this same account.[7]

The officer is full of praise for the King, describing him riding hither and thither to encourage his men. It also claims (contradicting all other reports) that Massey drove back Lambert's attack on Upton-upon-Severn. Note also that he confuses Lambert with Harrison.

Chester, 17 Sept. 1651
I believe you have too soon heard our misfortunes at Worcester; and it is possible there are amongst you that rather blame our proceedings then pity us. But if they knew the state of our Master's affairs when he was in Scotland and here, they would say otherwise. It is most certain that Cromwell would not at any time be drawn to hazard a battle in Scotland, but upon such great advantages as were no way reasonable to be given, which induced his Majesty (finding Cromwell to have passed the river Forth with most part of his forces, and engaged northward towards St. Johnston's, thereby giving us the advantage of foure or five days' time) to put in execution that which indeed was originally his design from the beginning of the campaign; namely, to march in

person with his army into England, not doubting but this his generous enterprise would give great encouragement and opportunity to his friends to rise, and free themselves from that yoke of tyrannye which lay so heavy on them.

Our army consisted of between ten and eleven thousand horse and foot, with sixteen leather guns, all absolutely under the command of his Majesty; who marched without any opposition, until he came to Appleby, where eleven or twelve troops of those horse which Harrison had left in England endeavoured to hinder our advancing, but were, without great difficulty, forced to retire; and so we went on with what diligence might be, and without any impeachment, unto Warrington, where we found their army, consisting of about nine thousand men united under Lambert and Harrison, possessed of the bridge, which they had almost broken; from which the King, at the head of his first troops, did beat them, with loss to them and great hazard to his own person. And, having made up the bridge with plankes, passed over his whole army, they retreating in such disorder, that besides their loss upon the retreat, at least three thousand of their men did that night disband. The King from thence continued his march to Worcester; they not daring to give him so much as one alarm all the way.

In Worcester, besides the garrison, his Majesty found five hundred horse, which Lambert had the night before sent in, which presently upon the approach of the army, quitted the place, leaving there the Earl of Shrewsbury, and diverse prisoners of note, which they had formerly taken. The city was neither fortified nor victualled, only an old broken wall, and a fort, in a manner slighted. His Majesty's intention was not to have staid there, but to march on towards London; but the army was so wearied with their hasty and continued march of three and twenty days (whereof it rested only one day at Penrith in Cumberland) that it was altogether impossible to advance, and no less necessary to rest and refresh them.

After near a week's stay in Worcester (in which time his Majesty used all endeavours to get into Gloucester, Hereford, and some other places; and likewise provided for the better arming and clothing of his souldiers), Cromwell appeared with his army near Perry-wood (about a mile from Worcester); and having drawn his left wing towards the river of Severn, his Majesty sent out a party of a thousand commanded foot and two hundred and fifty horse, to have fallen on them that night. But this design was betrayed by —— Gives, a townsman of Worcester (who was afterwards hanged), whereupon they drew of in the night to their body, leaving only some guards, which were beaten away. During the abode at Worcester, Major-Generall Massie was sent to try his credit about Glocester, and lay within a mile of Upton bridge, which was not so broken, but that the enemy's foot, for want of the placing of a sentinel, got over upon a piece of timber (laid only for the convenience of foot passengers), after which a body of their horse did also pass the ford; some of their foot got into the church of Upton. Whereupon Massie, having the alarm, came with some Horse, charged their cavalry, and beat them back over the river; then returning towards Upton, he found in the church those men who had possessed themselves of it; who fired upon him, and these shot him through the left hand upon diverse places of his Armes, and killed his horse under him. After which he returned to Worcester with his brigade.

Upon Tuesday, September 2, toward night (which was the day before the fight), his Majesty had intelligence that fifteen hundred horse were gone to Bewdely and that a very strong party of horse and foot and canon were gone to Upton – which made his Majesty the next morning to call a council of war on the top of the steeple at Worcester, whence the country round about might best be discovered, there to advise upon some action, while the enemy was thus divided and part of their forces gone farther off.

The result of this consultation was to divide the army into two parties; the one to goe upon the one side of Perry Wood, and the other on the other, reserving a body to fall on and assist where need should require. Whilest this was going to be put in execution, his Majesty discovered a body of the enemy's foot, about a thousand, with carriages of poles and planks and some canon, going towards the water-side (as was supposed, and proved afterwards true) with intention to make a bridge. And immediately after, espying some fire given at the bridge of Powick, his Majesty gave order to the Generall Officers to put the army in posture, and went himself in person out of the town, where he found the parties already engaged neare Powick, where the enemy were making two bridges to pass a part of their army over the rivers, Severn and Teyne, so as to get to the other side of the town of Worcester.

The King, leaving there two brigades of foot, making near two thousand men, returned to put in execution his first design of falling on the enemy at Perry Wood; and having led out the army, and engaged it himself, charging at the head thereof many several times in person, with great courage and success returned towards Powick, to command two brigades of foot to assist those who were already engaged upon that pass. After which, his Majesty went again towards the main body, which he already found disordered, and with some difficulty made them stand a while; but upon the enemy's second firing, they were so dispersed that they rallied no more, but gave back violently, and forced the King to make into the town.

The enemy, taking this advantage, fell close in with the rear of his Majesty's horse, and at the same time, with their foot, seized upon the mount, so that our horse were able to stand no longer without the walls; and the King, with much difficulty and danger, got into the town at Sudbury gate, about the shutting in of the evening. The enemy's foot entered the town before their horse, and our foot, in disorder threw downe their arms. Whereupon the enemy's foot fell to plunder; but the King's horse, which were left in the town, disputed it from street to street, and made great slaughter of the enemy, by reason of the greediness after pillage, insomuch that the streets were full of dead bodies of horse and men; till at last, over-mastered with numbers, they were forced downe to the Key, where many rendered themselves prisoners. Only Colonel Wogan about midnight broke thorough with fifty horse and marched after the King, who was some hours before gone out at St. Martins gate and marched northward that night with a body of about six hundred horse in disorder near thirty miles; where the next morning, finding the close pursuit of the enemy, and the country altogether unsecure, he consulted for his safety.

And of his royal person, I can give no farther account. But certainly a braver prince never lived, having in the day of the fight hazarded his person much more then any officer of his army, riding from regiment to regiment, and leading them on upon service with all the encouragement (calling every officer by his name) which the example and exhortation of a magnanimous general could afford; shewing so much steadiness of mind and undaunted courage, in such continual danger, that had not God covered his head, and wonderfully preserved his sacred person, he must, in all humane reason, needs have perished that day.

Duke Hamilton was shot in the first charge which he performed with great honour at Perry wood; where the King broke through and forced back their horse to their body of foot. The Duke, I hear, is since dead, upon the cutting off of his leg at Worcester.

We hope God almighty will preserve his Majesties sacred person to be an instrument of his glory in the performance of great things hereafter, though it did not please the Divine Power at this time to give him the victory: which in all likelihood he had obtained, had not the enemy so exceedingly overpowered him in numbers, they being (as their own party gave out) no lesse then threescore thousand, whereas his Majesties army was not in all eleven thousand fighting men, but so well governed as the like hath not been seen. For, in the whole march from Scotland to Worcester, they never took anything but what they paid for; and the discipline was so severe and so strictly observed, that divers were shot to death only for going out of their ranks to gather a few apples in an orchard as they passed, and another did undergo the same punishment only for taking a pint of beer without paying for it. It is a great comfort to us in this our calamity that his Majesty hath taken some private way (with only the Lord Wilmot) for his escape, for had he stayed with us, his person had inevitably fallen into the hands of the enemy.

On Thursday night (which was the day after the battle) our Lieutenant-Generals, Middleton and Lesley, left us, or lost us willingly; but were afterward taken and with Sir William Hemming brought prisoners hither. The Earl of Derby, Earl Lauderdale, Sir David Cunningham and Mr. Lane are prisoners here in the castle; and many others of quality are kept in private houses. They have already condemned some, and what will become of us, I yet know not.

4. LETTER FROM COLONEL ROBERT STAPLETON TO CAPTAIN GEORGE BISHOP: 8 SEPTEMBER 1651

This letter was published as a pamphlet after the battle and is of particular interest in giving a list of the prisoners taken at the battle.[8] It may have been this publication from which Lady Fanshawe received the news of her husband's capture (see above, p. 127).

N.B. 'Reformades' were officers from dispersed regiments.

A more full Relation of the great Victory Obtained by our Forces near Worcester . . . With an exact List of the Prize and prisoners of Lords, Knights . . .
Sir,
The account I gave you by the last Messenger, though it was rude and unpollished, yet it was a true one as to the narrative of the Victorie God hath blessed us with; only the particulars were wanting, which I have here inclosed. Our men went on very resolutely, and possess themselves of *Worcester* by eight of the clock on Wednesday night, onely there were about one thousand three hundred who fled to the Castle Mount, who surrendered themselves at mercy, next morning. The Mercy is highly seasonable and glorious; and though in the Field we kil'd more than we took Prisoners; Yet upon entering the Town after the Souldiers fury was over, there were multitudes Prisoners, as in the List inclosed you may see. We heare of many that are taken by Major Generall *Harrison*, Colonell *Lilburne*, and the Countrie people. I hope the Lord will deliver if not all of them, yet most into our hands, so that few shall escape. What shall we returne unto the Lord for his great kindnesse, his mercies never faile. I suppose we are now drawing a little neerer to you. The last news from *Scotland* is great also; Old *Lesley*, *Crawford*, *Linsey*, *Ogleby*, with divers of qualitie, besides three hundred taken that were making Levies to raise the Siege at *Dundee*. This is in great hast; but the full of all things that I know.
I am most faithfully yours,

Robert Stapylton
Worcester 5. 1651.

An exact List of the Prisoners taken.
Earle of *Darby*.
Earle of *Cleaveland*.
Earle of *Shrewesbury*.
Duke *Hamylton*.
Earle *Louderdale*.
Earle of *Rothis*.
Earle of *Cornwagh*.
Earle of *Kellsey*.
Lord *Sinclare*.
Sir *John Packington*.
Lord *Spyne*.
Sr *Charles Cunningham*.
Sir *Ralph Clare*.
Collonell *Graves*.
Mr *Richard Fanshaw*, the King of *Scots* Secretary.

Collonels of Horse.
Col. *William Hurry*.
Col. *William Kent*.
Col. *John Cheston*.
Col. *Benbow*.
Col. *Gibt Cambel*.
Col. *John Forbs*.
Col. Sr. *David Ogleby*.
Col. *Geor. Montgomery*.

Col. *John Shaw*.
Col. *James Ogleby*.
13 Collonels of Foot, whereof 3 are Reformades.
Col. S. *James Graham*.
Col. Sr *Tho. Orquaint*.
Col. *John Butler*.
Col. *Tho. Thomson*.
Col. Sr *Thomas Hume*.
9 Lieut. Collonels of Horse, whereof one a Reformade.
8 Lieut. Collonels of Foot.
8 Majors of Horse.
13 Majors of Foot.
37 Captaines of Horse.
72 Captaines of Foot, whereof 8 are Reformades.
55 Quarter Masters of Horse.
84 Lieut. of Foot.

Generall Officers.
Ma. Generall *Pitscotty*.
Ma. Gen. *Montgomery*.
James Weames Gen. of the Ordinance.
Archibald Waddall Adjutant Gen. of Foot.
Marshall *White*.
Sam. *Tavert* Quar. Ma. Gen. of the English Forces.
Alex. Harriot Waggon Ma. Generall.
76 Cornets of Horse.
99 Ensignes of Foot.
90 Quarter Masters.
30 Of the Kings Servants, whereof some are of quality.
9 Ministers.
9 Chirurgeons.
158 Colours.
The Kings Standard.
10000 Prisoners.
Above 2000, slaine.
All Armes, Bag and Baggage taken.
The Kings Coach and Horses, with much rich goods.
The Maior of *Worcester*.

Of Ours there was slaine.
Quarter Master Generall Moseley.
Captain Jones.
Captaine Howard wounded, and another Captaine.
100 Souldiers slaine, 300 wounded.

5. LETTER OF SIR EDWARD NICHOLAS TO LORD HATTON: 19 SEPTEMBER 1651

The Royalists in exile were eager for news and ready to accept any optimistic view of events in England. Hopes had been raised by initial stories of a great victory at Worcester; the full impact of the reality of the defeat was devastating.

Sir Edward Nicholas (1593–1669) was Secretary of State to King Charles, in exile in the Netherlands. This letter was written from Antwerp, sixteen days after the battle of Worcester.[9] The intense depression that many Royalists must have felt at the eventual news of the crushing defeat is clear. Treachery or cowardice are seen as the only possible explanations, together with bewilderment that their king could be so abandoned by the rest of his subjects. Nevertheless, there are practical matters to consider. The 58-year-old Sir Edward ponders as to whether the scale of the victory might mean that Parliament would be more inclined to allow exiles such as he to return home without penalty.

Yours of the 13 present found me here in a doleful condition upon the news that the K's being totally defeated and his person is in so very great danger.

It is doubtless an abominable shame and dishonour to all our nation that the K. should with so great peril and hazard bring into the midst of the kingdom so great an army and that so few English should rise to assist him or to divert the rebels. Albeit the presbyterians had the most encouragement to rise, yet the Royalists were in duty no less obliged; and even in policy, as well for their own preservation as for the restoration of his Majesty, they ought to have taken arms in his Majesty's assistance in so gallant an enterprise.

It is to the soldiery here a very riddle, I perceive, that 12,000 men should be taken prisoners in a fortified town, if there were not some great treachery or unpardonable cowardice in it.

It is conceived that upon the glorious victory Cromwell and his masters will become less rigorous than formerly to those that are under their subjection. And if they do so, it is believed all men will come in and submit to them. I know some men of good condition in the Low Countries that intend to go now over and make their peace, if they may be permitted upon good security to live quietly without having any oaths imposed upon them. I pray favour me with your advice what course you would have me to take, who, by my long attendance and with even insupportable contempt, have wasted myself and my poor fortune even to the last.

The Order of Battle

SCOTTISH

Few details survive as to the Scottish order of battle. It has therefore not been possible to place a considerable number of units that are documented as being at the battle. The allocation of the cavalry units is from a muster of 7 May 1651 and so may not entirely match the situation on the battlefield.

Castle

Rothes's Foot
Drummond's Foot

Fort Royal

Forbes's Foot

Powick

Keith's Foot (*c.* 700 men)

Teme and Severn confluence

under the command of Major General Pitscottie
Pitscottie's Foot
MacLeod's Foot
Neil MacNeil's Foot (fought on right flank of the MacLeods; predominantly Catholic)
Sleat's Foot (under Col. James MacDonald of Sleat; possibly amalgamated with MacLeod's)

Between Powick and St Johns

under the command of Major General Robert Montgomery

Three regiments of foot

2nd Cavalry Brigade

under the command of Montgomery
[?Montgomery's Horse – not clear whether his regiment was actually at Worcester]
Cranston's Horse
Dunfermline's Horse
Linlithgow's Horse

St Johns/Wickfield

a cavalry brigade
Dalzell's Foot

City

General of Artillery's Regt under James Wemyss of Caskierberran
presumably most of the Foot

Pitchcroft

1st Cavalry Brigade

under Lieutenant General Leslie
Leslie's Horse
Brechin's Horse
Craig of Riccarton's Horse
Rothes's Horse

East of city

7th Cavalry Brigade

under the Duke of Hamilton
A very mixed and small brigade which probably formed the nucleus of the left column assault on
Red Hill under the Duke of Hamilton.
Hamilton's Horse Troop (little more than a troop of gentry)
Buckingham's Horse (reformadoes)
Homes's Horse (probably only a single troop)

The King

Part of right column assault by King Charles
Lifeguard of Horse
Lifeguard of Foot

Upton-upon-Severn

Massey commanded at Upton and had previously been in command of the 5th Cavalry Brigade so it
is possible that the units he took there were drawn from this brigade.

5th Cavalry Brigade

under the command of Major General Massey
Massey's Horse (raised from English and Scots)
Stewart's Horse
Drummond's Horse

Other units known to have been at Worcester but location not known

Horse

Cavalry brigade information largely based on presence at Dunbar and muster of 7 May 1651. Most
of these units were probably based on the Pitchcroft with Leslie.

4th Cavalry Brigade

seems definitely to have served as a brigade at Worcester
Middleton's Horse
Erskine of Scotscraig's Horse
Mercer of Aldie's Horse (raised in Perthshire)
[Earl Marischal (led by Lt. Col. Sir William Keith of Ludquharn); may possibly have been
dispersed before Worcester]

6th Cavalry Brigade

under the Dutch commander Van Druschke
Van Druschke's Horse
James Forbes's Horse
Mauchline's Horse
Innes's Horse

Unbrigaded

Urry's Horse

Foot

Some of these would been to the south of the city but the rest would have been on the east side and within the walls.
Earl of Atholl
Master of Banff's Foot (*c.* 500 men)
Master of Caithness's Foot
Sir James Cambell of Lawer's Foot
Sir George Douglas of Kirkness's Foot
Col. James Grant's Foot (*c.* 300 men)
Master of Gray's Foot
Maj. Gen. James Holburne's Foot
Earl of Kellie's Foot (*c.* 960 men)
Lord Kintail's Foot (*c.* 980 men)
Col. John Lindsay of Edzell's Foot
Col. Harie Maule's Foot
Sir George Preston of Valleyfield's Foot
Col. William Gordon of Rothiemay's Foot (*c.* 400 men)
Col. Henry Sinclair's Foot
Col. Walter Forbes of Tolquhon's Foot (*c.* 600 men)
Lord George Spynie's Foot (*c.* 560 men)

Other clans

Frazer (*c.* 800 men)
Gunn
MacGregor
MacKay
MacKenzie
MacKinnon
MacNab
It seems probable that some units were basically grouped as clans, outside the usual regimental structure. This would help to explain some of the lack of sources.

PARLIAMENT

The present list is based upon accounts in contemporary letters and pamphlets (including Appendix 1.2 above). Even if all of these units were slightly below strength it would equate to the reported total of *c.* 30,000 men. As one-third of the troops were reported to be militia, many were probably referred to in the contemporary documents under the names of their colonel. The main militias to play an active part in the battle were from Essex and Cheshire.
[NMA = New Model Army unit]

West bank of the Severn (from Upton)

under the command of Major General Fleetwood

Left column

under the command of Major General Richard Deane
Cobbett's Foot (newly raised NMA)
Haynes's Foot (?militia)
Matthew's Foot (in reserve)
Fleetwood's Horse (NMA)

Right column

The field commander is not stated but was probably Fleetwood himself. This column formed the third assault wave across the River Teme.
Gibbon's Foot (newly raised NMA)
Marsh's Foot (?militia)
Blake's Foot (newly raised NMA)
Lord Grey's Foot (?militia)

Column to Bransford Bridge

Twistleton's Horse (NMA)
Kendrick's Dragoons (?militia)
Worcestershire Dragoons (militia)

Column to Bewdley

under the command of Colonel Blundell
Worcestershire Dragoons (five troops; militia)
Worcestershire Horse (militia)
Rich's Horse (two troops; NMA)
Barton's Horse (militia)

Reserve: Assault force across Bridge of Boats

The first two waves were from the New Model Army reserve from Red Hill, under the command of Oliver Cromwell

First wave

Lifeguard Horse (NMA)
Cromwell's Horse (NMA)
Hacker's Horse (NMA)
Ingoldsby's Foot (NMA)
Charles Fairfax's Foot (NMA)

Second wave

Goffe's Foot (NMA)
Deane's Foot (NMA)

Third wave

Right column from Upton (see above)

Red Hill

under the command of Major Generals Harrison and Lambert
Pride's Foot (NMA)
Cooper's Foot (NMA)
Lambert's Foot (NMA)
Duckenfield's Foot (newly raised NMA from Cheshire)
Cheshire Militia (three regiments under Colonels Bradshawe, Brooke and Croxton, in a brigade
    under the command of Duckenfield)
Essex Militia (three regiments under Colonels Cooke, Honywood and Matthews)
Worcestershire Militia (militia)
part of Surrey Militia (militia)
[later joined by Cobbett's Foot from the west bank of River Severn]
Train of artillery (NMA)
Whalley's Horse (NMA)
Tomlinson's Horse (NMA)
Harrison's Horse (NMA)
Lambert's Horse (NMA)
Saunders's Horse (NMA)
Desborough's Horse (NMA)
Rich's Horse (part of) (NMA)

MILITIAS SUMMONED TO THE MIDLANDS RENDEZVOUS BEFORE THE FINAL BATTLE

Not all of these units actually reached Worcester and some were incorporated in units under the name of the colonel. Five thousand of the militias were held in reserve at Coventry. In addition, other militia units (principally the Cheshire brigade) came south with Lambert's army. Units marked with an asterisk are documented as having fought at the battle. The sheer number of the counties that were mobilized indicates the organizational capabilities of the Council of State.

Northampton rendezvous

Leicestershire
Rutland
Northamptonshire*
Warwickshire
Oxfordshire
Lincolnshire (missed rendezvous and on 29 August sent to Mansfield)
Bedfordshire
Huntingdonshire
Buckinghamshire
Worcestershire* (order cancelled and the militia retreated to Gloucester before returning to the battle)
18 August ordered to Daventry for rendezvous on 23 August
19 August rendezvous changed to Northampton on 22 August

Oxford rendezvous

Sussex
Surrey* (not ready on 26 August; some units referred to in battle)
Hampshire

Berkshire
23 August ordered to Oxford
Norfolk
Suffolk*
Essex*
Cambridgeshire (not completed recruiting on 25 August)
Kent (Twistleton's Dragoons)
18 August ordered to rendezvous at St Albans on 26 August
19 August orders changed to rendezvous at Dunstable on 25 August
23 August orders changed to rendezvous at Buckingham
24 August orders changed to rendezvous at Oxford

Gloucester rendezvous

Gloucestershire
South Wales
Monmouthshire
Herefordshire
Wiltshire
20 August ordered to rendezvous at Gloucester on 25 August

St Albans

Middlesex
21 August ordered to St Albans by 23 August (presumably moved on to another rendezvous)

APPENDIX 3

Sites to Visit

Bransford Bridge (site of)

In the early stages of the battle on 3 September, Worcestershire dragoons raced to Bransford Bridge to cut off any retreat of the beleaguered Scots into Wales. The cavalry then pushed the Scottish army back into Worcester.

Broadway

Lygon Arms

Tradition holds that Cromwell stayed here during the campaign of 1651. Civil War period armour is mounted on the walls of the dining room.

Ombersley

Ombersley was the site of the first skirmish in Worcestershire in 1651 as the advancing Scots headed for Worcester. Captain Yarranton tried to delay the march but had to fall back quickly to Worcester.

Kings Arms

One of a number of places where King Charles is reputed (mistakenly) to have stopped during his flight from Worcester in 1651. In any event the fine seventeenth-century (and earlier) buildings in the village give a good impression of what the village would have looked like at the time of the Civil War.

Pershore

Pershore Bridge

The Parliamentary army marched across this fine fifteenth-century bridge on its way from Evesham to Worcester. Part of the bridge had collapsed and been repaired during the First Civil War in 1644.

Powick

Powick Bridge

The fifteenth-century bridge was the centre of the first major action in the Civil War and a key point in the battle of 1651. The two northern spans, across the mill race, have clearly been repaired and were probably those demolished during the battle of 1651.

Powick Church

Marks on the church tower are reputed to be the result of gunshot from the initial stages of the main battle on 3 September when the Parliamentary troops fought to dislodge the Scots and push them back over the River Teme.

Powick Ham

The opposing armies fought a desperate hand-to-hand combat along the lanes and hedgerows as the Scottish troops were forced back across Powick Bridge.

Walk along the River Teme

Walk beside the River Teme to the confluence with the Severn. The battle of 1651 raged along this river bank. Eventually Cromwell's cavalry were able to force a bridgehead across two pontoon bridges, one on the Teme and another just to the north on the Severn. The Scots were then forced to retreat past Manor Farm and into Worcester itself. The lane leading into Worcester was described as being lined with the bodies of the dead.

Upton-upon-Severn

Bridge over the River Severn (site of)

The bridge existing in the seventeenth century (south of the present bridge) has now been demolished. The crossing of the River Severn at Upton on 28 August was a critical factor in Cromwell's success in the battle of Worcester. The initial crossing was made by eighteen dragoons who had to shuffle across a plank laid across the partly demolished bridge. They then caused a diversion whilst the main force forded the river *c.* 150 m downstream. The bridge was then repaired so as to allow the rest of the Parliamentary army to cross over.

Church (now heritage centre)

The advance party of eighteen dragoons was forced to shelter in the church whilst under attack from Massey's men. The latter tried to burn the church down around them. Only the fourteenth-century tower of the church still survives. This has now been converted into a small heritage centre which contains a display on Upton in the Civil War.

Pool Brook

Part of a rectangular emplacement dug by Colonel Massey to protect the road to Worcester in 1651 is still visible from the road, in front of the stream. A ditch runs off this towards Hyde Lane and was also possibly part of the defences. This position was stormed by Lambert's dragoons on 28 August. The Parliamentary army then paused to regroup until the final assault on the city on 3 September.

Worcester

Cathedral

The Cathedral suffered from both Parliamentary and Royalist armies during the Civil War. It was used as a Royalist ammunition magazine and was then desecrated by Essex's army in 1642. Subsequently, Royalist troops stripped the lead off the roof to make into musket balls. The Cathedral was used to contain prisoners from the battle of 1651. The Duke of Hamilton is buried here.

City Walls, City Walls Road

Remains of the city walls and footings of St Martin's Gate are still visible. King Charles escaped through St Martin's Gate after the battle of 1651.

The Commandery, Sidbury Street

The Royalist HQ during the battle of 1651. This lay just outside the medieval defences of the city but within a new Civil War defence that led up to Fort Royal. The Royalist general, the Duke of Hamilton, died here of his wounds. Now a Civil War museum.

Fort Royal

Fort Royal Park contains the remains of the 1651 sconce. The outline of the large rectangular fort, with three of its four corner bastions to carry artillery, can still be easily made out on the ground.

The fort was built to help defend the city, but its capture during the battle allowed Cromwell's army to pound the city with cannon from close range. Up to 1,500 men were reported to have been killed when the Essex militia stormed the fort and massacred the garrison and those who had taken shelter there.

Guildhall

The seventeenth-century town hall has now been rebuilt. This was used to house prisoners after the battle and had to be fumigated subsequently. Note the statues of Charles I and Charles II flanking the doorway, with Cromwell depicted as the devil, pinned by his ears above the arch.

King Charles's House, New Street

Built in 1577, King Charles resided here before the battle and took refuge here just before escaping the battle of Worcester in 1651.

Perry Wood, 'Cromwell's Trenches' (off Humber Road)

On the north side of Perry Wood is an area of open park bounded by a disused watercourse. The landscape is much as it was in 1651 when the Duke of Hamilton stormed up the hillside here to attempt to seize the Parliamentary gun position. On the brow of the hill is a substantial V-shaped ditch linked to the watercourse that was dug to protect the gun positions. Fighting then spread into the woods until the Scots and Royalists were forced to retreat through lack of ammunition and in the face of overwhelming odds.

Pitchcroft (now the racecourse)

The Scottish cavalry formed up here during the battle of 1651. Their commander, David Leslie, refused to commit them to the battle until it was too late. The cavalry then broke northwards to try to escape.

Tamar Close, off Ronkswood Crescent

There is a rectangular earthwork here, measuring 73 × 82 m, which was probably constructed in 1646 as a sconce for artillery but may well have been reused in 1651. The surrounding ditch is clearly visible on three sides. That on the city side has probably been ploughed flat.

Viewpoint, A38 Tewkesbury Road (off the Malvern/Worcester roundabout)

This overlooks the site of the bridge of boats built by Cromwell's men to cross the Severn and attack the flank of the Scots during the battle of 1651. Despite the presence of modern roadworks, it is still possible to appreciate the character of the open countryside beside the Teme and Severn over which the battle was fought. A panoramic display of the battlefield is provided.

Whiteladies, Barbourne

Charles may have stayed here prior to the battle of Worcester. Tradition also has it that he changed his clothes here before his flight north after the battle.

APPENDIX 4

Chronology of the Third Civil War

Background
1649
January	Excise riots in Worcester
30 January	Execution of Charles I
5 February	Charles II proclaimed King in Scotland
17 March	Abolition of monarchy
19 March	Abolition of House of Lords
19 May	Declaration of the Commonwealth

Third Civil War
1650
2 January	Engagement Act (an oath of loyalty to the Commonwealth without King or House of Lords)
23 June	Charles II takes the Covenant
24 June	Charles II lands in Scotland
26 June	Thomas Fairfax resigns command of army in favour of Oliver Cromwell
22 July	Parliamentary army enters Scotland
16 August	Charles II forced to sign Declaration of his father's responsibility for the wars
3 September	**Battle of Dunbar**
4 October	Charles II tries to escape the clutches of the extreme Covenanters
30 November	Defeat of western Covenanters at **Hamilton**
24 December	**Surrender of Edinburgh Castle** to Cromwell

1651
1 January	Charles II crowned in Scotland
February	Cromwell taken ill
31 March	Col. James appointed commander of Worcestershire militia
17 April	Campaign in Scotland renewed
20 July	**Battle of Inverkeithing**: Scots defeated
31 July	Charles II begins the march south from Stirling
1 August	Charles II enters England; Cromwell at Perth
3 August	Harrison at Berwick
5 August	Cromwell at Leith with c. 10,000 men; Lambert separates to shadow the Scots; Harrison at Newcastle
6 August	Charles II approaches Carlisle
9 August	Lambert at Penrith, one day behind the Scots; Harrison at Ripon
11 August	Charles II near Preston; Harrison at Skipton; Earl of Derby lands at Castle Ruthin with 300 men

12 August	Charles II proclaimed King at Lancaster; Cromwell rests army at Ryton Haugh
13 August	London Trained Bands mobilize
14 August	Lambert and Harrison rendezvous at Haslemoor, Lancs, to shadow Scottish army with 12,000–14,000 men; Cromwell at Brancepeth (4 miles SW of Durham); **Stirling surrenders to Monck**
15 August	Lambert and Harrison at Bolton; Earl of Derby arrives in Lancashire
16 August	**Skirmish at Warrington**: Parliamentary forces refuse to be drawn into battle and the Scots cross the River Mersey; Cromwell at Catterick
17 August	Charles II at Stoke; Cromwell at Ripon
19 August	Charles II at Market Drayton; Lambert and Harrison at Uttoxeter; Cromwell at Ferrybridge
21 August	Charles II at Tong, Shropshire; Scottish army enters Worcestershire and passes through Kidderminster; Cromwell at Chesterfield; meeting between city council and County Committee agrees to surrender Worcester when the Scots arrive
22 August	Skirmish between Worcestershire Militia and Scots at **Ombersley**; Cromwell near Mansfield, Notts
	Scottish army enters Worcester; Cromwell at Rufford Abbey, Notts; Council of State passes over full military command to Cromwell
23 August	Cromwell at Leicester and Lutterworth (15 miles E of Coventry)
	King Charles enters Worcester
24 August	King hears Sunday service in Cathedral; Cromwell rendezvouses at Warwick with Fleetwood, Deane, Desborough and Grey; Essex, Norfolk, Suffolk and Cambridgeshire militias ordered to Oxford
25 August	**Battle of Wigan**: Earl of Derby defeated; 15,500 men of the London Trained Bands muster on Tothill Fields
26 August	Abortive Royalist muster on Pitchcroft; Cromwell at Stratford upon Avon; order published across country declaring 'Charles Stuart' and his supporters as rebels and traitors; Commissions of Martial Law issued in Lancashire, Chester, Shropshire and North Wales to try offenders
27 August	Cromwell and Fleetwood rendezvous at Evesham with an army of 30,000 men
28 August	**Skirmish at Upton-upon-Severn**: Lambert captures bridge; 12,000 Parliamentary troops cross River Severn
29 August	Opposing forces within 'half musket shot' on east side of Worcester; Scottish raiding party ambushed on Bund's Hill and Red Hill
31 August	Earl of Derby enters Worcester with survivors from battle of Wigan
1 September	**Monck takes Dundee**

3 September: Battle of Worcester

dawn	Fleetwood's two columns leave Upton-upon-Severn
c. 12 noon	Western column launch attack on Powick ridge
c. 2 p.m.	Eastern column reaches confluence of Teme and Severn
c. 3 p.m.	Cromwell launches attack across Bridge of Boats
c. 4 p.m.	King Charles attempts counter-attack on Red Hill
c. 5 p.m.	Fort Royal captured by Essex militia
c. 6 p.m.	King Charles escapes Worcester
c. 10 p.m.	Last of Royalists finally surrender
c. midnight	Colonel Wogan escapes the city with *c.* 50 men

The Royal Escape

3 September	King flees battlefield *c.* 6 p.m.
4 September	Escape party arrives at Whiteladies House, Boscobel, Shropshire at *c.* 3 p.m.; day spent hiding in the woods
	In the evening, to Francis Woolf at Madeley, Shropshire
5 September	Day spent in Mr Woolf's hayloft
6 September	Return to Boscobel House *c.* 3 a.m.; hid for the day in an oak tree in Boscobel Wood

7 September	To Moseley, Staffs (now West Midlands)
8 September	Boscobel searched by Parliamentary troops
9 September	To Bentley Hall, Staffs (now West Midlands)
10 September	Begins journey with Jane Lane; after a ride of *c.* 2 hours has horseshoe replaced at 'Long ——' (?Longborough); spends night at Long Marston, Warwickshire
11 September	At Cirencester, Gloucestershire
12 September	Arrives at Mr Norton's house, Abbots Leigh, nr Bristol
16 September	Departs for Trent, Somerset
22 September	Failed attempt to find ship at Charmouth, Dorset
6 October	Moves to Heale House, Wilts
12 October	Leaves for Hambledon, Hampshire at *c.* 2 a.m.
13 October	Arrives at George Inn, Brighton, Sussex
15 October	At 8 a.m. the King and Wilmot take ship for France [Execution of Earl of Derby]
16 October	**King lands in Normandy**

Notes

ABBREVIATIONS

BCA	Birmingham City Archives
BL	British Library
BM	British Museum
CAM	Committee for the Advancement of Money
CCC	Calendar of the Committee for Compounding
CJ	Commons Journal
CSPC	Calendar of State Papers Colonial
CSPD	Calendar of State Papers Domestic
HMC	Historic Manuscripts Commission
HWRO	Hereford and Worcester Record Office
Trans. Worcs. Archaeol. Soc.	*Transactions of the Worcester Archaeological Society*
Worcs. Hist. Soc.	Worcester Historical Society

Preface

1. C. Carlton, *Going to the Wars* (London, 1992), p. 340.
2. S.R. Gardiner, *History of the Commonwealth and Protectorate*, vol. 2 (1903, repr. Adlestrop, 1988), p. 47.
3. J. Buchan, *Oliver Cromwell* (London, 1941), p. 334.
4. J. Kenyon, *The Civil Wars in England* (London, 1988); M. Ashley, *The English Civil War* (Gloucester, 1990).
5. R. Holmes, *Worcester 1651* (Market Drayton, 1985); M. Atkin, *The Civil War in Worcestershire* (Stroud, 1995).
6. For example P. Young and R. Holmes, *The English Civil War* (London, 1974), pp. 310–14.
7. J.W. Willis-Bund, *The Civil War in Worcestershire 1642–1646 and the Scotch Invasion of 1651* (Birmingham, 1905); *The Battle of Worcester* (Worcester, 1913).

8. Letter from Cromwell to Lenthall, 4 September 1651 in W.C. Abbott, *The Writings and Speeches of Oliver Cromwell* (Oxford, 1939), Vol. 2, p. 462.

1. Background

1. J.W. Willis-Bund (ed.), *Diary of Henry Townshend of Elmley Lovett, 1640– 1663* (Worcs. Hist. Soc., 1920), vol. 2, p. 87.
2. BL E.266 (24): *Perfect Ocurrences*, 21 November 1645.
3. M. Atkin, *The Civil War in Worcestershire* (Stroud, 1995), pp. 105–16.
4. J.W. Willis-Bund (ed.), *Diary of Henry Townshend of Elmley Lovett, 1640–1663* (Worcs. Hist. Soc., 1915), vol. 1, p. 190.
5. BCA 398334 (HCC 590).
6. R.H. Silcock, *County Government in Worcestershire 1603–1660* (PhD thesis, University of London, 1974), p. 275.

7. I am grateful to Jenny Townshend for this information.
8. R. Baxter, *Reliquae Baxterianae* (London, 1696), part 1, p. 73.
9. T. Blount, *Boscobel* (1660), p. 145.

2. The Third Civil War

1. Letter from Cromwell to his wife, 4 September 1650 in W.C. Abbott, *The Writings and Speeches of Oliver Cromwell* (Oxford, 1939), vol. 2, p. 329.
2. M. Atkin, *The Civil War in Worcestershire* (Stroud, 1995), pp. 100–16
3. R. Baxter, *Reliquae Baxterianae* (London, 1696), part 1, p. 68.
4. Letter from Duke of Hamilton to Crofts, 8 August, in H. Cary, *Memorials of the English Civil War* (London, 1842), vol. 2, p. 305.
5. *The King's Narrative* in J. Hughes (ed.), *Boscobel Tracts* (London, 1830), p. 149.
6. B. Whitelock, *Memorials of the English Affairs* (1732), vol. 3, p. 503.
7. CCC 4 February 1652, p. 2948.
8. *Relation from the Queen Mother* (Letter of a Scottish prisoner at Chester to France, 17 September 1651), in W. Matthews, *Charles II's escape from Worcester* (London, 1967), pp. 29–30; Appendix 1.3.
9. *Letter from Colonel Whiteley to Sir Philip Musgrave* (12 August 1651) in Cary, *Memorials*, vol. 2, p. 321.
10. W.C. Trevelyan (ed.), 'Copies of Various Papers Relating to the Family of Thornton of Witton Castle in Northumberland', *Archaeologia Aeliana*, 1st series, ii (1832), pp. 95–6.
11. Major General Harrison to Committee of Yorkshire, 1 August 1651, in Cary, *Memorials*, vol. 2, p. 297.
12. *Letter from Edward Massey to Sir Edward Hyde*, 16 March 1659, in J. Thurloe, *A collection of the State Papers of John Thurloe Esq.* (London, 1742), vol. 7, p. 855.
13. *Mercurius Politicus*, 18 September 1650, quoted in Abbott, *Writings and Speeches*, vol. 2, note p. 333.
14. D. Stevenson, *Highland Warrior: Alasdair MacColla and the Civil Wars* (Edinburgh, 1994), p. 272.
15. W. Dunn Macray (ed.), *Clarendon's History of the Rebellion and Civil Wars in England* (Oxford, 1888), vol. 5, p. 188.
16. *Letters from Roundhead officers written from Scotland* (Edinburgh, 1866), pp. 26–7, 28.
17. Abbott, *Writings and Speeches*, vol. 2, p. 449.
18. *Perfect Diurnall*, 11–18 August 1651, in M. Stace (ed.), *Cromwelliana* (London, 1810), p. 109.
19. *Letter from Cromwell to Lenthall*, 4 August 1651, in Abbott, *Writings and Speeches*, vol. 2, p. 444.
20. *Letter from Lambert to Harrison*, 5 August 1651, in Cary, *Memorials*, vol. 2, p. 295.
21. CSPD 18 August 1651, p. 339.
22. *Letter from Cromwell to Lenthall*, 4 August 1651, in Abbott, *Writings and Speeches*, vol. 2, p. 444.
23. CSPD 27 August 1651, p. 378.
24. CSPD 30 August 1651, p. 391.
25. CSPD 27 August 1651, pp. 372, 379.
26. T. Blount, *Boscobel* (1660), p. 8.
27. *Letter from Cromwell to Harrison*, 3 May 1651, in Abbott, *Writings and Speeches*, vol. 2, p. 411.
28. *Letter from Cromwell to Lenthall*, 4 September 1651, in Abbott, *Writings and Speeches*, vol. 2, p. 462.
29. CSPD 22 August 1651, p. 353.
30. *Mercurius Politicus*, 4–11 September 1651.
31. HMC 14th Report, Appendix 9, p. 478; B. Whitelock, *Memorials of the English Affairs* (1732), vol. 3, p. 508.
32. CSPD 20 August 1654, p. 314.
33. *Letter from Lilburne to Cromwell*, 25 August 1651, in Cary, *Memorials*, vol. 2, p. 341.
34. Whitelock, *Memorials*, p. 503; CSPD 18 August 1651, p. 341.
35. CSPD 10 March 1653, p. 207.
36. CSPD 26 August 1651, p. 373.
37. CSPD 30 August 1651, p. 392.
38. S. Bond, *The Chamber Order Book of Worcester 1602–1650* (Worcs. Hist. Soc. new series 8, 1974), p. 458.
39. CSPD 13 January 1651, pp. 11–12.
40. HMC 13th Report, Appendix I, pp. 576–602.
41. M. Atkin, *Gloucester and the Civil War* (Stroud, 1992), pp. 126–30; CSPD 19 March 1651, p. 96.
42. CSPD 31 March 1651, p. 120.
43. HMC 12th Report, Appendix IX, p. 498.

3. The Armies

1. R. Wiseman, *Of Wounds, of Gun-shot Wounds, of Fractures and Luxations* (1686, repr. Bristol, 1977), p. 441.
2. I am grateful for discussion with Alan Turton over this and other matters.

3. See J. Litchfield, *The Pike* (Newbury, 1997), p. 12.
4. S. Reid, *Scots Armies of the 17th Century, vol. 3: The Royalist Armies 1639–46* (Leigh-on-sea, 1989), pp. 42–9. For a more traditional view see D. Stevenson, *King or Covenant? Voices from the Civil War* (East Lothian, 1996), pp. 138–9.
5. I am grateful for discussion with Alan Turton over this and other matters.
6. Reid, *Scots Armies*, esp. p. 53.
7. L. Hutchinson, *Memoirs of the Life of Colonel Hutchinson, Written by his Wife Lucy* (London, 1889), p. 348.
8. C.H. Firth, *Cromwell's Army* (London, 1992), p. 185.
9. Thanks to Dave Rayner (Yorkshire Historic Arms) for this information.
10. A.J. Rowland, *Military Encampments of the English Civil Wars 1639–1659* (Bristol, 1995), pp. 4–8.

4. *The Occupation of Worcester*

1. See P.J. Brown, 'The Military Career of Andrew Yarranton', *Trans. Worcs. Archaeol. Soc.*, xiii (1992), pp. 193–202.
2. CCC 3 April 1652, p. 567.
3. CSPD 15 August 1651, p. 332.
4. F.W. Joyce, *Tenbury: Some Records of its History* (Oxford, 1931), pp. 102–4.
5. CCC 10 March 1652, p. 556.
6. B. Whitelock, *Memorials of the English Affairs* (1732), p. 503.
7. *Letter from Cromwell to Colonel Cooper*, 6 September 1651, in W.C. Abbott, *The Writings and Speeches of Oliver Cromwell* (Oxford, 1939), vol. 2, p. 466.
8. *Letter to Council of State*, written from Gloucester, 23 August 1651, in H. Cary, *Memorials of the Civil War* (London, 1842), vol. 2, pp. 335–7.
9. Ibid.
10. Whitelock, *Memorials*, p. 504.
11. Clarendon, vol. 5, p. 181; R. Wiseman, *Of Wounds, of Gun-shot Wounds, of Fractures and Luxations* (1686, repr. Bristol, 1977), p. 408.
12. CSPD 24 August 1651, p. 363.
13. CCC 9 September 1651, p. 2867.
14. HMC 14th Report, Appendix 8, p. 188; CSPD 1656.
15. T. Blount, *Boscobel* (1660), p. 7.
16. Father Huddleston, 'Original Account . . .' (1682) in W. Matthews, *Charles II's Escape from Worcester* (London, 1967), p. 108.
17. Whitelock, *Memorials*, p. 504.
18. W. Dunn Macray (ed.), *Clarendon's History of the Rebellion and Civil Wars in England* (Oxford, 1888), vol. 5, p. 189.
19. S. Wells, *A History of the Drainage of the Great Level of the Fens Called Bedford Level* (London, 1830), vol. 1, p. 236.
20. J. Thompson, *The Other Army* (Leigh-on-Sea, no date), p. 1.
21. M. Atkin, *The Civil War in Worcestershire* (Stroud, 1995), p. 73.
22. Dunn Macray (ed.), *Clarendon's History*, vol. 5, p. 181.
23. H. Ellis, 'Letters from a Subaltern Officer in the Earl of Essex's Army', *Archaeologia*, xxxv (1853), p. 328.
24. Atkin, *The Civil War in Worcestershire*, pp. 62 and 111.
25. HMC 5th Report, Appendix, p. 299.
26. *Stapleton to Captain George Bishop*, 29 August 1651, in Cary, *Memorials*, p. 348.
27. Letter of Royalist prisoner in CSPD 17 September 1651, p. 437
28. Personal communication from Peter Reynolds, with thanks. Unfortunately, the records of the excavation are no longer available.
29. P. Barker, 'The Origins of Worcester', *Trans. Worcs. Archaeol. Soc.*, 3rd series, ii (1968–9), p. 99; R. Jackson, *Salvage Recording at King's School, Worcester* (County Archaeological Service Internal Report 97, 1991), pp. 3–4.
30. Barker, 'Origins', p. 102; M.O.H. Carver, 'Medieval Worcester', *Trans. Worcs. Archaeol. Soc.*, 3rd series, vii (1980), pp. 76, 81.
31. *Mercurius Politicus*, 30 August 1651; Cary, *Memorials*, p. 348.
32. Whitelock, *Memorials*, p. 506.
33. HWRO 850 Salwarpe, BA 1054/1.
34. HMC 5th Report, Appendix, p. 299.
35. *Perfect Diurnall*, 1–8 September.
36. J.W. Willis-Bund (ed.), *Diary of Henry Townshend of Elmley Lovett 1640–1663*, vol. 2 (Worcs. Hist. Soc., 1920), p. 244.
37. W.G. Leadbetter, *The Story of Bromsgrove* (Bromsgrove, 1949), p. 38.
38. Dunn Macray (ed.), *Clarendon's History*, vol. 5, p. 187.
39. Yarranton was subsequently accused of accepting bribes to take the men back into the militia and protect them from prosecution: Brown, 'Military Career', pp. 195–6.

40. CAM 9 September 1652, p. 1451.
41. T. Blount, *Boscobel* (1660), pp. 10–11.
42. CAM 27 October 1654, p. 1479.
43. CCC 27 November 1651, p. 1773.
44. CCC 28 October 1656, p. 1824.
45. HMC 10th Report, Appendix 6, pp. 175–6.
46. T.R. Nash, *Collections for the History of Worcestershire* (London, 1783), vol. 2 suppl., p. 89.
47. CCC 12 March 1652, p. 2898.
48. Dunn Macray (ed.), *Clarendon's History*, vol. 5, p. 187.
49. CCC 6 November 1651, p. 498.
50. CSPD 9 September 1651, p. 419.
51. J.W. Willis-Bund, *The Civil War in Worcestershire 1642–1646 and the Scotch Invasion of 1651* (Birmingham, 1905), p. 245.

5. *The Encirclement of the Scots*

1. L. Hutchinson, *Memoirs of the Life of Colonel Hutchinson, Written by his Wife Lucy* (London, 1889), p. 356.
2. Ibid.
3. R. Baxter, *Reliquae Baxtrianae* (London, 1696) pt 1, p. 66.
4. CSPD 25 August 1651, p. 368.
5. CSPD 23 August 1651, p. 361.
6. CSPD 25 August 1651, p. 369.
7. CSPD 20 August 1651, pp. 346, 348.
8. *Letter to William Lenthall*, 25 August 1651, in J. Washbourn, *Bibliotheca Gloucestrensis* (Gloucester, 1825), p. 403.
9. CSPD 25 August 1651, p. 368.
10. CSPD 18 August 1651, p. 339
11. CSPD 22 August 1651, p. 356.
12. Ibid., p. 355.
13. CSPD 27 August 1651, p. 376.
14. For other details of the Essex militia see D. Appleby, 'Essex Men at the Battle of Worcester', *English Civil War Times*, 52 (1997), pp. 24–8.
15. CSPD 2 September 1651, pp. 398–9.
16. CSPD 29 August 1651, pp. 384–5, 386–7.
17. CSPD 21 August 1651, p. 350.
18. CSPD 24 August 1651, p. 365.
19. CSPD 1 September 1651, p. 395.
20. HMC 5th Report, Appendix, p. 299.
21. Letter from one of Lambert's officers in B. Whitelock, *Memorials of the English Affairs* (1732), vol. 3, p. 340.
22. Robert Stapleton in *Perfect Diurnall*, 3 September 1651.
23. CSPD 29 August, 1651, p. 385.
24. *Letter from Royalist prisoner* in CSPD 17 September 1651, p. 436; *Letter from Robert Stapleton*, 29 August 1651, in H. Cary, *Memorials of the English Civil War* (London, 1842), vol. 2, p. 348.
25. CSPD 4 September 1651, p. 409.
26. A. MacFarlane (ed), *The Diary of Ralph Josselin* (London, 1976), p. 256, quoted in Appleby, 'Essex Men', p. 27.

6. *The Storm Breaks*

1. W. Dunn Macray (ed.), *Clarendon's History of the Rebellion and Civil Wars in England* (Oxford, 1888) vol. 5, p. 190.
2. T. Blount, *Boscobel* (1660), p. 15.
3. There is no contemporary reference to trench lines, as there was at the start of the siege of 1646.
4. Robert Stapleton in *Perfect Diurnall*, 1–8 September 1651.
5. *Ibbotson's Proceedings in Parliament*, p. 1560, quoted in V. Green, *History of Worcester*, vol. 1 (1797), p. 280.
6. B. Whitelock, *Memorials of the English Affairs* (1732), vol. 3, p. 505.
7. The widow of William Guise was awarded £200 and an annual pension of £200: Commons Journal, vii, 13.
8. Robert Stapleton in *Perfect Diurnall*, 3 September 1651; Dunn Macray (ed.), *Clarendon's History*, vol. 5, p. 189.
9. J. Washbourn, *Bibliotheca Gloucestrensis* (Gloucester, 1825), p. cxxii.
10. *Letter from Lilburne to Cromwell*, 25 August 1651, in H. Cary, *Memorials of the English Civil War* (London, 1842), vol. 2, p. 341.
11. *Letter from T. Scott and R. Salway to Council of State*, in Cary, *Memorials*, vol. 2, p. 364.
12. Robert Stapleton in *Perfect Diurnall*, 3 September 1651.
13. W. Dunn Macray (ed.), *Clarendon's History*, vol. 5, p. 190.
14. Ibid., p. 192.
15. HMC 10th Report, Appendix VI, p. 175.
16. *Letter from G. Downing to Lord ——*, in Cary, *Memorials*, vol. 2, p. 357.
17. *Letter from T. Scott to R. Salway to Council of State*, in Cary, *Memorials*, vol. 2, pp. 362–4.
18. C. Carlton, *Going to the Wars* (London, 1992), p. 132.
19. *Letter from Cromwell to Lenthall*, 3 September 1651, in W.C. Abbott, *The Writings and Speeches of Oliver Cromwell* (Oxford, 1939), vol. 2, p. 461.

7. The Final Phase

1. *Letter from Cromwell to Lenthall*, 4 September 1651 in W.C. Abbott, *The Writings and Speeches of Oliver Cromwell* (Oxford, 1939), vol. 2, p. 462.
2. T. Blount, *Boscobel* (1660), p. 18 simply says that he took off his armour because it was 'heavy and troublesome'. The more detailed account, reflecting his dress at least at the end of the battle, is in *An Exact Narrative and Relation* (1660) in W. Matthews, *Charles II's Escape from Worcester* (London, 1967), p. 88.
3. *Letter from T. Scott and R. Salway to Council of State*, in H. Cary, *Memorials of the English Civil War* (London, 1842), vol. 2, p. 363.
4. HMC 10th Report, Appendix VI, p. 175.
5. Cary, *Memorials*, vol. 2, p. 363.
6. HMC 10th Report, Appendix VI, p. 175.
7. Hamilton to Lady Hamilton, Commandery Museum, Worcester.
8. *Relation of the defeat of the King's army at Worcester, 3 September 1651*, in CSPD 17 September 1651, p. 437.
9. Robert Stapleton in *Perfect Diurnall*, 3 September 1651.
10. *Mercurius Politicus*, 4–11 September 1651.
11. *Letter from T. Scott and R. Salway to Lenthall*, 3 September 1651, in Cary, *Memorials*, vol. 2, p. 354.
12. *Letter of a Scottish prisoner*, in J. Hughes (ed.), *Boscobel Tracts* (London, 1830), p. 144; *Relation of the defeat of the King's army at Worcester, 3 September 1651*, in CSPD 17 September 1651, p. 437.
13. W. Dunn Macray (ed.), *Clarendon's History of the Rebellion and Civil Wars in England* (Oxford, 1888), vol. 5, p. 191.
14. HMC 10th Report, Appendix VI p. 175.
15. *An Exact Narrative and Relation (1660)* in Matthews, *Charles II's Escape*, p. 86.
16. D. Stevenson, *King or Covenant? Voices from the Civil War* (East Lothian, 1996), p. 9.
17. *Commons Journal*, vii, pp. 12, 13.
18. *The King's account of his escape (1680)* in Matthews, *Charles II's Escape*, p. 38.
19. *Letter from Cromwell to Lenthall*, 3 September 1651, in Abbott, *Writings and Speeches*, vol. 2, p. 461 and Appendix 1.1.
20. Robert Stapleton in *Perfect Diurnall*, 3 September 1651.

8. Aftermath

1. On 16 December, Parliament voted compensation to the widows, ranging from £200 for the wife of a captain to £20 for a private's wife: *Commons Journal*, vii.
2. Essex Record Office Q/SBa2/78, quoted in D. Appleby, 'Essex Men at the Battle of Worcester', *English Civil War Times*, 52 (1997), p. 28.
3. R. Baxter, *Reliquae Baxtrianae* (London, 1696) pt 1, p. 67.
4. Baxter, *Reliquae Baxtrianae*, pt 1, p. 69.
5. W. Dunn Macray (ed.), *Clarendon's History of the Rebellion and Civil Wars in England* (Oxford, 1888) vol. 5, p. 191.
6. *Memoirs of Captain John Hodgson* (Pontefract, 1994), p. 30.; CSPD 8 October 1651, p. 470.
7. B. Whitelock, *Memorials of the English Affairs* (1732), vol. 3, p. 508.
8. Letter in CSPD 17 September 1651, p. 437.
9. HWRO *Audit of the City Accounts 1640–1669.*
10. D. Stevenson, *King or Covenant? Voices from the Civil War* (East Lothian, 1996), p. 124; *Dictionary of National Biography*, vol. 20, p. 48.
11. HMC 10th Report, Appendix VI, p. 175.
12. *Letter of 6 September from Harrison*, cited in J.W. Willis-Bund, *The Civil War in Worcestershire 1642–1646 and the Scotch Invasion of 1651* (Birmingham, 1905), p. 251; Whitelock, *Memorials*, vol. 3, p. 508.
13. Whitelock, *Memorials*, vol. 3, p. 348; HWRO *Audit of the City Accounts 1640–1669.*
14. R. Wiseman, *Wounds, of Gun-shot Wounds, of Fractures and Luxations* (1686, repr. Bristol, 1977), p. 401.
15. Ibid., p. 420.
16. St Michael Bedwardine, *Churchwardens' Accounts 1651–2*, ff111, 112, 113d.
17. C. Beardsmore, 'City Walls Road: Summary Report of the Archaeology', *Worcestershire Archaeology Newsletter*, 17 (1976), p. 21.
18. HMC 5th Report, Appendix, p. 299; HMC 10th Report, Appendix VI, p. 175.
19. *Letter from Cromwell to Lenthall*, 8 September 1651, in W.C. Abbott, *The Writings and Speeches of Oliver Cromwell* (Oxford, 1939), vol. 2, p. 467; CJ VII 1651–9, p. 103.

20. R.D. Hunt (ed.), 'Henry Townshend's Notes of the Office of a Justice of the Peace, 1661–3', *Worcs. Hist. Soc. Miscellany* II (1967), new series, vol. 5, p. 83.
21. J. Washbourn, *Bibliotheca Gloucestrensis* (Gloucester, 1825), p. cxxiv.
22. *Perfect Diurnall*, 15–23 September 1651, in M. Stace (ed.),*Cromwelliana* (London, 1810), p. 116.
23. CSPD 16 December 1656, p. 197.
24. *Perfect Diurnall*, 6 September 1651.
25. Appleby, 'Essex Men', p. 28.
26. CSPD 8 September 1654, p. 596.
27. CCC 19 September 1651, p. 483.
28. CCC 12 November 1651, p. 501; CCC 24 September 1651, pp. 483–4.
29. CCC 30 September 1651, p. 485; CCC 11 November 1651, p. 500.
30. D.R. Guttery, *The Great Civil War in Midlands Parishes* (Birmingham, 1950), p. 17.
31. CSPD 29 June 1652, p. 307; CSPD 3 August 1652, p. 354.
32. CSPD 17 December, 1651, p. 67; CSPD 12 January 1652, p. 98; CSPD 19 January 1652, p. 549.
33. Hunt, 'Henry Townshend's Notes', p. 114.
34. CSPD 15 March 1653, p. 215.
35. W. Bray (ed.), *Diary of John Evelyn*, vol. 1 (London, 1907), p. 299; HMC 14th Report, Appendix VIII, p. 189.

9. The Fate of the Prisoners

1. *Personal communication*, Erica Enslin-Franklin.
2. CSPD 22 January 1656, p. 126.
3. B. Whitelock, *Memorials of the English Affairs* (1732), vol. 3, p. 516.
4. Harrison to Parliament, 31 October 1650, in *Parliamentary History*, xix, pp. 417–21.
5. BM Add. Mss 31955, transcript of Pepys Mss 2141: copy in HWRO 899.31. Whitgreave describes possibly the same men as coming to the door asking for provisions and dressings for their wounds: A. Fea, *After Worcester Fight* (London, 1904), Tract III, p. 165.
6. Sir James Turner, *Memoirs of his Life and Times 1630–72* (Edinburgh, 1829), p. 96, quoted in C. Carlton, *Going to the Wars* (London, 1992), p. 336.
7. *Memoirs of Lady Fanshawe* (1830), pp. 113–17.
8. Whitelock, *Memorials*, vol. 3, p. 512.
9. CSPD 26 September 1651, p. 449; CSPD 17 December 1651, p. 67.
10. *Letter from Cromwell to Cotton*, 2 October 1651, in W.C. Abbott, *The Writings and Speeches of Oliver Cromwell* (Oxford, 1939), vol. 2, p. 482.
11. HMC 5th Report, Appendix, p. 611.
12. CSPD 1 September 1654, p. 353.
13. CSPD 4 September 1655, p. 314.
14. CSPC 10 September 1651, p. 360.
15. *Personal communication*, William F. Cummins.
16. CSPC 21 October 1651, p. 363.
17. CSPD 17 October 1651, p. 480.
18. CSPD 23 October 1650, p. 397; CSPC 26 September 1651, p. 361.
19. Whitelock, *Memorials*, vol. 3, p. 510.
20. CSPD 2 December 1651, p. 44.
21. Ibid.
22. C. Boyer (ed.), *Ships' Passenger Lists: National and New England (1600–1825)* (California, 1977), p. 154.
23. C.E. Banks, *Accounts of Lynn Iron Works*, fol. 29 (Baker Library, Harvard University) quoted in *Proceedings of the Massachusetts Historical Society*, lxi (1928), p. 23.
24. Ibid., p. 24.
25. Carlton, *Going to the Wars*, p. 337.
26. BL E1833, cited in P.W. Coldham, *Emigrants in Chains*, p. 115.
27. *Letter from Cotton to Cromwell*, 28 July 1651, in Boyer, *Ships' Passenger Lists*, p. 157.
28. Ibid., p. 161.
29. 'Letters written by Mr Moray . . . from Ware River in Montjack Bay, Virginia, Feb. 1 1665', *William and Mary Quarterly*, 2nd series no. 3 (July 1922), p. 160.
30. Lord Braybrooke (ed.), *Diary of Samuel Pepys* (London, 1906), vol. 1, p. 408.
31. Some of the correspondence of this company was published in S. Wells, *A History of the Drainage of the Great Level of the Fens Called Bedford Level*, vol. 1 (London, 1830).
32. Wells, *History of the Drainage*, p. 228.
33. Ibid., p. 232.
34. Ibid., p. 233.
35. Ibid., pp. 229–31: 666 yards of white kersey were ordered to make up the smocks, at a price not to exceed 2s 3d per yard.
36. Ibid., p. 233.
37. Ibid., p. 237.
38. Ibid., p. 241 (for 24 December 1651): a

hassack was a turf cut, moulded and dried for fuel.

39. T. Craddock, *History of Wisbech and the Fens* (Wisbech, 1849), pp. 147–8.
40. Ibid., p. 241.
41. Ibid., p. 243.
42. CSPD 17 December 1651, p. 67; CSPD 2 August 1652, p. 353.
43. CSPC 19 October 1654, p. 419.
44. Carlton, *Going to the Wars*, p. 337.
45. CSPD, 1 November 1651, p. 2.

10. The King's Escape

1. A. Fea, *After Worcester Fight* (London, 1904), Tract 1, pp. 5–44.
2. T. Blount, *Boscobel* (1660).
3. Fea, *After Worcester Fight*, Tract 1, p. 6.
4. Ibid., p. 10.
5. Blount, *Boscobel*, p. 42.
6. Blount, *Boscobel*, p. 48.
7. Father Huddleston, 'Original Account . . .' (1682) in W. Matthews, *Charles II's Escape from Worcester* (London, 1967, p. 112.
8. Fea, *After Worcester Fight*, Tract 1, p. 29.
9. Fea, *The Flight of the King*, Tract III, p. 166.
10. J.F. Downes, quoted in A. Frazer, *King Charles II* (London, 1979), p. 122 note.
11. *Letter Book*, Rawlinson MSS.
12. Fea, *The Flight of the King*, Tract IV, p. 190.
13. R. Ollard, *The Escape of Charles II after the battle of Worcester* (London 1986), p. 95.
14. Blount, *Boscobel*, p. 82.
15. Fea, *The Flight of the King*, Tract IV, pp. 227, 200.
16. Alford Deposition, in W. Matthews, *Charles II's Escape from Worcester* (London, 1967), p. 128.
17. Fea, *The Flight of the King*, Tract IV, pp. 189, 193.
18. Blount, *Boscobel*, p. 90.
19. Blount, *Boscobel*, p. 93.
20. *Calendar State Papers Venetian*, vol. 28 (1647–52), p. 202.
21. Blount, *Boscobel*, pp. 97–8.

11. Later Events

1. *Calendar State Papers Venetian*, vol. 28 (1647–52), p. 200.
2. B. Whitelock, *Memorials of the English Affairs* (1732), vol. 3, p. 618.

3. CSPD 2 February 1655, p. 31; CSPD 15 June 1655, p. 207.
4. J.W. Willis-Bund (ed.), *Diary of Henry Townshend of Elmley Lovett, 1640–63* (Worcs. Hist. Soc., 1915), pp. 30, 33.
5. W.C. Abbott, *The Writings and Speeches of Oliver Cromwell* (Oxford, 1939), vol. 4, pp. 671–2.
6. CSPD 31 October 1655, p. 409.
7. R. Baxter, *Reliquae Baxterianae*, pt 1 (London, 1696), pp. 97–8.
8. D.W. Rannie, 'Cromwell's Major Generals', *English Historical Review*, x (1895), pp. 471–506.
9. The story was originated by Colonel Lindsay, one of Cromwell's own officers, in order to excuse his desertion from the battle.
10. CSPD 15 August 1659, p. 111.
11. CCC, p. 2898.
12. CSPD 14 September 1659, p. 195.
13. CSPD 4 January 1660, p. 298.
14. *Letter from Cromwell to Lenthall*, 4 September 1651, in Abbott, *Writings and Speeches*, vol. 2, p. 463.
15. V. Collet, 'The Trial of Sir Thomas Streete', *Trans. Worcs. Archaeol. Soc.*, xxxiv (1957), p. 70.
16. W. Bray (ed.), *Diary of John Evelyn*, vol. 1 (London, 1907), p. 341.
17. J.W. Willis-Bund (ed.), *Diary of Henry Townshend of Elmley Lovett, 1640–1663*, vol. 1 (Worcs. Hist. Soc.), p. 36.
18. Ibid, pp. 71, 75.
19. *HMC Various Collections*, vol. 1, 1909, p. 137.
20. Essex Record Office Q/SO1, f.13v, quoted in D. Appleby, 'Essex Men at the Battle of Worcester', *English Civil War Times*, 52 (1997), p. 28.
21. Lord Braybrooke (ed.), *Diary of Samuel Pepys*, vol. 1 (London, 1906), p. 63.
22. E. Heath Agnew, *Roundhead to Royalist: A Biography of Colonel John Birch* (Hereford, 1977), p. 187.
23. HMC 14th Report, Appendix 8, p. 190.
24. CCC 12 May 1652, p. 2069.
25. HWRO 110, BA 1 90/23; 93/25; 98/8–10.
26. R. Ollard, *The Escape of Charles II after the Battle of Worcester* (London, 1986), p. 140.
27. CSPD 22 July 1668, p. 499.
28. Camden Society Publication, 1851.
29. Townshend, vol. 1, p. 37.

Appendix 1

1. M. Atkin, *The Civil War in Worcestershire* (Stroud, 1995), pp. 168–9.
2. M. Stace (ed.), *Cromwelliana* (London, 1810), p. 110.
3. J. Raymond (ed.), *Making of the News* (Moreton-in-Marsh, 1993), pp. 117–21.
4. HWRO 899:31 BA3669/2 (v).
5. J. Hughes (ed.), *Boscobel Tracts* (London, 1830), pp. 138–46.
6. W. Matthews, *Charles II's Escape from Worcester* (London, 1967), pp. 25–31.
7. CSPD 17 September 1651, pp. 436–7.
8. HWRO 899:31 BA 3669/2 (vi).
9. Published in C.E. Green, 'Charles II and the Battle of Worcester', *English Historical Review*, v (1890), pp. 114–18.

Bibliography

Abbott, W.C., *The Writings and Speeches of Oliver Cromwell*, vols 2 and 4 (Oxford, 1939)

Agnew, E. Heath, *Roundhead to Royalist: A Biography of Colonel John Birch* (1977)

Anon., 'Charles II and the Battle of Worcester', *English Historical Review*, v (1890)

Appleby, D., 'Essex Men at the Battle of Worcester', *English Civil War Times*, 52 (1997), pp. 24–8

Ashley, M., *The English Civil War* (Gloucester, 1990)

Atkin, M., *Gloucester and the Civil War* (Stroud, 1992)

Atkin, M., *The Civil War in Worcestershire* (Stroud, 1995)

Barker, P., 'The Origins of Worcester', *Trans. Worcs. Archaeol. Soc.* 3rd series, ii (1968–9)

Baxter, R., *Reliquae Baxterianae* (London 1696), part 1

Beardsmore, C., 'City Walls Road: Summary Report of the Archaeology', *Worcestershire Archaeology Newsletter*, xvii (1976)

Blount, T., *Boscobel* (1660)

Bond, S., *The Chamber Order Book of Worcester 1602–1650* (Worcs. Hist. Soc., new series 8, 1974)

Boyer, C. (ed.), *Ships' Passenger Lists: National and New England (1600–1825)* (California, 1977)

Bray, W. (ed.), *Diary of John Evelyn*, vol. 1 (Everyman, 1907)

Brown, P.J., 'The Military Career of Andrew Yarranton', *Trans. Worcs. Archaeol. Soc.*, xiii (1992), pp. 193–202

Buchan, J., *Oliver Cromwell* (London, 1941)

Carlton, C., *Going to the Wars* (London, 1992)

Carver, M.O.H., 'Medieval Worcester', *Trans. Worcs. Archaeol. Soc.*, vii (1980)

Cary, H., *Memorials of the Civil War*, vol. 2 (London, 1842)

Coldham, P.W., *Emigrants in Chains* (Stroud, 1992)

Collet, V., 'The Trial of Sir Thomas Streete', *Trans. Worcs. Archaeol. Soc.*, xxxiv (1957)

Craddock, T., *History of Wisbech and the Fens* (Wisbech, 1849)

Ellis, H., 'Letters from a Subaltern Officer in the Earl of Essex's Army', *Archaeologia*, xxxv (1853)

Fanshawe, Lady, *Memoirs of Lady Fanshawe* (1830)

Fea, A., *After Worcester Fight* (London 1904)

Fea, A., *The Flight of the King* (London, 1904)

Firth, C.H., *Cromwell's Army* (London, 1992)

Frazer, A., *King Charles II* (London, 1979)

Gardiner, S.R., *History of the Commonwealth and Protectorate*, vol. 2 (1903, repr. Adlestrop, 1988)

Green, V., *History of Worcester*, vol. 1 (1797)

Guttery, D.R., *The Great Civil War in Midlands Parishes* (Birmingham, 1950)

Hodgson, J., *Memoirs of Captain John Hodgson* (Pontefract, 1994)

Holmes, R., *Worcester 1651* (Market Drayton, 1985)

Hughes, J. (ed.), *Boscobel Tracts* (London, 1830)

Hunt, R.D. (ed.), 'Henry Townshend's Notes of the Office of a Justice of the Peace, 1661–3', *Worcs. Hist. Soc. Miscellany II* (1967), new series 5

Hutchinson, L., *Memoirs of the Life of Colonel Hutchinson, Written by his Wife Lucy* (London, 1889)

Jackson, R., *Salvage Recording at King's School, Worcester* (County Archaeological Service Internal Report 97, 1991)

Joyce, F.W., *Tenbury: Some Records of its History* (Oxford, 1931)

Kenyon, J., *The Civil Wars in England* (London, 1988)

Leadbetter, W.G., *The Story of Bromsgrove* (Bromsgrove, 1949)

'Letters Written by Mr Moray . . . from Ware River in Montjack Bay, Virginia, Feb. 1 1665', *William and Mary Quarterly*, 2nd series (July 1922), no. 3, p. 160.

Litchfield, J., *The Pike* (Newbury, 1997)

MacFarlane, A. (ed.), *The Diary of Ralph Josselin* (London, 1976)

Macray, W. Dunn (ed.), *The History of the Rebellion and Civil Wars in England* (Oxford, 1888), vol. 5

Matthews, W., *Charles II's Escape from Worcester* (London, 1967)

Nash, T.R., *Collections for the History of Worcestershire* (London, 1783)

Ollard, R., *The Escape of Charles II after the battle of Worcester* (London 1986)

Rannie, D.W., 'Cromwell's Major Generals', *English Historical Review*, x, (1895), pp. 471–506

Raymond, J. (ed.), *Making of the News* (Moreton-in-Marsh, 1993)

Reid, S., *Scots Armies of the 17th Century*, vol. 3: *The Royalist Armies 1639–46* (Leigh-on-sea, 1989)

Rowland, A.J., *Military Encampments of the English Civil Wars 1639–1659* (Bristol, 1995)

Silcock, R.H., *County Government in Worcestershire 1603–1660* (PhD thesis, University of London, 1974)

Stace, M. (ed.), *Cromwelliana* (London, 1810)

Stevenson, D., *Highland Warrior: Alasdair MacColla and the Civil Wars* (Edinburgh, 1994)

Stevenson, D., *King or Covenant? Voices from the Civil War* (East Lothian, 1996)

Thompson, J., *The Other Army* (Leigh-on-Sea, no date)

Thurloe, J., *A collection of the State Papers of John Thurloe Esq.* (London, 1742)

Trevelyan, W.C. (ed.), 'Copies of Various Papers Relating to the Family of Thornton of Witton Castle in Northumberland', *Archaeologia Aeliana*, 1st series, ii (1832)

Turner, Sir J., *Memoirs of his Life and Times 1630–72* (Edinburgh, 1829)

Ward, R., *Animadversions of Warre* (1639)

Washbourn, J., *Bibliotheca Gloucestrensis* (Gloucester, 1825)

Wells, S., *A History of the Drainage of the Great Level of the Fens Called Bedford Level*, vol. 1 (London, 1830)

Whitelock, B., *Memorials of the English Affairs* (1682, repr. Oxford, 1853)

Willis-Bund, J.W., *The Civil War in Worcestershire 1642–1646 and the Scotch Invasion of 1651* (Birmingham, 1905)

Willis-Bund, J.W., *The Battle of Worcester* (Worcester, 1913)

Willis-Bund, J.W. (ed.), *Diary of Henry Townshend of Elmley Lovett, 1640-1663*, 2 vols (Worcs. Hist. Soc., 1915 and 20)

Wiseman, R., *Wounds, of Gun-shot Wounds, of Fractures and Luxations* (1686, repr. Bristol, 1977)

Young, P. and Holmes, R., *The English Civil War* (London, 1974)

In recent years the activities of seventeenth-century re-enactment societies have done much to bring the history of the Civil War to life.

National

English Civil War Society
70 Hallgate, Howden, North Humberside, DN14 7ST
http://jpbooks.com/ecws

Sealed Knot
PO Box 2000, Nottingham, NO2 5LH
http://www.sealedknot.org.uk

Local

Worcester Militia
c/o The Commandery, Sidbury, Worcester WR1 2HU.

Index

Page numbers in *italics* refer to illustrations.